4-15-76

Scarcity and Control in Socialism

Scarcity and Control in Socialism

Essays on East European Planning

Phillip J. Bryson
The University of Arizona

Lexington Books
D.C. Heath and Company
Lexington, Massachusetts
Toronto   London

Library of Congress Cataloging in Publication Data

Bryson, Phillip J
   Scarcity and control in socialism.

   Includes bibliographical references and index.
   1. Europe, Eastern—Economic policy. 2. Decentralization in management—Europe, Eastern. I. Title.
HC244.B79   338.947   75-36012
ISBN 0-669-00375-1

Published simultaneously in Canada

Printed in the United States of America

International Standard Book Number: 0-669-00375-1

Library of Congress Catalog Card Number: 75-36012

To Pat, whose system of
economy has made ours a
happy home.

Contents

List of Figures and Tables

Figures

Tables

Preface

This book is the result of an extended study on the fundamental issues of socialist economics. I was induced by professional considerations to publish most of these chapters earlier but am convinced that their republication here is more than justified. Chapters 3, 5, and 7 were published in sources not readily accessible to a general audience in the United States. Chapters 1 and 2 were written especially for this book and have not appeared elsewhere. Most importantly, the final product does not represent a collection of loosely related essays combined as an afterthought; rather, it is a collection of individual parts into a preconceived whole; hopefully, it will prove to be greater than the sum of its parts.

My initial objective was to develop two chapters for each basic topic—one designed to survey, illustrate, and describe important issues and institutions and one designed to present my own contribution (of an analytical nature, where possible) to each basic topic. I am hopeful that the style and methodology of the survey chapters (1, 2, 5, 6, 9, and 10) recommend them to a nonspecialized audience. Moreover, since the methodological terrain of socialist economics is not restricted to professionals armed with highly quantitative weapons, anyone who has had some exposure to price theory should not find the other materials particularly foreboding.

Because a substantial amount of time went into researching most of the individual topics, the total research effort was a protracted one that indebted me to numerous individuals and several institutions. It goes without saying that I am obliged, however reluctantly, to accept the blame for deficiencies remaining in the final product. If there are any merits to appreciate, however, I must share their enjoyment with a number of appreciated colleagues and friends. Jozef M. van Brabant and Erich Klinkmueller provided particularly extensive assistance. In earlier publication, the materials presented in chapters 3 and 11 were coauthored by van Brabant; another article appearing here as chapters 9 and 10 was coauthored by Klinkmueller. I am grateful to them for permitting me to publish these materials here as a part of the combined study.

The study would have been unthinkable without grant assistance from the Alexander von Humboldt Foundation in Bonn, the Division of Economic and Business Research of the University of Arizona, and the Graduate College Committee for Faculty Research Support in the Humanities and Social Sciences of The University of Arizona.

Permission to utilize materials previously published is gratefully acknowledged to *Weltwirtschaftliches Archiv, Survey, Revue d'Études Comparatives Est-Ouest, Kyklos,* and *Konjunkturpolitik.*

Valuable assistance was provided by a number of individuals kind enough to discuss planning issues with me, to read drafts of one or more of the chapters, and to offer helpful comments. Listed in alphabetical order, I am indebted to Dennis R. Cox, Louis G. Gasper, Clark A. Hawkins, Edward A. Hewett, Gert Leptin, Heinrich Machowski, Manfred Melzer, Jean E. Weber, and Donald A. Wells.

A large share of the work was completed during a pleasant stay in Berlin from May 1973 to January 1975. The members of the Department of Economics at the East European Institute of the Free University of Berlin provided not only professional assistance but also encouragement and friendship to myself and my family. Several contributed directly to the study and have already been mentioned. A most helpful and capable librarian, Annemarie Genske, likewise deserves express thanks.

Finally, I cannot avoid grateful mention of Barbara Sears, Mary Chavez, and some highly proficient typists at the Division of Economic and Business Research of the University of Arizona.

I do not claim guilty to the traditional sin of manuscript producers, i.e., of having neglected my family during the preparation of this book. They are far too special to be neglected; nor have they neglected to be a continual source of inspiration and encouragement to me. I appreciate and love them for kinds of assistance no others could give.

P.J.B.

**Part I
The Domestic Socialist
Economy**

1

Introduction:
The Nature of Centralist
Administration in Socialism

Soviet-Type Bureaucratization

Some years ago, a Western economist published an article on economic planning in the U.S.S.R. that opened with the warning that the Soviet planning bureaucracy would grow thirty-six-fold by 1980 and require the services of the entire Soviet population, unless a radical planning reform was initiated. The article was published in a respectable journal, and the projection reported was actually made by Victor Glushkov, a recognized Soviet academician.[1] Still, the contention struck me (at the time, a student just developing an interest in the planned economies) as little short of sensationalism; it seemed incredible that a scholar could take such a statement seriously.

Undeniably, scientists are not always above using their professional status as the basis for crusades to combat what they perceive to be crises. To some extent, the statement in question may have been so motivated. Nevertheless, the article went on to paint (and document) a rather dismal picture of the progress of bureaucratization in Soviet economic planning.

It is not surprising that these warnings were being voiced in a period in which various reforms were being contemplated. Especially in the last half of the 1960s, a number of reform measures were initiated in the U.S.S.R. and throughout East Europe, apparently in response to the pleas of both theoreticians and practitioners for some greater degree of decentralization of economic decision making.

Clearly, one need not fear at this point that the planning apparatus in the Soviet Union will have mushroomed to the forecasted level by 1980. This happy prospect is not, however, because the reform movement of the 1960s was remarkably successful. Rather, one must simply infer, from the kinds of evidence to be presented in this book, that Glushkov's prediction was indeed overly dramatized.

Nevertheless, even if Glushkov stretched a point in order to make one, his warning was not uncalled for. Even though reform efforts were made, they were less skillfully executed than conceived. No significant decentralization of decision-making authority was achieved in the planning modifications undertaken; the essentials of the system were left unchanged. Indeed, it can even be argued that the innovations developed in the attempt to achieve greater efficiency incentives actually added to the degree of

3

centralization and the complexity of administrative institutions prevailing in the system. It has been observed that these innovations have helped "to swell the administrative bureaucracy, which has increased nearly one-third since 1965."[2]

In the course of this study, frequent reference will have to be made to the bureaucratic administrative procedures of Soviet-type planning. It will be helpful to have some appreciation of the nature of allocation processes when economic activity is the exclusive function of administrative committees and agencies, i.e., when markets are not permitted to grease the flows of economic activity to any substantial degree at all.[3] Hopefully, such an appreciation can be achieved through an investigation into the principal allocation mechanisms utilized by socialist planners.

Balances and Balancing

This chapter will be devoted to a descriptive investigation of the primary tool of the committee economy, viz., planning balances. The principal species of this planning genre, the "material balance," will be of greatest importance for the discussion. It is to be hoped that the reader will already have acquired an appreciation for the automaticity of freely functioning markets. Whatever their failings may be, markets represent a most facile mechanism of coordination for economic decision making by diverse individual agents.

A system of balances is utilized in centralized socialist planning in the formulation and verification of the national plan, as well as in ensuring its fulfillment. The Soviet economist, Mikhail Bor, has categorized such balances according to types: (a) manpower; (b) financial; and (c) those for the material elements of production, consumption, and accumulation.[4]

Bor indicates that system (c) is most highly developed. It includes balances of natural resources, balances of productive capacity, balances of fixed assets, and material balances proper. The latter are divided into balances of the means of production and balances of consumer goods. Though Bor writes that material balances are drawn up for "industrial and agricultural goods of key significance for the major economic tasks of the state plan," he mentions that the use of this planning tool is acquiring ever greater importance in the Union Republics, economic areas, regions, territories, and cities.[5]

Material Balances and Planning

In the planning process, Gosplan or the central planning agency of the relevant East European country develops aggregated targets for output, labor, investment, and so on. Planners at the ministerial level generate more detailed assignments for their individual branches and pass these down to the enterprises. The relevant authority makes sure that these imperatives correspond with the latest available figures on productive capacity and, also, the established "technical-progressive norms," that regulate the maximum permissible expenditure of output.[6]

The enterprises then respond with their own estimates of possibilities. As is widely known, a sort of bargaining process occurs between enterprises and planners as agents attempt to put themselves in more favorable positions to earn bonuses given for fulfillment or overfulfillment of plan targets. Enterprises tend to minimize their output potential and to pad their requests for inputs, while planners attempt to extract at least maximal outputs and reduce input requirement estimates to at least minimal levels. In any case, the result is an estimate of productive potential which Gosplan or the planning agency eventually puts into a material balance.

Material balancing has been described basically as a trial-and-error method of equating the supplies and demands of various industries.[7] This "primary method" (*Hauptmethode*) of economic planning in socialism is treated more sympathetically by its proponents as a "confrontation of economic production with requirements, where balancing makes it possible to reveal and establish the requirements of equilibrium and proportionality."[8]

As suggested by its name, a material balance is essentially a balance sheet listing both the "sources" or "resources" (supply) for a given industry on the one hand and the "distribution," "allocation," or "uses" (demand) for that industry on the other hand. (See Table 1-1.)

After demands and supplies are calculated in this ex ante juxtaposition, a comparison of the balances of related industries will make potential bottlenecks and shortages apparent. Then, the process of adjustment can begin. Traditionally, planning has been "taut" in socialist countries, i.e., inventories are held at minimal levels, estimates of productivity improvements are optimistic, and output goals are not always realistic. With planning performed in this spirit, it often becomes apparent, early in the process, that various inputs will be in short supply. Committees will, therefore, find it necessary to substitute surplus items for deficit materials, call for greater productive effort on the part of enterprises, attempt to reduce stated input requirements, investigate the possibility of expanding imports to open bottlenecks, and so on.

Montias points out that it would be necessary to go through most of this procedure numerous times before the material balances could simultaneously be closed. Each time, the relevant planning committee or ministry

Table 1-1
Material Balance

Sources	Distribution
Production supplied by the industry	Production and operational needs
Total imports from (a) socialist countries and (b) capitalist countries	Construction
	Market fund (final consumer goods)
Inventories and carry-over at suppliers, at the beginning of the year	Exports to (a) socialist countries (b) capitalist countries
Supplies from other sources	Permanent state reserves (inventories for national disaster purposes)
	Operational reserves and inventories at year end

would have to calculate the input requirements of subordinate enterprises using the output targets given by the latest version of the yearly plan.[9] When the process had been completed, assignments would be passed down to the producing units and contracts and purchasing authorizations drawn up.

Clearly, the achievement of consistency in such a procedure would require an iterative approach, i.e., several rounds of adjustment and recalculation. In each round of balancing, the revelation of shortages calls for another round of recalculation to further diminish inconsistencies.

Balancing and Input-Output Analysis

If the planning process ceases before numerous iterations achieve consistency, production bottlenecks will make it impossible for some firms scheduled to receive the shortage items to meet their delivery quotas. A second wave of shortages begins to work its way through the productive system when the customers of these enterprises fail to receive scheduled productive inputs. It was Montias who first showed that every new set of output targets obtained in this iterative manner would come closer to the consistent set of targets that would be generated by the direct inversion of the technology matrix of input-output analysis.[10]

In recent years, the Soviet theoretician has become abundantly aware of the relationship of the iterative balancing approach to the mathematical approach of input-output analysis.[11] The Soviets are aware that the input-output approach is potentially far superior to material balancing as a planning device. The proposition is especially apparent when one compares the two sides of the material balance with the two sides of the basic input-output equation. Note that the planning task consists of adjusting the two sides of the balance to produce an equality between the total supply X_i and the total allocation $x_{ij} + x_i$.[12] In material balance terms we have:

Resources		*Allocation*
Production		Production and operational needs = x_{ij}
Imports	X_i	
Reserve and inventories		Market fund
		Exports $\left.\vphantom{\begin{array}{c}a\\b\\c\end{array}}\right\} x_i$
		Reserve and inventories

This is simply a tabular representation of the input-output expression:

$$X_i = \sum_{j=1}^{n} x_{ij} + x_i \qquad i = 1, \ldots n$$

So whereas the two methodologies are conceptually the same, the input-output approach is much more amenable to quantification and analytical manipulation.

Unfortunately, however, the Soviet Union to this juncture has been unable to use mathematical models, including input-output analysis, as anything more than adjuncts to the classical approach. For a long time after its development, of course, the input-output technique was avoided on the grounds that it was developed as a part of bourgeois economics, which implied, of course, that it was ideologically unsavory, if not taboo. But even since the ideological stigma began to wane, input-output tables generated in relative abundance are used merely to check on the consistency and feasibility of preliminary planning targets and to improve the planning norms used in calculating material balances. Despite high level political support for mathematical planning and frequent complaints from technicians that their models are not being utilized, nothing has been done to move the material balance from its place as the primary planning implement of socialism.[13]

The primary reason for the inability of input-output planning to drive balancing from the planning field is that the scope of desired planning activity is so large. Partly because the number of commodities subject to balancing oscillates, Western analysts have given widely divergent estimates of the extent of balancing activity. It is clear, however, that the total number of balances compiled is very large:[14] up to a figure well in excess of 1,000 for those balanced by Gosplan itself and up to a total of nearly 30,000 for the entire planning apparatus at all levels. It would be manifestly impossible to do quantitative work with any matrix of so many cells.

8

Other Planning Deficiencies

The limited assistance the material balancing system can claim from input-output methodology is not the only weakness in the system. The system is likewise plagued by (a) overambitious scope, (b) bad data, (c) insufficient planning time and capacity to carry out the successive iterations that consistent plans would require, and (d) increasingly complex production processes that make the economy less amenable to planning by balances.

Overambitiousness has had several implications historically. Because the scope of the planning operation is too extensive, the multitude of balances compiled at levels below the central planning agency are seldom integrated into the final plan. The press of time and capacity results in the use of unrealistic technical norms not reflective of current technology.

Both in the planning process and in the implementation of the plan, it is essential to accurately assess the levels of available inventories of supplies held by planning agencies and supply enterprises. Getting accurate inventory data is, however, very difficult. This is so not only for reasons associated with standard mechanical problems of data gathering, accounting methods, etc., but also because firms benefit from concealing their supply hoards in order to claim higher supply rations.[15]

Because the data transmission and processing requirements are great, it appears that there is no time in drawing up the plan to permit intercommittee communication and the successive iterations that would assure consistency.[16]

Montias reasons that the growing complexity of the industrial structure would tend to require more iterations of the balancing process to reach acceptable estimates of gross outputs.[17] The relevance of this simple, ex ante reasoning is borne out by repeated socialist attempts, in the past fifteen years or so, to develop and modify planning institutions to cope with increasingly sophisticated interindustrial relationships. In spite of the continued growth of the planning bureaucracy and increasing use of electronic computers, the committee method of planning seems unable to cope with the demands placed on it.

Ameliorative Aspects of the Planning Process

At this point, it would be difficult not to face the question: How, then, can the bureaucratic endeavor be made to function at all? A number of redeeming factors deserve discussion. In the first place, all commodities are not balanced—rather, only the more basic ones that determine the structure and development of the economy. Though the number may run into the thousands, it does not, at least, run into the millions. Additionally, the balances that are constructed can be kept manageable by countenancing a fairly high level of aggregation of information. The greater the detail one might insist upon, the greater the danger that the planning apparatus may be swamped with data.

Further simplification can be achieved by assigning a large number of material balances to administrative units at lower levels in the planning hierarchy.[18] Though (as indicated above) this implies some difficulty in integrating the balancing outputs of lower planning levels into the total effort, it at least permits the center to manage the determination of basic industrial proportions.

Aside from these planning accommodations designed to avoid a breakdown of the bureaucratic mechanism under the weight of excessive ambition, the Soviets also maintain a State Reserve of productive inputs that serves as a protection against national calamity, whether natural or plan-made.[19]

There is an additional Reserve of the Council of Ministers that serves as an operational reserve. In the course of the plan period, certain firms will run short of inputs because they have filled their quotas early. Such firms could continue to produce given the availability of extra inputs. Other enterprises may fail to receive scheduled deliveries because of supply failures elsewhere in the system. The reserves of the ministerial council can be dispensed to such firms to avoid breakdowns and inefficiency.

The final factor that permits continued functioning in spite of perennial planning errors is the traditional willingness to sacrifice production in nonpriority sectors when bottlenecks or supply shortages arise in the course of the plan period. In the face of the threat of a breakdown, one simply retreats from the original targets. If necessary, the low-priority sectors will bear the shortages. This may also have negative implications, of course, for shortages encountered in nonpriority sectors could work through the system and also affect high-priority sectors indirectly.[20]

Interestingly, Soviet writers point to extensive planning efforts statistically to investigate the budgets and expenditures of a large sample (50,000) of Soviet families, so that the orientation of production plans and the services of the industrial community can be based upon their preferences and needs.[21] However, production based upon these needs is the first that is sacrificed when plans prove to have been overambitious and outputs in higher priority sectors are being threatened.

In summary, the overextension of planning capacity in the socialist economies has resulted in this traditional outcome: plan consistency and target fulfillment are generally achieved only for the high-priority industries. This is primarily an upshot of the fact that the planning endeavor is dependent upon artificial, bureaucratic forms of resource allocation. The automaticity of market processes, though scarcely noticed (and perhaps little appreciated) by agents in market economies, spares nonplanning economies a substantial investment of resources that would have otherwise been required by a planning apparatus.

Additional Sources of Bureaucratization

It should be observed, however, that the material balance methodology is by no means the only source of bureaucratization in socialist economic administration. Two others are worthy of mention, not only because they are illustrative, but also because they are of recent origin and give insight into some important contemporary trends in Soviet-type planning.

The first source is the attempt to achieve greater microefficiency through the adoption of an increasingly numerous set of planning indicators. In the name of economic reformism, productivity is to be increased, new technologies are to be adopted, new products and old products of better quality are to be produced, and so on. All of these things are to be achieved by (a) devising statistical measures to assess performance in the light of plan objectives, (b) utilizing such indicators in the plan, and (c) tying a set of economic "levers" or incentives directly to the desired achievements. Rather than streamlining older procedures, this process simply makes planning a more detailed endeavor than it was before the reforms.[22]

It can be argued, naturally, that the arrival of the computer age makes it feasible to extend the scope of planning, and it is true that the use of computers has facilitated the planning effort in the Soviet Union. Unfortunately, it is no less true that the increased capacity computers offer can represent a dangerous temptation to the bureaucratic mentality. This brings us to the second source of increased bureaucratization, viz., the current Soviet "mania" for long-term forecasting and the practice of computerizing "everything that seems to be susceptible of computerization."[23] The Soviet Union is currently involved in an attempt to establish a network of computerized information processes and to integrate it into the planning process. Schroeder anticipates that this forecasting-computerization undertaking will simply have the effect of inundating the planning bodies under an avalanche of reports. Since it will be too massive to process and assimilate, it will most likely just be ignored.[24]

A little reflection on the part of the citizen of a market society should put the basic planning dilemma into perspective. The attempt to control or at least strongly to influence the decisions of myriads of buyers and sellers in a complex economy represents a frighteningly vast undertaking. This is especially so when it is undertaken by committee, administrative types who are far removed from the preferences, the information, and the incentives of the actual economic agents. In the Soviet-type economy, the latter are granted no opportunity to establish in the (at least quasicompetitive) market environment efficient resource allocation patterns.

With this background, it now becomes our interesting task to investigate the impacts of centralized planning. It should prove rewarding to examine the effects and implications of command allocation practices in the important subprocesses of the economy, viz., in economic organization, pricing, and investment as well as in international economic relations.

Notes

1. The article was Leon Smolinski's, "What Next in Soviet Planning?" *Foreign Affairs,* vol. 42, no. 4 (July 1964), pp. 602-613. Glushkov was, at that time, head of the Soviet program of research in cybernetics.

2. See Gertrude E. Schroeder, "Recent Developments in Soviet Planning and Incentives," *Soviet Economic Prospects for the Seventies,* Joint Economic Committee, Washington, D.C., 1973, p. 38.

3. It has been argued that even some economists willing to claim expertise in the matter, fail to recognize the substantive differences in the nature of centrally administered socialist planning and the centralized planning conducted internally by large corporations within the "new industrial state" described by John Kenneth Galbraith. Ota Šik, the spiritual father of economic reform in Czechoslovakia, has accused Galbraith of this failing. See George R. Urban, "A Conversation with Ota Šik," *Survey,* vol. 19, no. 2 (Spring 1973), pp. 252-253.

In that part of the U.S. economy that is largely noncompetitive and planned in the Galbraithian sense, industrial planning committees are not institutionally removed across several hierarchical levels from required planning information, but have direct access to such information.

The question of information flows, coordination, and economic control will be taken up in Chapters 2 and 3.

4. See Mikhail Bor, *Aims and Methods of Soviet Planning* (London: Lawrence and Wishart, 1967), p. 66. These kinds of balances are enlarged upon by Hans Fuelle, *Leitung und Planung der Volkswirtschaft* (East Berlin: Verlag die Wirtschaft, 1973), pp. 68-69; and N.A. Tsagolov, ed., *Kurs Politicheskoi Ekonomii,* vol. II, Sotsializm (Moscow: Ekonomika, 1974), pp. 487-489. Fuelle's discussion is worthwhile, for he indicates the degree of comprehensiveness left implicit in Bor's "financial balance" category. This would have to include, for example, the balance of pay-

ments, the national budget, etc. Interestingly, the habit of thinking about all economic activity in terms of balances may have its drawbacks. Fuelle's discussion of the balance of payments has a strong mercantilistic tone, as is typical of East European thought, for it favors the maintenance of a balance of trade with each individual trade partner.

5. Ibid., p. 67.

6. J.M. Montias also discusses the process in these terms. See his article, "Planning with Material Balances in Soviet-Type Economies," *The American Economic Review,* vol. 49, no. 5 (December 1959), p. 107.

7. See Robert W. Campbell, *Soviet-Type Economies: Performance and Evolution* (London: Macmillan, 1974), p. 36.

8. Fuelle, *Leitung und Planung,* op. cit., p. 59.

9. Montias, "Planning with Material Balances," op. cit., p. 965.

10. See ibid., esp. p. 968. Because input-output analysis is fundamental to the standard kit of tools of contemporary economics students, there is no point in developing the idea here. Putting production data for the basic sectors of the economy into a matrix (so that one can read off all the required production inputs of a given industry from a column of the matrix and all the outputs of a given industry from a row of the matrix) is a convenient way of organizing information. Moreover, by manipulating the matrix to solve for unknowns, one can account for both the direct and indirect technical relationships existing in the industrial productive system. For the original contribution, see Wassily Leontief, *The Structure of the American Economy, 1919-1939* 2nd ed. (New York: Oxford, 1951). The uninitiated might profitably refer to William H. Miernyk, *The Elements of Input-Output Analysis* (New York: Random House, 1965) or R. Dorfman, P.A. Samuelson, and R. Solow, *Linear Programming and Economic Analysis* (New York: McGraw-Hill, 1958).

11. If evidence were necessary, the reader might profitably be referred to A. Efimov et al., *La Planification Scientifique en URSS* (Moscow: Progress Publishers, 1973). This source indicates that input-output analysis and mathematical programming are analytical extensions and improvements of balances.

12. This expression of the conceptual relationship between balancing and input-output methodologies is the pedagogical device of Nicolas Spulber. See his *The Soviet Economy: Structure, Principles, Problems* (New York: Norton, 1969).

13. For a reasonably detailed discussion, see Schroeder, op. cit.

14. Compare Michael Ellman, "The Consistency of Soviet Plans," *Scottish Journal of Political Economy,* Vol. 16, No. 1 (February 1969), pp. 50-74; Herbert S. Levine, "The Centralized Planning of Supply in Soviet Industry," *Comparisons of the United States and Soviet*

Economies, JEC (Washington, D.C.: U.S. Government Printing Office, 1959); Schroeder, "Recent Developments," op. cit.; and Campbell, *Soviet-Type Economies,* op. cit.

15. See Montias, "Planning with Material Balances," op. cit., p. 979.

16. Levine says there seems to be no "set order of communication such as first section A makes its changes, then section B, etc.; all sections work simultaneously." He indicates that it was rare for even three or four iterations to be performed when Gosplan wished to trace the effects of a correction in an output target. See "The Centralized Planning," op. cit., p. 267.

17. Montias, "Planning with Material Balances," op. cit., p. 971.

18. Fuelle shows the following possibly representative breakdown for balancing assignments in East German planning. The Ministerial Council draws up 300 balances, the National Planning Commission is responsible for 550, the ministeries and other state organs for 1000, and the industrial associations and producing units for 2800. See *Leitung und Planung,* op. cit., pp. 63-64.

19. Levine uses the term "manmade" in his discussion of the reserves. See "The Centralized Planning," op. cit., p. 265.

20. For a concrete example, see Richard L. Carson, *Comparative Economic Systems* (New York: Macmillan, 1973), p. 302. In the plan for 1966-1970, a target of 750,000 units was established for the automobile industry. By early 1970, it had been revised downward to less than half the original figure. Many other original plan goals were likewise unmet, yet, as Carson suggests, the overall plan for industrial output was fulfilled, which implies a dramatic above-plan performance in defence-oriented industries.

21. Or at least upon the planner's perceptions of such needs, assuming his interpretation is not colored by his own preferences. For a sympathetic treatment of the problem, see A. Efimov et al., *La Planification Scientifique,* op. cit., p. 103.

22. Schroeder, op. cit., p. 37, comments aptly on the phenomenon: "The more detailed and technical these (plan) parameters are made, the more difficult it is to obtain consistency among them. Thus, the task of internal plan coordination becomes more complicated. Finally, the attempt to enforce efficiency and technological progress via plan indicators increases the degree of centralization."

23. The terms in quotation marks belong to Schroeder, ibid., p. 36.

24. Ibid., p. 37. Schroeder's overall assessment is worth quoting: "The task of coordinating all this activity is staggering. The grand scheme could, of course, be quietly abandoned when the costs mount, as were some of Stalin's canals. More likely, however, the time schedules for the projected systems and their numerous sub-systems will merely be pushed continually

forward, like the schedules of typical Soviet construction projects. The system's designers will be able to cite the immense, real difficulties and complexities involved, but in true bureaucratic fashion they will also be able to cite their calculations of the large resource savings that the new systems will bring about.''

2 Economic Organization I: The Question of Optimal Decentralization

The economic reforms of the 1960s were instigated in part because East European policymakers perceived that command processes had been characterized by an excessive degree of centralization. The persisting phenomena of unfulfilled targets, declining growth rates, and of ubiquitous inefficiencies rendered reform inevitable.

The task of reorganizing economic activity has not been and will not become an easy one. Grossman contends that in a given economic environment with specific societal goals, however these may be determined, the chief systemic difficulty of operating a command economy lies in determining and achieving the optimal degree of decentralization.[1]

In Eastern Europe the search for a satisfactory degree of decentralization was viewed in the reform era as a possible means of harmonizing the interests, goals, and plans of economic agents in the aggregate. Even to many socialists, it became apparent, before the advent of the "New Economic Systems," that the highest degree of central control and decision making could not force socialist enterprises to perform in a fashion beneficial to the national economy.

The view developed that whereas bureaucratization was a necessary evil, overbureaucratization certainly was not. According to this view, the latter phenomenon exists where an institutional framework is provided for economic processes that would fare better without it. In these terms, the traditional Soviet-type economy was described.[2]

If efficiency were to be achieved, institutions would have to be structured so that managerial decisions could be based on the goals of the enterprise itself and on information available at the enterprise level. To the greatest extent possible, such decisions must be responsive to the changing economic milieu and in correspondence with the sectoral and national objectives expressed in the plan.

Some Eastern Europeans became convinced in the 1960s that even though mathematical planning techniques may serve as an auxiliary means for improving central control and coordination, they cannot serve as a substitute for purposive enterprise behavior in harmony with the plan. Effective decision making at the periphery came to be recognized in some cases as the essence of the economic process.[3] Therefore, achieving optimal centralization is sometimes viewed as the key to plan-supportive enterprise performance and, consequently, more satisfactory aggregate economic performance.

Unfortunately, the problem of organizational innovation found no satisfactory resolution in the reform decade. Planners lacked the capacity and/or will to implement the decentralization innovations developed in the 1960s. By 1970, it was becoming apparent that the inconsistency of application of reform measures and the reluctance of planners to relinquish their grips on control mechanisms were causing the reform endeavor to abort. Economic theories that tended to imply the necessity of reducing or weakening the role of the state and the planning apparatus were more frequently denounced as "revisionist."[4] The traditional Soviet-type economy survived the onslaught of reform ideology, for in spite of the production of much literature, reforms were ultimately abandoned, downgraded, neglected,[5] or (in the case of Czechoslovakia) simply strangled.

It should not be forgotten, of course, that rationality on the part of planners does not require the pursuit of economic optimality. It may be that planners merely attempt to optimize their own preference functions, trading off the prerogatives of political control and the welfare gains of decentralization. Economic optimality may, according to this view, simply be sacrificed to other priorities.[6]

Edward Ames has argued, in a related manner, that in light of the potential role of traditional financial impulses in socialism—e.g., of money, credit, and noncentrally planned investments—the party has actively had to prohibit an ascension to power of the financial sector at the expense of the central planning committee.[7] So here again, the maintenance of control can be viewed as an end in itself.

Still, the problem of economic organization remains of long-term fundamental importance to the socialist economy. Though the planning literature of the bloc may seek new panaceas to persistent organizational difficulties, the phenomenon of overcentralization remains a stark fact of life.

It does not seem reasonable to assume that the centralization-decentralization pendulum has swung for the last time. Eventually, the pressures of suboptimal performance will require new reorganizational measures. This is not to deny, of course, that time can be won simply by intensifying interstate economic relationships within the bloc, seeking increased contacts with the West, and simply tolerating substantial welfare losses due to bureaucracy. However, the high efficiency costs of such a strategy can only be borne so long; then, the question of organization must receive renewed attention. To what extent does greater efficiency require less central control? What is the optimal degree of decentralization? How is it to be achieved? In this chapter, an investigation will be made of the theoretical approaches already developed, then some additional suggestions will be offered.

Definitions

The level of economic centralization has traditionally been treated in terms of information flows and of the particular organizational levels at which various kinds of decisions are made. Hurwicz emphasizes the informational aspects of decentralization, focusing on the characteristics of the transmission of information and upon the nature of the messages transmitted. In his view, an economic process is informationally decentralized if it is operational (with each message describing a set of conceivable resource transfers) and anonymous (with instructions applying to firms of a general class rather than to specific units).[8]

Marschak favors the view that a process is centralized if an outside observer is able, on the basis of signals transmitted between economic agents, to reproduce a process generated by the system.[9] Again the emphasis is upon information—in this case, that which is available to the outside observer.

Another possibility is to define centralization as Zielinski and Lange do, viz., with respect to the way in which economic control is achieved—whether by administrative statute or by market parameters.[10] Parameters are commodity and factor prices, interest rates, depreciation rates, and so on. Statutes (sometimes referred to as "methods of accounting") are directives designed to control activity at a given level in the organizational hierarchy. Complete decentralization would be defined as direction solely by parametric economic forces, while the opposite organizational extreme would have the plan directed strictly by statutes. The variety of possible hybrid forms constitutes a whole spectrum of possibilities. Industrial associations, for example, may be managed exclusively by parameters while enterprises subordinated to them may be controlled solely by directives. The organizational structure in which enterprises are managed by parameters would be classified as more decentralized than one in which industrial associations are controlled by parametric means while other levels of the hierarchy are subject to control by statute.

In this chapter, a disaggregative approach to the problem of decentralization will be attempted; it will incorporate some of the elements of the traditional analysis of organizations and investigate some of the costs and benefits of centralization in specific decision-making areas. It will be shown that the optimal degree of centralization of decision-making authority can best be pursued by investigating the nature of decisions made at various levels in the organizational hierarchy.

First, however, it is necessary from the viewpoint of the command economy to ask: Why decentralize? If decentralization is necessary, how much is desirable? To mention the beneficial aspects of the respective possibilities is to make clear two facts: (a) that the benefits of pushing an economy to either organizational extreme can be obtained only at the cost of losing other highly desirable outcomes and (b) that the actual decision can be an agonizing one, given the necessity for some favorable balance and the hope for an optimal one.

The Benefits of Economic Centralization and Decentralization

The advantages of the centralization of economic decision making have been extensively discussed and require only brief mention.[11] Centralized planning is most likely to insure that the regime's values (which may or may not correspond to the individual consumer's and citizen's preferences) will be enforced. Resources can, with facility, be mobilized and deployed on a large scale. Externalities can be internalized: where it is doubtful that two independent enterprises, for example, would pursue complementary investment projects because uncertainty exists for each party as to the decision of the other, a decision made at the center would instigate appropriate action. The economic process as a whole, as well as individual economic undertakings, are more susceptible through centralization to the overview (*Übersehbarkeit*) of those responsible for establishing societal goals. Centralization makes it possible to eliminate much duplication in decision making in those areas where operations are uniform and susceptible to the formulation of general decision rules.

In the case of a command society, there are some economies inevitably incurred in centralizing and incorporating into the plan activities related to both the economic and the noneconomic spheres of human activity. In East Germany, and to some extent in other bloc states, since many "extra-economic" (cultural, educational, or public health) activities are closely tied to the material production and financial systems and are dependent upon the fulfillment of the plan, they have been drawn into the sphere of central control. Moreover, when incentives are planned rather than left free to respond to market-environmental conditions, not only self-interest, but the broad spectrum of human drives, can allegedly be harnessed to the mechanisms of economic activity.[12]

The beneficial effects of decentralization are likewise generally known, though often left implicit in the literature. To a significant extent, they are associated with the shorter lines of communication (and the consequent greater speed and fidelity of information transmission), the reduced cost of information processing, and the greater responsiveness to changing economic conditions that decentralization assures. Decision making at lower levels permits resolution of conflict at those levels and also provides incentive for greater initiative and ingenuity in managerial performance.

It is not merely that enterprise managers often have better information than that available to the center. It has even been argued that most inefficiencies are not the result of managerial inadequacies or an ineffective incentive system; instead, they are often merely due to poor planning decisions reached by the directors. Bad performance at this level is not protected by institutional safeguards, and planners can fall prey to their poor foresight and insufficient grasp of efficiency concepts.[13]

Finally, if central authority wished merely to engage in perspective (long-term) economic planning and to focus greater attention on noneconomic, humanistic problems, it could rely on market mechanisms to coordinate current economic activity (as Czechoslovakian economists committed to the "New Course" wished to do).[14]

With regard to the optimal organization to guarantee innovation and technological progress, the issue is by no means clear. The degree of desirable decentralization is still being debated and valid points are made on both sides. Some types of knowledge simply cannot efficiently be relayed to the central planner: as an example, decisions connected with innovation appear to be subject to this difficulty. Moreover, without some degree of decentralization, the incentive to innovate is alleged virtually to disappear.

On the other hand, the Eastern Europeans are impressed with the as yet unproved argument that technological progress requires large-scale operations. If industries are organized into associations, the (imagined) requisite scale is achieved. Though they are endowed with significant economic powers, these associations appear to be amenable to the central controls that prove to be less easily applied to fragmented units. Indeed, central control is probably essential if monopolistic actions on the part of the associations are to be avoided. Additionally, under centralized direction of the economy, where technological knowledge is a collective possession rather than private property, there will likely be fewer legal barriers to free dispersion of that knowledge.[15]

The largely abortive reform movement taught us that one of the main difficulties with decentralization is its actual introduction into the system. One can find in socialist literature advocates of gradualism and also supporters of rapid implementation of sweeping reforms.[16] Marschak has referred to this matter as the "fundamental dilemma of reform." When incremental measures are relied upon, the uncertainties of major change are avoided; however, reliance upon small steps may lead to impatience, premature dissatisfaction, and disillusionment. As small steps are undertaken the available empirical information used to evaluate progress may provide misleading clues as to the performance that will be achievable only after the reformed allocation mechanisms have been completely implemented. In short, when incremental measures are applied, the danger exists that the reform will be terminated or despaired of before it could be expected to achieve necessary change.[17]

Decentralization of Decision Making by Economic Function

An awareness of the benefits and costs of various degrees of decision-making centralization is, by itself, of little assistance to those responsible for organizing particular economic activities or institutions. Balassa and Tinbergen, however, have made contributions to the analysis of optimal centralization that render the specific tasks of organization more manageable.

Balassa has shown that the optimum degree of decentralization will vary from industry to industry, depending on the size and structure of each (with centralization of information, for example, preferable in atomistic ones).[18]

In discussing the optimum regime, Tinbergen speaks of various levels of decision making, observing that decisions should be made at a level high enough to make the external effects of those decisions negligible. He reminds us that there is a whole range of different economic functions requiring policy decisions and that each of these has its unique optimum level of decision-making centralization.[19]

Some of the principal decision-making functions that are encountered at various organizational levels include price setting, the types and extent of sales effort, the level of investment and types of investment projects, the pricing and allocation of factors of production, the volume of imports for use in production and for final consumption, expenditures for innovation, the types and assortment of differentiated products, the range of quality of goods and services, and the share of national production sold abroad.

Care must be taken, of course, when we speak of individual levels of appropriate centralization for individual economic functions, since these functions continually interact as part of a general equilibrium system. Consider, as an extreme example, the investment function. It is widely known that planners most keenly desire to keep investment processes under firm central control.[20]

Even if the structure of investments were irrelevant to planners, it is doubtful that satisfactory control could be achieved merely by attempting to control the level of investments. To control the aggregate level of investment is to influence the level of consumption. Keeping the volume of consumer goods below that desired by the populace would generate inflationary pressures and could lead to balance-of-payments difficulties. These would be aggravated should individuals attempt to import the consumer goods sacrificed to the domestic growth effort, for they would have to compete for the foreign exchange also required by investors for capital goods imports. State authorities would probably attempt to eliminate the instability inherent in that situation, even if they overcame the inclination to control scarce foreign exchange to secure high-priority investments. These considerations are especially crucial in the smaller, more trade-dependent nations of Eastern Europe.

Under the much more realistic assumption that planners are also interested in influencing the *structure* of investments, it is even more difficult to ignore vital interactions of economic functions. One cannot promote the development of priority industries simply by providing investment funds. Other resources, especially labor, must be attracted, so it becomes appropriate to influence the structure of wages. Likewise, other resource-furnishing industries have to be developed, or arrangements for purchasing essential resources from beyond national boundaries have to be made.

Supplying labor in selected industries with greater stocks of capital can often be achieved only after various research and development problems have been solved. Likewise, the need for particular kinds of manpower training may be required. Socialists are aware that developing any kind of growth factor requires and, at the same time, furthers the concomitant development of all other growth factors.[21]

It is, therefore, apparent that even though individual economic functions can be positively influenced by either more or less central planning, account has to be taken (either by an iterative approach or by trial-and-error methods) of general equilibrium interactions among the totality of economic functions.

The extent to which centralization is favorable varies by function, and it is apparent that the best performance of the system can be achieved only if planners and managers are able, in each case, to perceive the optimal degree of centralization. For any given economic activity, this will clearly be a function of (a) planners' tastes, (b) the economic milieu or environment (consumers' tastes, production functions, etc.), and (c) the level of centralization of other related economic activities.[22]

Mere cognizance of the requirements of optimal centralization, however, is not enough to achieve planning efficiency. Potential conflicts between the goals, priorities, and methods favored by policymakers at different levels must be overcome through effective organizational methods and authority patterns. The planners must also be willing, having already recognized the need for various degrees of decentralization in the decision areas mentioned, to accede to systemic needs by actually relinquishing some of their political and economic prerogatives.[a]

---

[a]The Czechoslovakian invasion should teach us (if the reforms in progress in the last decade did not) that, for political reasons alone, decentralization could prove most difficult.

Difficulties may prove to be greatest where decentralization is most needed, which is probably in the area of pricing.[23] Given the current state of planning technology and computer capacity, pricing that can cope with the needs of a dynamic industrial order can be achieved only through decentralization. The day may come when a continuous process of calculating shadow prices will be feasible so that price distortions and rigidity no longer represent an unsurmountable barrier to economic calculation and acceptable performance.[24] That day has not arrived yet, however, and many analysts remain doubtful that it will ever come.

An excellent example of the double-edged sword of centralization can be seen in the problem of factor pricing. On the one hand, substantial benefits of efficient allocation accrue to completely decentralized organization, for the enterprise manager is in the best position to know prevailing scarcity conditions and and the prices he should be willing to pay for factors. On the other hand, centralizing this decision under inflationary conditions may make it easier to keep wage increases from exceeding increases in industrial productivity.

It has already been mentioned, with regard to innovation, that certain benefits accrue to the centralization of decision-making authority. An accretion to these benefits, however, can be achieved by an appropriate mix of policies, some of which require decentralized decision making.

If this analysis is correct, one view of the economic reforms is that in each area of decision making, central authorities should have been seeking to discover to what extent they must loosen the reins of control. We now have some clues as to how they should proceed the next time reorganization activity comes into vogue.

The Model of Optimal Decentralization: A Classic Minimization Problem

Decisions must be made with respect to the degree of decentralization that will provide the greatest effectiveness (defined in terms of the degree to which a given institutional arrangement can meet the goals of the plan) for each organizational function. Then, plan makers responsible for the organization of economic institutions are confronted with a classic minimization problem. They must minimize the deviation of the degree of centralization actually obtaining in the economic system from an ideal level of decentralization that would assure the achievement of planners' objectives.[b]

---

[b] Clearly, the conceptual nature of the problem should be emphasized here. All of the costs and benefits of centralization and decentralization are not quantifiable, and data for such a problem could not be generated from a simple computer program. The methodology described can only serve as a general format to be kept in mind in the planning process.

Conceptually, then, given a particular economic environment and planners' goals, a schedule is made of the decision-making tasks in ascending order of the degree of centralization each task requires. Two points will be associated with each planning task in the ranking: the first, Ca, will represent the actual degree of centralization inherent in the prevailing economic organization; the second, $\hat{C}a$, will represent the ideal degree of centralization (that most likely to permit plan fulfillment). The objective is simply the minimization of the sum of the squared errors, $\Sigma(Ca_i - \hat{C}a_i)^2$. The subscript i, of course, represents decision-making functions $(1, 2, \ldots n)$.

Expressed in this fashion, the problem is precisely analogous to the deviation of the normal equations of bivariate linear or curvilinear regression. Reference can be made to any of the standard works of economic statistics or econometrics. Beginning with the expression $Ca = \alpha + \beta \hat{C}a + u$, and wishing to estimate the α and β that give the line of best fit, we minimize the sum of the squared errors, ξ, for the expression:

$$\xi = \sum_{i=1}^{n} (Ca_i - \alpha - \beta \hat{C}a_i)^2$$

The process involves little more than expanding this equation, differentiating partially with respect to α and β, setting the results equal to zero for the two resulting equations, and checking to verify that a minimum (rather than a maximum) has indeed been found.

The slope and level of the function are determined by both the economic environment (technology, the capacity for informational transfer, motivation and skill or managerial talent, etc.) and the goals of planners. It is unlikely that the function would be linear; given planners' preferences for a high degree of control, a generalized parabolic function seems more reasonable. A parabolic curve represents a monotonically increasing function, which can be expressed in this instance as

$$Ca = \alpha Cr^\beta$$

Since the function is positively accelerated, $0 < \beta < 1$. It can be linearized by taking logarithms of both sides:

$$\log Ca = \log \alpha + \beta \log Cr$$

where $\log Ca$ is a linear function of $\log Cr$.

Individual points on the curvilinear function would express the appropriate planner's objective, i.e., the degree of centralization at which there is a correspondence of the marginal costs and benefits associated with the centralization of individual planning tasks. Obviously, the relative prices that would have to be available in order actually to calculate marginal costs and benefits simply are not available. In some cases, this is because inadequate pricing systems are applied in Eastern Europe; and, in other cases, it is because it is not apparent how the various costs and benefits could be expressed in pecuniary terms. The relevant (rather amorphous) benefits would have to be pursued on the basis of the planner's (often intuitive) calculations of organizational effectiveness.

This calculation problem is an important element of the planner's dilemma. It means we must consider three possible levels of centralization: the actual level, the planner's target level, and the ideal level. A miscalculation of the ideal level of centralization will mean a deviation of Ca from $\hat{C}a$, even if the actual degree of centralization achieved corresponds to the planner's target level.

Expressing the optimal degree of centralization of an economic function in terms of an equality of marginal values implies, of course, subscription to a diminishing marginal productivity theory of national economic control. Under a given organizational technology (with the availability of particular managerial skills, information, and computational technology, etc.), it is apparent that the state can manage only so much. The marginal effectiveness of control diminishes as control extends over more areas. This seemed to be the logic of reformers, too, who desired to limit their direct influence in the 1960s to the "structurally determining" sectors.

The point representing the actual degree of centralization achieved will deviate to some extent from the relevant target point on the curve, even though planners strive to structure the economy's institutional development so that the deviation is minimal. To the extent that organizational arrangements deviate from the optimum, dissatisfaction or "organizational tension"[25] will tend to increase, with the degree of restiveness serving as motivation for correction or reform.

Though organizational tension likewise is not susceptible to quantitative measurement, successful planners must perceive to some degree the extent to which economic organization is failing to satisfy the expectations of the economy's power structure. The intensity of the sense of failure associated with expressions of discontent appearing in various forms— crude though such indicators may be—can be read as a signal (once organizational tension exceeds a given threshold point) that reorganization may be imminent.

Evaluating the Success of Decentralization

In the attempt to achieve a quantitative evaluation of the effects of economic organization on the performance of economic systems, clear-cut success is extremely elusive. Marschak's analysis of Yugoslavian performance before and after centralization is a good example of the problems involved. His laudable attempt yielded results that he himself described as "staggeringly obscure."[26] The weakness of economic theory and economic measurement in this area is, as Marschak suggests, a major challenge to systems economists.

A recent study by Gisser and Jonas seems to rise to the challenge and is of particular interest here because it emphasizes opportunities lost by the Soviet Union because of overcentralization.[27] They divide the Soviet economy into agricultural and nonagricultural sectors, each approximated by a Cobb-Douglas production function. Utilizing special output, labor and capital indices permits comparison of actual Soviet historical growth to a Bukharinian alternative hypothesis of Soviet growth. They assume that, in the absence of collectivization, a free farm sector would have enjoyed a "more evenly distributed disembodied technical change over time," one which would have followed the Western pattern.[28]

Gisser and Jonas base their analysis on the notion that the process of out-migration from the farm represents a "channel through which progress in the agricultural sector can be 'exported' to the industrial sector."[29] Their calculations indicate that its absorption there would permit generation of a growth rate higher than that actually achieved in the industrialization period. Even if there had been no change in farm out-migration, projected hypothetical results were as good as those the Soviet Union enjoyed historically.

Other worthwhile endeavors have been made to illuminate the nature of economic growth in Soviet-type economies.[30] Usually, as in the Gisser-Jonas study, a Cobb-Douglas or sometimes a Constant Elasticity of Substitution (CES) production function is specified, utilizing a geometric weighting of factor inputs. The estimations, based upon output indices, give a rough indication of growth rates and the relative contributions of capital, labor, and technology (or the "residual"). It is scarcely ever possible, however, to apply this sort of quantitative analysis to one country in two different periods—before and after a major reorganizational endeavor has been attempted—as Marschak did for Yugoslavia.

It would seem unfortunate, however, not to have more disaggregative indicators of organizational success, especially given the desirability of investigating individual decision-making functions as an approach to the problem of optimal economic centralization. Where organizational effects can be investigated, studies of economic progress in subglobal performance areas would represent a most welcome contribution to the literature on socialist economics. In addition to the question of growth as a measure of effectiveness, it would, therefore, also be desirable to inquire into the extent to which an innovative spirit (or lack of the same) characterizes enterprise managers. It would likewise be worthwhile to analyze such things as improvements in product quality and product differentiation, the growth of international trade within the bloc and beyond, and the extent to which productive factors are underemployed.

The blueprint for analytical action hinted at in the preceding paragraph

implies some measures of organizational performance that are not susceptible to quantitative evaluation. Moreover, as was suggested earlier, to the
extent that optimal decentralization of economic decision making eludes
the planners, "organizational tension" (implying the possibility of reorganization) will be generated within the system. There is likewise, of
course, no satisfactory quantitative measure of organizational tension in
the command economy.

Nevertheless, Brzeski suggests that considerations of *Realpolitik* are of
paramount importance in the pursuit of optimal planning organization.[31]
Model building, he indicates, is the farthest thing from the minds of communist leaders attempting to reorganize their economies. Even if they were
so inclined, they lack the information that would be necessary objectively
to analyze the organizational options open to them—information on the
productivity of an organizational form; its breaking-in characteristics; its
"decay function" (the rate at which organizational structures disintegrate
because of widespread "cynical disbelief in the permanence of institutions,
procedures, and positions" prevailing in Soviet-type economies);[32] and the
costs of organizational changeover.

If Brzeski is right in postulating that communist leaders have never
attempted to achieve optimality in economic performance (basically, according to the *Realpolitik* analysis, because they have never com-
prehended it), cataclysmic overhaul of the economic organization has
always been and must always be political in nature.[33] If that is the case, and
reorganization is a function of the preferences of the planners (such preferences being but loosely linked to economic growth indicators), quantitative
analysis cannot, even if successful, tell us all we need to know with regard
to the prospects of an organizational structure prevailing at a given point in
time.

It would seem preferable to pursue understanding of organizational
centralization in command systems by paying attention not merely to
(a) the growth indicators, but also to (b) disaggregative, subglobal indicators (both quantitative and qualitative) of economic performance and
(c) the degree of "organizational tension" (the conditions of *Realpolitik*) to
which economic decision makers in the country under investigation are
exposed.

Notes

1. Cf. Gregory Grossman, "Notes for a Theory of the Command
Economy," *Soviet Studies*, vol. 15, no. 2 (October 1963), p. 107.

2. This description is still used by some socialists of reform bent. See
Bela Csikos-Nagy, *Socialist Economic Policy* (London: Longman, 1973),

pp. 82-83. Overbureaucratization, incidentally, is merely to be understood as a traditional phenomenon occurring in the postrevolution phase during the proletariat's consolidation of power. However, "at a later stage in the process of stabilization of the socialist society, decentralization should come to the fore. This is a sign that the . . . organizational structure is . . . in a position to adjust to criteria of economic rationality."

3. Cf. Edward Lipinski, "The Theory of the Socialist Enterprise," in *Economic Development for Eastern Europe*, Michael Kaser, ed., (New York: St. Martin's, 1968), p. 294.

4. Two East German writers refer, for example, to suggestions to decentralize substantial decision-making powers to the industrial association level as revisionism. If the socialist state cannot directly intervene, the "power instrument of the labor class" would be irresponsibly weakened, its class character completely negated, and the objective requirements of socialism frustrated. See Rudi Weidauer and Albert Wetzel, *Sozialistische Leitung im Betrieb und Kombinat*, 2nd ed. (East Berlin: Verlag die wirtschaft, 1974), p. 26. This book is proof that a study on organization can be written in East Germany without a single mention of economic reform, either in the guise of the New Economic System or its successor, the Economic System of Socialism.

5. A positive view of the limited extent of the reforms has been given (apparently almost as an offhand comment) by Joseph C. Brada. He says, "Indeed, the relatively minor scope of the reforms may be an advantage since there are likely to be many unforeseen negative repercussions from their introduction." See his "Allocative Efficiency and the System of Economic Management in Some Socialist Countries," *Kyklos*, vol. 27, no. 2 (1974), p. 273. The remark is somewhat humorous (or painful, depending on where one's sympathies lie) because it is only too true. The advantage of an automobile that has ceased to run is that one is unlikely to have an accident in it.

6. For an analysis of this phenomenon in the area of foreign trade, see Chapter 8.

7. Ames holds that the potential impact of financial forces arises from the Soviet Credit Reform of 1930, since which time (traditional views of Eastern and Western economists notwithstanding) the standard physical allocation techniques applied in the Soviet sphere have been under the threat of attack. These views were hinted at in his article, "The Structure of General Equilibrium in a Planned Economy," *Jahrbuch der Wirtschaft Osteuropas*, Band 1 (Wien-Munchen: Gunter Olzog Verlag, 1970), pp. 15-61, but developed more specifically in "Theorie de la Planification Économique," *Revue d'Économie Politique,* vol. 84, no. 3, May/June 1974), pp. 364-398.

8. Leonid Hurwicz, "On the Concept and Possibility of Informational Decentralization," *American Economic Review*, vol. 59, no. 2 (May 1969), pp. 513-524. Also see his "Efficiency of Decentralized Structures," in *Value and Plan*, Gregory Grossman, ed. (Berkeley: University of California Press, 1960), pp. 176-183.

9. Thomas Marschak, "On the Comparison of Centralized and Decentralized Economies," *American Economic Review*, vol. 59, no. 2 (May 1969), pp. 525-532. A later, more sophisticated formulation of the "outside observer" concept can be found in Marschak's "Decentralizing the Command Economy: The Study of a Pragmatic Strategy for Reformers," in *Plan and Market*, Morris Bornstein, ed. (New Haven: Yale University Press, 1973), see pp. 39-47.

10. See. J. G. Zielinski, *On the Theory of Socialist Planning* (Ibadan: Oxford University Press, 1968), pp. 103-110. For one unable to read Polish, it is difficult to know to what extent the ideas presented in these lectures belong to Zielinski. He cites a paper of Lange's available only in Polish and declares himself "greatly indebted" to Professor Lange.

11. Cf. Grossman, "Notes for a Theory," op. cit., pp. 112-114.

12. See Robert A. Solo, *Economic Organizations and Social Systems* (New York: Bobbs-Merrill, 1967), p. 59. Perhaps much should be made of this (though not here), for economic and social life can take on an entirely different complexion in an environment in which numerous institutions are designed merely to function as molders of good attitudes and generators of dedication to the "victory of socialism." For reference to some serious studies on the methodology of generating nonpecuniary incentives see Hannelore Hamel, *Das sowjetische Herrschaftsprinzip des demokratischen Zentralismus in der Wirtschaftsordnung Mitteldeutschlands*, (Berlin: Duncker & Humblot, 1966), pp. 165-167.

13. An exponent of this view is Alan Abouchar. See his "Inefficiency and Reform in the Soviet Economy," *Soviet Studies*, vol. 25, no. 1 (July 1973), pp. 66-76.

14. Ludek Rychetnik and Oldrich Kyn, "Optimal Central Planning in 'Competitive Socialism'," *Czechoslovak Economic Papers*, 10, Prague, 1968, p. 33, optimistically claim that when "the major part of current economic coordination is done by market mechanism . . . the center can concentrate on perspective planning and, at the same time, shift its attention from economic to the humanistic role." They hold that "only an economic mechanism, based on a combination of perspective planning and market mechanism, is adequate for the needs of a developed socialist society."

15. For a commendable description of the respective advantages of centralization and decentralization in the progressive economy, see Solo, *Economic Organizations* op. cit., chapters 12 and 13.

16. Weidauer and Wetzel, *Sozialistische Leitung*, op. cit., p. 215, claim in a single paragraph that (a) organization changes introduced in rapid, short-term succession or introduced simultaneously must be avoided and (b) carefully prepared changes should be so implemented that the new organization functions in short order.

17. Marschak, "Decentralizing the Command Economy," op. cit., p. 60.

18. Bela Balassa, "Strategic Theory and its Applications: Discussion," *American Economic Review*, vol. 59, no. 2 (May 1969), p. 536.

19. Jan Tinbergen, "Some Suggestions on a Modern Theory of the Optimum Regime," in *Socialism, Capitalism and Economic Growth: Essays Presented to Maurice Dobb*, by C. H. Feinstein, ed. (New York: Cambridge, 1967), pp. 130-131.

20. Marschak, "Decentralizing the Command Economy," p. 55, says that decentralizing investment decisions "comes last and is likely to be very incomplete, the center retaining at least some control over the direction of enterprise investment." Further (p. 58), he explains that "too much seems at stake, and the consequences of investment mistakes must be lived with too long, to trust the matter to many separate agents, to the self-policing induced by profits or other incentives, and to the imperfect controls a weakened central agency can impose."

21. Sigrid Maier and Martliese Mehnert, "Intensivierung des volkswirtschaftlichen Reproduktionsprozesses und sozialistische Akkumulation," *Wirtschaftswissenschaft*, vol. 19, no. 8 (August 1971), p. 1156.

22. John M. Montias refers to (a) as the set of policies planners effect, to (b) likewise as the environment, and (c) as system rules and organizational patterns. The vector of outcomes observed in any given period is a function of these variables in his model. See his paper, "A Framework for Theoretical Analysis of Economic Reforms in Soviet-type Economies," in *Plan and Market*, op. cit., pp. 65-122.

23. See Chapter 4.

24. Whether or not a top-level optimum can be achieved, it has been shown that there is some point in attempting to achieve more satisfactory performance through incremental planning measures, the theory of second best notwithstanding. Under certain conditions, a more efficient operation can be accomplished by optimizing in certain sectors, even though a top-level optimum is not possible. See E. J. Mishan, "Second Thoughts on Second Best," *Oxford Economic Papers*, 14 (October 1962), pp. 205-217, reprinted in his *Welfare Economics: Ten Introductory Essays*, Second Ed. (New York: Random House, 1969).

25. Cf. Alexander Gerschenkron, *Economic Backwardness in Historical Perspective* (New York: Praeger, 1962).

26. Thomas A. Marschak, "Centralized Versus Decentralized Resource Allocation: The Yugoslav 'Laboratory'," *Quarterly Journal of Economics*, vol. 82, no. 4 (November 1968), pp. 561-587. This article is an answer to the often voiced lament that systems economists are prone either to discuss theory in a vacuum or to discuss particular cases without references to theory.

27. Micha Gisser and Paul Jonas, "Soviet Growth in Absence of Centralized Planning: A Hypothetical Alternative," *Journal of Political Economy*, vol. 82, no. 2, Part I (March/April 1974), pp. 333-351.

28. Ibid., p. 341.

29. Ibid., p. 342.

30. Cf. Evsey D. Domar, "On the Measurement of Technical Change," *Economic Journal*, vol. 71, no. 284 (December 1961), pp. 709-729; E. R. Brubaker, "Synthetic Factor Shares, the Elasticity of Substitution, and the Residual in Soviet Growth," *Review of Economics and Statistics*, vol. 52, no. 1 (February 1970), pp. 100-104; and the extensive work done in the Joint Economic Committee's *Economic Developments in Countries of Eastern Europe: A Compendium of Papers* (Washington, D.C.: U.S. Government Printing Office, 1970). especially see Thad P. Alton, "Economic Structure and Growth in Eastern Europe."

31. Andrzej Brzeski, "Social Engineering and Realpolitik in Communist Economic Reorganization," in *Essays in Socialism and Planning in Honor of Carl Landauer*, Gregory Grossman, ed. (Englewood Cliffs, New Jersey: Prentice-Hall, 1970), see pp. 159ff.

32. Ibid., p. 157. To develop the organization model, it was necessary, of course, to abstract from some of these problems which Brzeski discusses at length.

33. Along the same lines, "marketization" schemes are seen as a symptom of the decomposition of politics in communist states as much as an attempt to rationalize economies. After all, Brzeski says, though these economies are doing badly, they are not performing disastrously. See ibid., p. 176.

3

Economic Organization II: On Information Flows and Organizational Effectiveness

When the market ceases to play a prime role in resources allocation, it is evident that substitutes must be sought to perform the functions of prices, wages, profits, and other market signals. These information sources will not be generated automatically by central economic planning as they are in systems permitting at least quasi-free interaction of supply and demand forces.

In socialism, information is transmitted to various economic agents by directives, success indicators, and other messages. One need reflect but little on the weighty functions of these information forms to comprehend the reason for the extensive organizational undertakings of the planned economies. Consider, for example, success indicators as an informational proxy for profits. Success indicators alone must (a) indicate the effectiveness of enterprise performance to directors, (b) serve as a choice criterion for enterprise managers, (c) indicate where (and in what magnitude) managerial bonuses are appropriate, and (d) permit the regulation of the availability of capital to enterprises.[1] When committees perform economic functions otherwise carried out by markets, an administrative task of tremendous magnitude is implied.

To this point, the socialists have made no known attempts to measure the administrative costs of establishing large bureaucratic systems to service their economies' information needs. Naturally, the publication of any such attempt would be an ideological (not to mention a public relations) absurdity. It is apparent, from the published statistical works of the socialist countries, that appropriate data are not collected for such a purpose. Even for internal planning purposes, it is highly improbable that such measurements are made.

If one had data revealing the economic costs of central planning, one would wish to compare it to comparable data for alternative forms of economic organization. Since such data are also unavailable for nonsocialist economies, their generation could service nothing more than the hope that other countries would follow suit or that such measures might at least make intertemporal comparisons possible later.

The material in this chapter was originally published with Jozef M. van Brabant as coauthor as "L'Industrie Socialiste de l'Information: Evaluer l'Efficience de l'Organisation dans les Économies Centralement Planifiées" ("The Socialist Information Industry: Measures of Organizational Effectiveness in Centrally Planned Economies") *Revue d'Études Comparatives Est-Ouest*, vol. 6, no. 4, pp. 45-63.

For these reasons, one would scarcely expect the Soviet Union to research the question of comparative bureaucratic efficiency. Still, Soviet theoreticians have shown rather keen interest in recent years in determining what systems of economic information might be developed and implemented to achieve optimal economic performance.[2]

This is not to deny that Soviet-type planners generally neither understand nor pursue concepts of optimality and that analysis remains largely in the domain of the mathematical school. Nevertheless, information theory has recently been productive of suggestions that are receiving wide attention.

The distinguished N.P. Federenko advocates continued improvement of measuring and classifying economic information, of organizing it for use in programming models, of evaluating informational organization through a "unified system of normative economics," of unifying economic documentation, and of elaborating and coordinating information systems throughout the economy.[3] This seems to represent a step toward an analysis of organizational efficiency.

It is the purpose of this chapter to propose some conceptual and practical measures of the effectiveness of organizations and of the degree of centralization prevailing in them. Though the question of economic reform no longer has the appeal it had in the 1960s, the need for continued improvement in managing the centrally administered economy remains apparent. Measurements of organizational effectiveness also remain important simply because planners still need to know where they are and where they are capable of going.

The attempt to determine the actual extent of central control prevailing in the economy can produce additional benefits. To measure centralization is to illuminate the nature of the exchange of information between the center and the periphery and to discover the level in the hierarchy at which decision-making authority for various economic functions is located. Above all, however, planners must be aware of the costs of organizing the economy according to a given format, and they must be able to evaluate the potential savings or losses associated with incremental or major organizational change.

Crude Information Flow Measurements and the Degree of Centralization

Measures of varying degrees of sophistication are possible. At the outset, some of the more fundamental ones will be treated. As has been mentioned, measures currently under discussion by specialists and additional ones to be suggested here often defy calculation. Some intuitive perception of the situation pertaining in a socialist economy will often suffice, however, for purposes of economic control. As a consequence, even purely conceptual measures are worth discussing, and some would also be worthy of implementation.

Any proposed centralization measurement must have reference to the flows of information requisite to economic decision making. Hurwicz refers to interlevel (vertical) informational flows as "messages,"[4] while Brzeski aptly calls intralevel (horizontal) exchanges "elaborations."[5]

Messages are defined as "proposals, bids, plans, information about technology or preferences," and a later paper by Hurwicz develops the notion that messages are a function of the environment and of previous messages. A probabilistic model could be constructed developing the rules and relations of information communication, thus accounting for uncertainty in planning processes.[6] To this point, the question of uncertainty, though always of some importance, seems much less pressing for the command environment than for the nonsocialist milieu. The very inflexibility that guarantees inefficiency in planning also assures a high degree of stability and a relatively innocuous degree of uncertainty.

The relative absence of formalized "horizontal" messages has been explained by Kornai, who indicates that information of this type is referred to as "market relations" in traditional economics.[7]

It might be possible, on the basis of the number of messages of average length[8] and of the type of message sent, to establish the degree of centralization prevailing in an economy. There are three basic types of information flows, viz., indicatory, regulatory, and auditory.

Indicatory messages represent the transmission of information or requests for information required in the planning process. Where the economy is characterized by a high degree of homogeneity of outputs and production processes (so that operations can to a large extent be based upon decision rules), relatively few indicatory messages might provide optimal efficiency; generally speaking, however, highly centralized economies require the transmission of large quantities of such information.

Regulatory or command messages are also prime informational characteristics of the Soviet-type economy. These can take the form of specific (or in Hurwiczian terminology, nonanonymous) instructions (e.g., directives regarding the quantity of a certain type of productive resource allocated to a specific enterprise), or they can be transmissions of general (anonymous) information directed to all firms of a given class. The Lange-Lerner rules are of the latter type.

Auditory messages are ex post transmissions of information, the processing of which is designed to answer the question of whether economic activity has conformed to the plan. The requests for transmissions and processing of auditory messages will generally be based upon statistical sampling techniques, but even this aspect of command control requires great effort and cost.[9]

Letting mi represent the sum of indicatory messages, mr regulatory messages, and ma auditory messages, the total volume of information transmitted can be given by $mi + mr + ma = mt$. Since, as was mentioned before, the Soviet-type economy requires extensive flows of information, one is tempted to measure centralization by the ratio mi/mt. Since all types of messages are sent in greater number in the command economy, however, this measure may prove to be an inadequate indicator. It is difficult to say a priori whether mr and ma will grow more or less rapidly than mi as the degree of central control increases. As a starter, it might make more sense to consider the ratio of regulatory messages to the total, mr/mt.

A more precise measure of central intervention might be developed in terms of the type of regulatory messages transmitted. If mr_g represents general directives (parameters) and mr_s represents specific nonanonymous messages (administrative orders), the ratio $mr_s/(mr_s + mr_g)$ or mr_s/mr, may give some indication as to the likelihood that difficulties of control can be expected to develop in the bureaucracy.

This measure may also give some indication as to whether or not a particular industry can be decentralized so that most decisions can be made at the association level. Lipinski has observed that the optimal size of an institution depends on the most favorable and rational division of functions. An association that has heterogeneous production outputs and functions must be decentralized.[10] This says nothing more than that one must be able to hold the ratio of specific regulatory messages to total regulatory messages rather low if centralization is to be effective.

Although these ratios may give some indication as to the informational aspects of the organization of the economic system, they fail to incorporate a clear indication as to the locus of decision-making power in the organization hierarchy. Perhaps the seat of authority for particular economic tasks and decisions can be located, at least in conceptual terms, by a measure of the regulatory messages that are transmitted and by the number of organizational levels (tiers) over which each regulatory message must be relayed.

An index of the degree of centralization prevailing over time I_c could be developed along these lines. Letting mr_0 represent regulatory messages in the base period, mr_t represent regulatory messages in the current period, LT represent the number of levels over which any decision must be relayed before reaching the enterprise, and letting j $(j = 1, 2, \ldots, n)$ represent the enterprise for which the message is designated, an indication of the increase or decrease in distances messages travel through the hierarchy would be given by

$$I_c = \frac{\sum (LT)_t (mr_j)_0}{\sum (LT)_0 (mr_j)_0}$$

An indication of the accretion of messages transmitted over given levels in successive time periods would be given by

$$I'_c = \frac{\sum(mr)_t \, (LT)_0}{\sum(mr)_0 \, (LT)_0}$$

1902934

An approach to the measurement of centralization through horizontal information flows would address itself to the utilization of message "elaborations," *me*. To the extent that horizontal links are lacking in a system, contacts between units at the same level in the planning hierarchy can be made only through higher levels—in an ascending then descending route from one enterprise to another or from one industrial association to another. In agreement with works cited above by Kornai and Brzeski, Zielinski holds that the degree of centralization corresponds to the number of horizontal links, or the measure *me/mt*; the smaller this ratio, the more centralized the organization is.[11]

Given the unavailability of the appropriate statistical data, these measures remain of strictly conceptual value. Planners must proceed, nevertheless, in their endeavors to organize efficiently. How this can best be done remains a question to decision makers in socialist economies, while the process of trial and error continues. If anything like efficient operation is to be achieved, the organizational effort must be enlightened by knowledge of the economic structure. Reorganizing institutions to improve performance will require, in each area of economic decision making, some reasonable estimate of the flow of information and degree of decentralization (prevailing and desired) as given by the decentralization ratios and indices discussed.

Before leaving the matter of simple ratio measures of the degree of centralization, it seems worthwhile to mention some possibilities that could be undertaken quite easily in practice. Such measurements would not only be entirely feasible—they could be undertaken with facility.

Measuring the productivity of economic control need not be complicated. The socialists have long undertaken measures of labor and agricultural productivity.[a] Why not take the ratio of national output to the number of individuals employed in generating, transmitting, and processing information? Then, it would be simple to make international comparisons of output per economic bureaucrat or planning official.

Another interesting measure of bureaucratic productivity would be the ratio of total labor to bureaucratic labor, i.e., all workers involved in the planning effort. It would be delightful to know how many workers a single Soviet bureaucrat can service. A comparable measure could be made, of

---

[a] Every sophomore can memorize how many Soviet citizens can be fed by each Soviet farmer. Extending the notion of productivity to the information industry also seems sophomorically simple.

course, for Western countries: the ratio of the total labor force to the total number of administrators in economics ministries, government agencies involved in economic affairs, and so on. Not only could one develop control productivity statistics for the economy as a whole, but it would be of interest to make interindustrial comparisons, generating these ratios for individual sectors of the economy.

General Equilibrium Measurements of Centralization and of Information Flows

This section will return to conceptual measurements likely to remain unfeasible in practice. Hopefully, though, they will be of didactic value for planners and students of the centrally administered economy.[12] Since the approach of this section will be more sophisticated, suggested measurements would require a greater planning investment than those discussed previously.

Again the notion of messages will be fundamental to the endeavor to determine the magnitudes and implications of planning information flows. A Leontief model of the economy's informational inputs and outputs will be developed, and its focus will be on indicatory messages. Similar systems, however, could be constructed equally well for regulatory and auditory messages.

It is unthinkable that complete information could be transmitted about production sets, resource endowments, and indifference maps. Nevertheless, as Hurwicz has pointed out, planning participants can process messages as complex as those "occurring in a Walrasian market process," which is to say that proposed input-output vectors and price vectors can indeed be transmitted.[13]

It will not be possible to treat the quality (accuracy, thoroughness, etc.) of messages in the information flow. Indirectly, of course, poor quality will often require greater volumes of information than would otherwise be necessary. Moreover, inadequate quality is reflected in a reduced level of total output with given resources and in a lower degree of satisfaction of economic agents with the final outputs.[14] Though this consideration is a matter of general knowledge, it is not apparent how one might attempt to incorporate it into a quantitative system.

For the informational input-output model, a five-tier hierarchy will be assumed, the tiers of which will be represented by subscripts: enterprises e, groups of enterprises or industrial associations g, ministries m, the central planning agency c, and the top economic directors or the relevant party members d.

The structure of the model is traditional. Total information required is the sum of information flows lubricating current productive processes and the final demand for information required for future plans. Assuming that there is an interindustry proportionality that is stable,[b] let $\overline{mi}$ represent the vector of gross informational requirements, A the technology (information) matrix, and $\overline{mp}$ the vector of net informational output or of final demand for planning purposes. This vector gives information required for current final use of private consumers, social consumers, and "investments" or information required to improve the planning process. In summary notation, $\overline{mi}$ = $A\overline{mi} + \overline{mp}$.

The technology matrix has elements a_{ij}, where the subscript i denotes the source and j is the destination of informational inputs. The input coefficients are assumed fixed at a given period of time and reflect planning information associated with production technology. Rather than writing out the full technology matrix, it has been partitioned into its components according to informational tiers. The basic construction is as shown below:

$$
\begin{bmatrix} mi_e \\ mi_g \\ mi_m \\ mi_c \\ mi_d \end{bmatrix} = \begin{bmatrix} A_{ii} & A_{ik} & A_{in} & ap_i & aq_i \\ A_{ki} & A_{kk} & A_{kn} & ap_k & aq_k \\ A_{ni} & A_{nk} & A_{nn} & ap_n & aq_n \\ \overline{ap}_i & \overline{ap}_k & \overline{ap}_n & ap_p & ap_q \\ \overline{aq}_i & \overline{aq}_k & \overline{aq}_n & aq_p & aq_q \end{bmatrix} \begin{bmatrix} mi_e \\ mi_g \\ mi_m \\ mi_c \\ mi_d \end{bmatrix} + \begin{bmatrix} mp_e \\ mp_g \\ mp_m \\ mp_c \\ mp_d \end{bmatrix}
$$

In the construction of the technology matrix, top directors (e.g., central committee of the party) and the central planning agency are each considered as single economic entities (decision makers or information processors). Subscripts in the information matrix are $(1, 2, \ldots, i)$ for enterprises, $(j \ldots k)$ for groups, and $(1 \ldots n)$ for ministries. Matrices include A_{ii} (of order i), A_{ik} [of order i-by-$(k - i)$], A_{in} [of order i-by-$(n - k)$], and A_{ki} [of order $(k - i)$-by-i]. Column vectors include ap_i (or length i) and aq_i (of length i). Row vectors are $\overline{ap}_i$ (of length i), $\overline{ap}_k$ (of length i), and so on. Scalars are ap_p, ap_q, aq_p, and aq_q.

As always, given some desired or required output of information, one can solve the system through matrix inversion and determine what net informational inputs will be necessary. On the other hand, one might equally well determine, on the basis of given information, transmitting and processing technology and some feasible volume of informational inputs in relation to how much informational output can be achieved.

One can conceptualize the present information system as one infor-

---

[b] This stability is more likely to be achieved if the message flows are measured in terms of their monetary costs, i.e., the costs of bureaucratic labor, etc., involved in generating, transmitting, and processing information.

mally approximating the system presented here. Using the same notation, $m = Am + mp$, planners begin any given planning period with a desired set of final informational outputs mp' corresponding to a desired set of physical outputs. They will estimate initially the amount of information m' that appears to be necessary to guarantee satisfaction of these final demands. Probably mp' and m' in the initial plan will be inconsistent. A solution, however, can be reached by iteration. Given m' and mp', the equation above implies a new set of gross informational outputs m'' by the relation $m'' = Am' + mp'$. Now, one continually substitutes more appropriate m values, converging to an equilibrium in a few iterations (so that $Am' + mp' = m'' = m' = m$). This mode of exposition is Michael Montias'.[15]

In a strictly centralized system of planning, communications are carried on only vertically between successive tiers. As a matter of principle, then, there will be no intratier communication, and each tier will communicate only with subordinate and superordinate tiers in the hierarchy. Assume, for example, that enterprise 1 is subordinated to association j, and enterprise 5 is subordinated to association k. Both of these associations are subordinated to ministry 1. Any necessary communication between enterprises 1 and 5 must be routed upwards over association j to the ministry and back down over association k to enterprise 5. Should two enterprises belonging to different ministries be forced to communicate, messages must be routed all the way to the central planning level.

In practice, the elements of the information matrix that reflect intratier communication and communication between elements vertically unrelated in the information system will actually assume nonzero values on occasion. This occurs in fact only because *tolkachi*-type operations perform informal allocatory (and, therefore, informational) functions.[c]

As a result of *tolkachi*-type operations, enterprises are able to communicate (a) with other enterprises; (b) (probably) with other industries; (c) (definitely) with ministries, and if the enterprise is of particular importance (*e.g.*, one engaged in armaments production), it will have direct access; (d) to the central planning board; and (e) (possibly) with the central committee.

Putting the information flow of the command economy into this general equilibrium framework provides not only a good overview of the structure of information exchanges, but it permits us to observe how the system and planners can respond to disproportionalities (whether breakdowns or overfulfillment of plan targets) as they occur. In the more unfortunate case of a breakdown, it matters little whether a bottleneck appears in the production process or whether the information flow per se is afflicted. Both events

---

[c] *Tolkachi* are the "pushers" or "expeditors" who perform functions outside formal hierarchical lines. Doubtlessly, apart from *tolkachi*, other informal channels of communication exist.

work simply to render obsolete the planning information generated and processed during the preparation of the plan.

Minor problems arise constantly, of course, and the existence of *tolkachi* assures that sufficient flexibility is maintained in the system to prevent it from experiencing rigor mortis.

Should a disporportionality occur (*e.g.*, a crop failure or a bumper crop), the planning agency can regroup its forces. Information flows can be reestimated from previous plans, from simple extrapolations, and so on. New information can be collected and processed, though it may be necessary to sacrifice some precision for haste. Plans tend to be available only at late dates in the first place, and when a breakdown occurs, the process must be expedited if the information is not to be too late to be of any value whatsoever.

Above all, it is significant that, when a disproportionality occurs and the signals broadcasted by the plan become false, any resultant dislocations are general equilibrium disturbances. Those industries that receive direct inputs from the bottleneck or unexpectedly abundant industry are the primary victims of planning information that has become erroneous. These industries, however, furnish other secondary industries, which likewise experience the lack of correspondence between plan information and actual input deliveries.

Evidently, the interesting thing about a breakdown is not that it occurs, but what response it evokes from directors and planning agencies. If a disproportionality occurs in the Stalinist system, there will generally be no perceived need to generate information for a completely new matrix. Though the burden of formulating new plans may be greater initially, implementation is facilitated in the Stalinist economy, since orders can be dispatched from the center directly to all vertical branches. The process is not quite so simple if horizontal links exist, for in this case it is not possible for planners to send a message (''primary input'') to a particular industry; it will have to let all operative cells communicate again.

In the contemporary socialist model, the ''unbiased planner'' would reprocess information and reproportion production possibilities, permitting the effects of disproportionalities to spread themselves more or less evenly across the system. The traditional planning response in the socialist countries has been a biased one, however. After a breakdown, for example, a disproportionate reduction of available resources has usually been arranged for the nonpriority (consumer goods) industries. The so-called priority (''structurally determining'') industries will be spared from the effects of the breakdown as far as possible. In this case, planners will not attempt to obtain a new, complete information matrix, but will settle for a flow of instructions only to the industries most directly concerned.

Attention has been focused here on the indicatory information system.

The regulatory and auditory systems are somewhat less complex, but are of no smaller importance for the socialist economy. To compare the costs and benefits of organizational systems, one would have to consider the aggregate of flows.

Qualitative Models of Comparative Information Systems

Four basic models of economic organization and information deserve attention. Two are conceptual (perhaps utopian), while two represent general practice in the socialist and nonsocialist worlds. The most decentralized is the Walrasian model, and the successively more centralized approaches are Galbraithian mixed, Libermanesque reform, and Leninist-Stalinist models.

The informational requirements of these models differ substantially. The least demanding is the Walrasian model, which is of interest almost strictly to economists whose analysis requires some ideal form as a benchmark. It is a world without a planning or regulatory hierarchy in which all information is transmitted on price tags.[16]

The most demanding model, in terms of the informational requirements arising from the prevailing degree of centralization, is the Leninist-Stalinist economy. As observed in the previous section, the informational matrix is complementary to the system of production-consumption planning: all information is concentrated at the highest levels of the planning hierarchy, i.e., the central planning board is guided by the central committee, with the preferences of the latter faithfully expressed in processes directed by the former. All flows of information are decided upon and guided by these highest hierarchical tiers; no horizontal communication is permitted.

The Stalinist system referred to earlier is now more appropriately designated "Leninist-Stalinist" because of the ideal of omnipresent and absolute planning that remains an important part of Soviet thought, even though the Leninist vision of a single economic plan for the socialist world is still rather purely eschatological. Nevertheless, the goal of total planning for the Soviet economy permeates Russian literature.

Two models of informational decentralization more descriptive of reality are between the extremes already mentioned. The first of these, the Galbraithian mixed system, is as well known to educated Western citizens as the Walrasian system to Western economists. Here the basic market signals remain, though they are often drowned out by institutionally administered noise in the regulation of economic information and activity. In this model, we observe the beginnings of the bureaucratization of life, for numerous agencies begin to carry out planning functions that are even favored by corporations.

With reference to the informational model presented earlier, the Galbraithian framework can also be described in terms of hierarchical tiers. For purposes of simplification, let the highest tier include both executive and legislative branches (in European terms, "government" and "parliament"). Government agencies and administrative bureaucracies are the second level, and industrial groups or associations follow. At the lowest level, individual firms round out the Western economic hierarchy. Explicit reference should be made to three points that exemplify the significant informational differences between the Galbraithian and Libermanesque models.

It is noteworthy that, in the political economy of the nonsocialist world, industrial groups (and even large enterprises) pursuing their own interests are not restricted to initiatives directed at the inertia of the bureaucracy. Direct information flows between industrial and executive legislative tiers (nonzero values for the vectors aq_k and $\overline{a}\overline{q}_k$ in the model) are of great significance in achieving policies that express the preferences, not only of political, but also of corporate powers.

Second, the mixed system of the Western world is characterized by a number of bureaucratic institutions that have evolved to accommodate the extraction of tax revenues from the private sectors. (This is a problem, of course, that need not arise in socialism.) Since the industrial tier is able to pursue its interests sometimes directly at the top level of the hierarchy, as was indicated above, they have been able to gain a complex network of fiscal concessions. However, the government's granting these concessions does not reduce the need for funds for public purposes. An extended struggle is therefore carried on for tax revenues.[17]

The final point to be mentioned here is that, in the nonsocialist economy, government agencies and administrative bureaucracies plan a less direct role in economic processes. Their function is basically to provide norms of acceptable behavior or "rules of the game" within which firms are able to operate on their own initiative. Often, in fact, Western bureaucratic clout can only be wielded by selectively issuing threats of punishment or other intervention. Information flows may sometimes, therefore, be sparse but esoteric (through an opportune press release, for example). In the socialist world, there is a tendency to engage in more extensive "petty tutelage," i.e., direct intervention.

The Libermanesque reform model represents, for the former Stalinist world, a significant movement away from centralism. This model, as will become apparent, is also distinctly different from the Galbraithian world.[18]

The current socialist planning system is described here as Libermanesque because we wish to avoid the impression that all of the elements of Liberman's proposals have been achieved in East European reform endeavors. Nor have the reforms achieved any uniform degree of decentralization, either of the type advocated by Liberman or other reformers in East Europe.

The previous section analyzed the manner in which messages are generated, transmitted, and processed in socialism. In terms of the information model presented there, planning reforms have led to an increase in the number of nonzero elements in the technology (information) matrix over the number pertaining in earlier, more purely Leninist-Stalinist systems. As is known, this is much less true for the Soviet Union than for Hungary.

In spite of potentially substantial differences in the informational structure of the various East European systems, they have retained certain common characteristics. An increase, for instance, in decision-making authority at the level of the industrial association was a common phenomenon of the reforms. Here, too, differences from country to country are a matter of degree. Rather than merely serving as a relay station, associations now generate a greater volume of their own information, though it is still based upon general directives from the center. The reduction of the number of planning norms utilized implies a substantial increase in information flows in the matrix A_{ki} and a reduction in those of row vectors $\overline{ap}_k$ and $\overline{ap}_i$.

Complementary to this development has been the increase in the volume of interenterprise and interassociation communications. Whereas, under the Leninist-Stalinist system, the matrices A_{ii} and A_{kk} were nearly empty, they now have a greater number of nonzero elements. This is again much more true of Hungary and Czechoslovakia than of, say, East Germany and the Soviet Union.

The focus to this point has mainly been on the flows of indicatory information. It should not be forgotten, however, that the function of regulatory and auditory flows is also of importance and differs among systems and countries. With regard to regulatory and auditory information, Western bureaucracies have substantially fewer prerogatives and are expected to function with far less thoroughness than could be the case under central planning. The Western bureaucracy can satisfy its needs largely with statistical sampling techniques. The tendency in central planning is for the bureaucracy to spread itself rather uniformly over decision-making processes, thereby embroiling itself in information flows that are much more difficult to manage.

Toward a More Libermanesque Socialist World

The transition of the Soviet-type economy from traditionalism to a more Libermanesque world is an extended, continuing, and fascinating process. The ultimate shape of the East European reforms is clearly contingent on the configurations of reform in the Soviet Union. It is noteworthy that questions of an optimal information system have been of keen interest in recent Soviet planning discussions.

The question of optimal information processes goes back to the 1960s, when many Russian theoreticians were preoccupied with the implementation of revolutionizing ideas and possibilities stemming from mathematical programming. The drive in this decade toward institutionalized automation in planning has seen the Soviets adopt the "Automated System of Plan Computation," which is designed to achieve complete national planning "at every level of control on which it is being performed."[19]

Federenko, director of the Central Mathematical Economics Institute (U.S.S.R. Academy of Sciences), has argued that, in an era of technological explosion (in which, for example, Mars will be "assimilated"), it is necessary to resort to systematic analysis in which practically everything is subject to central computation and programming.[20]

In spite of substantial optimism, some Soviets are distinctly reserved in their appraisal of the possibilities of computation. The "theory of the optimal functioning of the economy" was recently attacked by N. Baibakov, Chairman of the State Planning Committee. He found it unthinkable that "all of the present planning techniques will be replaced solely by economic-mathematical model building."[21]

Federenko has countered that the "theory of optimal functioning" is really nothing more than the "refinement of the theory and methodology of economic planning, of economic theory as a whole."[22] He also admits that more work needs to be done on it. Moreover, he would probably not be inclined to reject considerations presented by advocates of moderation—such as Volkonsky, one of the pioneers in the theory of optimal planning for large-scale systems. On the basis of informational considerations, Volkonsky maintains that sufficient flexibility and processes of optimal pricing and planning cannot be achieved in a fully centralist system. With regard to information processes, he holds that a rational degree of decentralization would depend, on the one hand, on the volume of information to be processed in the plan construction and, on the other hand, on the costs of and technology for processing such information.[23]

In fairness, Federenko himself is on record with the admission that no quantity of electronic calculating machines and no number of methodological refinements of programming can take account of all the dynamics and of all the interactions among variables in economic life. This is particularly true, he observes, because of the occurrence of all the continuous new possibilities "generated by the creative activity of tens of millions of people engaged in the productive process."[24]

In short, the Soviet goal of "computopia" for the intermediate run, at least, cannot be considered a realistic prospect. It is, therefore, necessary for socialists to continue either to reckon with the need to accept the informational limitations inherent in the contemporary socialist planning system or to extend the techniques of decentralization.

A Feasible Suggestion for General Equilibrium Information Analysis

Though the socialist countries currently do not gather the data that would be required to program information flows as suggested earlier, and though such data probably couldn't be collected if planners desired to do so, it would still be possible to undertake a quantitative investigation of information processes.

The analysis would not be as precise as that implied by the previously suggested models broken down for indicatory, regulatory, and auditory messages. Still, one could empirically determine the structure of the information industry and, at the same time, determine administrative and planning costs, thereby making interspatial and intertemporal comparisons possible.

The information industry could simply be treated as a separate sector to be incorporated into a normal input-output model for the whole economy. Since one has no tangible outputs for the information sector, the analysis could be conducted in value terms utilizing transaction matrices for all (including information) outputs produced.

One could construct the system with $n + 2$ industries: the normal n industries, an industry of households, and a "control" or information industry producing administrative communications.[25] The households purchase products from other industries and supply labor (the volume depending on the wage rate) for physical production in the n industries and for informational outputs for the $n + 2$th industry, the planning apparatus.[26]

Information produced and supplied, both to other industries and to the planning hierarchy, could be quantified according (primarily) to the labor costs of its production. It should be administratively feasible to establish information production costs incurred in transmitting messages to other industries for current production purposes, to planning agencies for current production purposes, and to the central planning apparatus for the purpose of preparing forthcoming plans.

Economists have long asserted that high information costs and inefficient central management represent a most important drawback for socialist economies. The very fact that reforms were undertaken in the 1960s indicates the growing awareness of East European economic directors of inadequacies in the centralized planning system.

Conceptual and practical measures of informational costs, such as those discussed in this chapter, should clearly represent more than a matter of intellectual curiosity. It is inconsistent that societies hoping to achieve nearly complete planning of national life would attempt to operate planning mechanisms and implement planning reforms without at least general knowledge of their informational characteristics and costs. In our view, the proposals suggested here are at least a first step in bringing to fruition the theoretical work already done on economic organization. They could also permit greater understanding of the socialist information industry.

Notes

1. Janusz G. Zielinski's extensive discussion of this matter can be found in his "Le systeme d'information de l'entreprise socialiste," *Revue de L'Est*, vol. 2, no. 2 (April 1971), pp. 19-61.

2. Much of this work has been done by and under the direction of N. P. Federenko. See, for example, his *O Razrabotke Sistemy Optimalnogo Funktsionirovania Ekonomiki*, Moscow, 1968.

3. Ibid., p. 208.

4. Leonid Hurwicz, "Efficiency of Decentralized Structures," in *Value and Plan*, Gregory Grossman, ed. (Berkeley: University of California Press, 1960), pp. 176-183.

5. See Andrzej Brzeski, "Social Engineering and Realpolitik in Communist Economic Reorganization," in *Essays in Socialism and Planning in Honor of Carl Landauer*, Gregory Grossman, ed. (Englewood Cliffs, New Jersey: Prentice-Hall, 1970), p. 153.

Harry Nick, one of the more prolific GDR economists, has emphasized the important function of horizontal information transfers as well. As an economy becomes more complex, Nick holds, it can greatly benefit from some degree of centralization at the association or industrial level. Then important technological information can be passed on horizontally to all the enterprises that could benefit from the information. Where information is private property, of course, one firm can often retain the sole right to its benefits—a temporary monopoly profit. See "Zu einigen problemen der Wirtschaftsorganisation als einem Wachstumsfaktor der sozialistischen produktion," *Wirtschaftswissenschaft*, vol. 18, no. 1 (January 1970), pp. 49-54.

6. Leonid Hurwicz, "Centralization and Decentralization in Economic Processes," *Jahrbuch der Wirtschaft Osteuropas, Yearbook of East European Economics*, vol. 3 (Munich-Vienna: Gunter Olzog Verlag, 1972), pp. 90-91.

7. Janos Kornai, *Anti-Equilibrium: On Economic Systems Theory and*

the Tasks of Research (Amsterdam-London: North-Holland, 1971), p. 83.

8. Or, in other words, on the basis of the number of message elements in a Hurwiczian code system. See his "On the Concept and Possibility of Informational Decentralization," *The American Economic Review*, vol. 59, no. 2 (May 1969), pp. 515-516.

9. Note the profit verification rule prevailing in most socialist countries. Hayek refers to the costs of auditory operations. He insists that "every calculation by an outsider who believes that he can do better will have to be examined and approved by the authority, which in this connection will have to take over all the functions of the entrepreneur." See his "Socialist Calculation: The Competitive 'Solution'," *Economica*, New Series, vol. 7, no. 26 (May 1940), pp. 125-149. Reprinted in Morris Bornstein, ed., *Comparative Economic Systems: Models and Cases*, Revised ed. (Homewood, Illinois: Irwin, 1969), p. 89. On p. 92, Hayek says it seems fairly clear that "the planning authority will be able to exercise its function of controlling and directing investment only if it is in a position to check and repeat all the calculations of the entrepreneur."

10. Edward Lipinski, "The Theory of the Socialist Enterprise," in *Economic Development for Eastern Europe*, Michael Kaser, ed. (New York: St. Martin's, 1968), p. 297.

11. J.G. Zielinski, *On the Theory of Socialist Planning* (Ibadan: Oxford University Press, 1968), pp. 107-108.

12. In a subsequent section entitled "A Feasible Suggestion . . .," however, measurement techniques will be suggested that will be subject to calculation and practical use.

13. See Hurwicz, "Centralization and Decentralization," op. cit., p. 104.

14. See Antonio Camacho's "Centralization and Decentralization of Decision Making Mechanisms: A General Model," *Jahrbuch der Wirtschaft Osteuropas, Yearbook of East European Economics*, vol. 3 (Munich-Vienna: Gunter Olzog Verlag, 1972), pp. 45-66. On this point he cites Hayek's paper, "The Use of Knowledge in Society," *The American Economic Review*, vol. 35 (1945), pp. 519-530.

15. See Michael Montias, "Planning with Material Balances in Soviet-type Economies," *The American Economic Review* vol. 49, (December 1959), pp. 963-985.

16. Hurwicz says this system is opposite to the centralized economy, for in the "Walrasian price adjustment economy . . . there is no directing group (hence no hierarchy) and all units are autonomous." See his "Centralization and Decentralization," op. cit., p. 101. Kornai says (with his own emphasis): "*The world of Walras is a strictly single-level economic system.*" See his *Anti-Equilibrium*, op. cit., p. 86.

17. This represents no new phenomenon in capitalism. It was observed some time ago by Joseph A. Schumpeter, *Capitalism, Socialism and Democracy* (New York: Harper & Brothers, 1942), chap. 17.

18. It is Šik who reminds us that Galbraith has never had the opportunity to live in or attempt to direct a centrally-planned economy, and that he can, therefore, perhaps, be forgiven for his view that the world is of homogeneous bureaucratic composition. See George R. Urban, "A Conversation with Ota Šik," *Survey*, vol. 19, no. 2 (1973), pp. 250-270.

19. Economists are indebted to Alfred Zauberman for his close tracking of these events and of the mathematical school's writings. The quote here is from his "Notes on Systematic Approach to Large Scale, Decentralization, and Related Matters," *Jahrbuch der Wirtschaft Osteuropas, Yearbook of East European Economies*, vol. 4 (Munich-Vienna: Gunter Olzog Verlag, 1973), p. 140.

20. Ibid., p. 141.

21. When one comprehends scientifically the nature of planning, "one can only stand amazed at the conception developed by some economists," Baibakov holds. See his "Dalneishee Sovershenstvovanie Planirovania Vazhneishaya Narodnokhozyaistvennaya Zadacha," *Planovoe Khozyaistvo*, no. 3 (March 1974), p. 11. Interestingly, Baibakov's proposed solution is for economists to work more on developing the theory and methodology of planning by material (as well as by value and labor) balances. He says (p. 12) that "the further development and improvement of economic balances, their mathematization not excluded, of course, is of the greatest importance." What Baibakov fails to realize is that planning by balances is nothing more than programming without computers and without theory. Programming, as has long been recognized, is merely the analytical extension of planning by balances. See Montias, "Planning with Material Balances," op. cit.

22. See his "Sovremennye Zadachi Ekonomicheskoi Nauki," *Voprosy Ekonomiki*, no. 2 (1974), pp. 19-31.

23. Zauberman, *Jahrbuch der Wirtschaft Osteuropas*, op. cit., p. 167, quotes Volkonsky's article, "Optimalnoye planirovanye v usloviakh bolshoi razmernosti," *Ekonomika i Matematicheskiye Metody*, no. 2 (1965).

24. Federenko, *O Razrabotke*, op cit., pp. 241, 242. The message is not negative with regard to programming; it is merely realistic. He warns that successful competition with capitalism will require continual, creative implementation of the remarkable developments in planning and programming that have occurred in the past decade or two.

25. This distinction is clearly related to Kornai's classification of "real" institutions (those specializing in production, investment, marketing and purchasing) and "control" institutions (those specializing in proc-

essing and transmitting information, decision making, etc.). Control organizations are merely considered as those higher in the planning hierarchy. See Kornai, *Anti-Equilibrium*, op. cit., pp. 76-77.

26. The theoretical requisites for constructing such a model (though no suggestions are made, of course, regarding an information sector) can be found in the standard texts. R.G.D. Allen's discussions on "InterIndustry Relations" and "The Walras-Leontief Closed System" develop, for example, the relevant analysis. See his *Mathematical Economics* (London: Macmillan, 1960), pp. 343-370.

4

Pricing I:
Toward a Theory of Socialist
Pricing

In prereform socialist countries, pricing was a strictly ancillary problem of resource allocation. The central task of socialist planners was to develop material balances and to issue disaggregated production commands for individual enterprises. Prices were of secondary importance, since they were mere surrogates for the command directives of centralized resource allocation.

That inflexible prices failed to represent scarcity values and that they were the source of considerable distortion and inefficiency in Soviet-type economies is well known not only to Western economists. The economic reforms and the associated price revisions of the 1960s are clear evidence of the socialist admission of antereform pricing inadequacy.[1] A decade of price revision and the concomitant discussion throughout the bloc regarding the nature of "correct" socialist pricing produced no peremptory solutions. The evolutionary nature of economic reform and the state of the art of economic planning have not been such as to eliminate the necessity for improvement.

There are four principal directions in which East European functionaries can direct pricing institutions: (a) as in the traditional planned economy, pricing decisions could remain highly centralized and of secondary importance to the crude process of allocation by balances; (b) decision-making power could be retained entirely at the center, with mathematical programming generating "shadow prices" designed to guarantee efficient allocation; (c) pricing could be decentralized so that most of the actual planning would be done at the industrial level, though basic commodities would remain directly subject to central control and all decisions would be subject to central review; and (d) pricing could become the unconstrained function of free markets, so that the plan would be concerned only with investment policy, the provision of public goods, and so on. Hybrid possibilities combining elements of each of these four approaches could also be discussed, of course, but these represent the core of

The material in this and in the following chapter was revised from two articles: "Dynamic Price Planning in Command Economies: A Partial Equilibrium Approach," *Weltwirtschaftliches Archiv*, vol. 109, no. 3 (December 1973), pp. 495-513 and "La Fixation des Prix en Allemagne de l'Est: Les Occasions Manquées d'Une Reforme Avortée" (East German Pricing: The Lost Opportunities of Miscarried Reform), *Revue d'Études Comparatives Est-Ouest*, vol. 6, no. 2 (1974), pp. 137-154.

the serious elements of the reform discussion in socialist countries. Needless to say, the theoretical views emerging in East Europe, as pertaining to details and particulars, have varied considerably from country to country, though the clear outlines of several broad fronts of attack have appeared. Points of convergence of thought will be of interest here, since points of divergence are too numerous and sometimes too trivial to justify treatment.

The first approach is clearly unacceptable to East European planners, though bureaucratic inertia favoring that approach remains strong in the Soviet Union and, consequently, has potential impact upon bloc planners.

The second possibility holds the greatest appeal for many economists in the Soviet Union, for, as a general equilibrium approach, it offers the opportunity potentially to revolutionize economic planning—to utilize the most sophisticated quantitative techniques available and to achieve a high level of economic efficiency. However, limitations on the availability of statistical data and the capacity of computers minimize the possibilities of achieving the programming of complete economies.

The fourth approach is given no serious consideration by decision makers in contemporary East Europe, though it will be seen below that a part of the reform discussion did focus on the plan *and* the market.

The most pressing need of command planning at this juncture is for an operational approach to the third possibility—a partial equilibrium method by which dynamic (or at least more flexible) prices could be established at the periphery for nonbasic commodities. The prices of the most crucial ("structurally determining") products will, of course, generally remain securely within the jurisdiction of central authorities, who can thus maintain what they consider to be sufficient control over the economy. However, some guidelines are sought by which other industries (and sometimes individual enterprises) can establish their own prices in a manner that is socialistically acceptable, i.e., that does not circumvent planners' objectives.

After the next section treats the basic objectives and possibilities of central control over pricing, a brief discussion of current socialist price-planning theory will be provided. An effort will then be made to show the nature of the modifications required in socialist pricing theory to achieve "quasi-optimality" as defined by Baumol and Bradford. The final section treats the incorporation of quality and technology considerations into the quasi-optimality analysis and the establishment of a methodology for determining the equilibrium price.

Price as a Control Lever for Decentralized Industries

The state of the art of economic planning and the preferences of contemporary socialist planners together assure nonoptimal outcomes for economic performance in the reformed command economies. The thrust of reform endeavors was that, for a few crucial industries, a general equilibrium approach would be pursued. Input-output information supplements the crude material balance allocation technique for industries producing priority ("structurally determining") commodities.[a]

For most other industries, decentralization of pricing decisions was advocated. Rather flexible guidelines were to be established for industrial associations or even individual enterprises, and pricing, once again, was to become a more than passive mechanism in the allocation process. Such prices are described as "economic levers" rather than mere surrogates for the coefficients of physical allocations. They contain an element of "profit" that empowers enterprise or industrial association managers to accumulate funds to finance investment projects internally or to dispense bonuses to managers and workers.

Reform economists generally wished to eschew the traditional model of rigid, highly centralized allocations by balances. For most, the programmed economy rather than the market economy is the objective, though it will for some time remain beyond the frontier of planning possibilities. Socialists are still struggling, however, to find out where in the evolutionary process of command planning they are now. It is clear that the institutional arrangements by which some degree of pricing decentralization is to be achieved have not yet reached a final equilibrium, though the spirit of experimentation exuded by reform literature has been replaced by more cautious writings.

With regard to the dynamic features of pricing innovations, they take two basic forms: first, changes in production costs, product quality, technological modernity, and consumer preferences are permitted to enter at least indirectly into pricing calculation and second, pricing decisions are delegated to the periphery, where they can be reviewed periodically and altered in response to dynamic change in the economy. The objective of this section is to develop optimal pricing formulae for peripheral-level decision makers (incorporating some innovations socialists have introduced) that would permit better dynamic performance of command economies.

An unspecified supply price function, would relate the supply price P_s of a given output to the relevant variables as follows:

$$P_s = f(c, v, s_e, s_p, Q, A) \tag{4.1}$$

where we let s_p = surplus value for public revenues, s_e = surplus value for enterprise revenues, Q = product quality, and A = product technological age (some index of modernity or obsolescence).

---

[a] "Structurally determining" commodities are the most crucial in an economy's output mix and those whose prices are, therefore, most instrumental in determining the structure of relative prices of final consumers and producers goods throughout the economy.

It is unlikely that any extensive efforts will be made in the near future by the central planners, industrial associations, or individual enterprises of command systems to determine the demand schedules that would apply to their outputs.[2] It will, therefore, be assumed that industrial associations will be concerned with the quantity demanded, q_d, at a given price (rather than a whole demand schedule), which in practice may be estimated rather crudely. The basic functional demand relationship, however, would be given by:

$$q_d = f(\bar{p}, EF, ip) \tag{4.2}$$

where $\bar{p}$ represents the preferred price of the peripheral decision maker, given his tastes and objectives, EF is the equilibrating factor by which the price will be adjusted to eliminate excess queuing or inventory buildup (adjustment can be made in part, of course, by changing production volume, redefining what constitutes acceptable inventory levels, etc.), and ip represents (potentially competitive) prices in international markets.

Before specifying the particular forms these functions appear to be assuming in the socialist countries, it would be helpful to discuss some of the implications of the fact that these pricing formulae are being developed for peripheral, decision-making units *not* producing structurally determining commodities.

For the structurally determining commodities, a partial equilibrium analysis would be insufficient because the impact of interindustrial effects would have serious ramifications in numerous basic industries; input-output analysis or linear programming would be essential for efficient allocation.

The quantity demanded of good 1, namely, would in a general equilibrium framework be a function of all other prices:

$$q_{d1} = f_1(p_1, p_2, p_3, \ldots, p_n; ip_1, ip_2, \ldots, ip_n)$$

where the subscripts represent different commodities.

An investigation of the dynamic and stability properties of a general equilibrium system would require that such a function be combined with (similar) expressions of demand for all other commodities. All such functions would then be differentiated totally with respect to p_1, and (with the help of matrix algebra) the impacts of a change in p_1 upon all substitute and complement goods, no matter how remotely related, could be traced through the system.

Where good 1 is not a structurally determining commodity, however, and where the relevant country's exports and imports of good 1 represent a negligible share of the entire quantity supplied and demanded in world markets, the analysis is simpler. With general equilibrium effects assumed to be negligible, i.e.,

$$q_d \neq f(p_2, p_3, \ldots, p_n; \, ip_1, ip_2, \ldots, ip_n)$$

and assuming the basic demand relationship to be given by

$$q_{d1} = f(p_1, t_1, EF)$$

where t represents consumer tastes, the effects of a change in the price of good 1 can be investigated without reference to other prices. Differentiating totally,

$$\frac{dq_d}{dp_1} = \frac{\partial q_d}{\partial p_1} + \frac{\partial q_d}{\partial t} \cdot \frac{dt}{dp_1} + \frac{\partial q_d}{\partial EF} \cdot \frac{dEF}{dp_1}$$

we are able to isolate the effects sought for in terms of industry 1 alone.

An investigation of dynamic central planning for a basic industry must account for the authoritarian control one can expect to find in such an industry. If growth is being encouraged (e.g., as in the capital goods industries of Soviet-type economies), state-stimulated demand would, in most cases, result in an upward drift of price as the industrial output expands (though significant economies of scale might in some instances permit a steady or even declining price).

On the other hand, authoritarian control can also be invoked to prevent the expansion of an industry. Constrained industrial growth is best achieved by limiting the growth of supply. Were planners to attempt merely to restrain demand, the restricted output would be accompanied by an artificially low price. This could result in strong pressures to augment domestic supply with imports or to expand production and might also encourage the development of black markets. Such problems have traditionally been avoided by the imposition of a high turnover tax. The artificially high price that results represents an imposed distortion of the price structure. Constrained supply, on the other hand, results in a somewhat higher, but not so artificially distorted, price for the restricted industrial output.

Though authoritarian control is necessary in industries requiring general equilibrium planning, the nonstructurally determining industries need only be given some flexibly structured planning guidelines. Those industries that can be granted considerable discretionary administrative powers can be termed *supervised drift* industries.

The growing supervised drift industry or enterprise expects, over time, to confront expanding demand. On the basis of centrally issued guidelines, the manager can determine his supply schedule at any given point in time. He then estimates a quantity demanded that coincides with a point on his supply schedule and attempts to sell that quantity of output at the associated price. If queues or inventories develop, he adjusts the price upward or downward along the supply schedule until he finds the point at which the unknown demand curve intersects the supply curve.[3]

It may be, of course, that the peripheral unit or the central authority will pursue particular growth or revenue goals which would imply different behavior. Moreover, the possibility of central intervention in the economic planning of nonbasic industries or enterprises is not to be overlooked, especially if the extent of general equilibrium programming is modest relative to the objectives and size of the planning bureaucracy.

If it turns out, for example, that, over time, some nonbasic industry confronts a less buoyant demand than anticipated, it might not reduce the price and the quantity offered. It might (of its own volition or by interdiction of central autority) choose instead to adopt a constrained-growth policy, i.e., to leave the price as set and simply reduce the supply (offering less at each possible price, including the prevailing one, of course).

In a case where actual demand in a supervised drift industry is found to be stronger than anticipated, the price might likewise not be adjusted upward along the supply schedule. The central planners or managers with sales maximization preferences might attempt to satisfy this demand by opting for an expansion of the industry's capacity. An induced-growth policy (offering a greater quantity of output at the prevailing price) would be appropriate, for example, for an import-substitution industry.

Having pursued the general character of price planning in authoritarian control and supervised drift industries, we are prepared to investigate the particulars of pricing rules that have been developed by and for command economies.

The Nature of Traditional Socialist Pricing

Orthodox Marxist economists in bloc countries have been described by Bornstein as the "surplus product markup school."[4] The basic idea to which they subscribe is that prices should represent the "value" or (average) cost of production plus a uniform, proportional markup appropriately termed "surplus product" (*Mehrwert*). The prime costs of production (the sum of the costs for variable capital v and constant capital c) include direct and indirect labor, materials (including power and fuel), depreciation allowances, and overhead expenses. Rent and interest payments on capital have not been included, though interest on short-term bank loans has. The surplus value markup m generally aims at providing the enterprise with a 5-10 percent return on total prime costs.

Much discussion has been conducted among socialist economists as to the nature of a proper Marxian markup. Three different proposals have dominated the discussions in East Germany[b] and the Soviet Union: prime

---

[b] Since East Germany will be the main case study of Chapter 5, terms and practices discussed here will usually be those prevailing in that country. These usually correspond to practice in the U.S.S.R., however.

cost-related (*Selbstkostenbezogene*) prices, capital-related (*Produktionsfondsbezogene* or *Kapitalbezogene*) prices, and wage-related (*Lohnbezogene*) prices.[5] In the following discussion, let

p = price of the commodity

c = constant capital used per unit of output (material costs plus depreciation)

v = variable capital used per unit of output (labor costs, i.e., the wage bill)

m_i = the given markup ($i = 1, 2, 3$)

K = the ratio of the stock of total fixed and working capital used in production to total output

In the case of wage-related (*Lohnbezogene*) prices, the markup is applied to variable capital (or the labor input) and the price of a commodity can be reckoned as

$$p = c + v + v(m_1)$$

Though this formulation's emphasis on variable capital holds appeal for Marxian orthodoxy (holding as it does the relation between profits and wages constant in all sectors and basing profits upon the use of that factor which alone supposedly "creates value"), it is disadvantageous in that it overvalues labor-intensive products. This, of course, provides the enterprise with an incentive to adopt labor-intensive processes, discouraging technical progress. Additionally, when labor-intensive commodities are relatively high priced, demand is distorted to some extent in the direction of capital-intensive products. Although output distortion of this type would have been constrained by the very limited degree of reliance on market allocation as to have been rather negligible in the past, it is nevertheless to be expected that choices of technique (input substitution processes) would have been more severely distorted under this price type.

Prime cost-related (*Selbstkostenbezogene*) prices imply a markup based on the total of prime costs rather than just "living labor," so that the following pricing rule is applied:

$$p = c + v + (c + v)m_2$$

This pricing rule was originally adopted as the basis of industrial price reform in the German Democratic Republic (GDR). Formerly, the percentage markup had been based on total prime costs (*Selbstkosten*), so that enterprises faced an incentive to use expensive materials and excessively material-intensive inputs or inputs of high cost from other enterprises. After the introduction of the reform, however, the profit markup was based strictly on the value added by the firm, i.e., upon total costs minus the costs of purchased inputs from other enterprises. Since no interest costs are included in value added, this turns out mainly to be labor cost v, which is quite Marxian in spirit.

Problems inevitably arise under this method, too. Because interest charges are ignored in cost calculations, production costs for capital-intensive industries are too low. So long as capital costs are insufficiently recognized, labor-intensive industries prove to be more profitable. Because resources will automatically flow away from capital-intensive industries as a consequence of their being unable to finance their own investment, constrained technical progress may be a concomitant of this distortion in resource allocation.

In response to such difficulties, East German planners turned to capital-related (*Fondsbezogene* or *Kapitalbezogene*) prices, which had for some time been the preference of most East German economists. The rule here is

$$p = c + v + K(m_3)$$

This technique permits capital-intensive industries to obtain sufficient sales revenues for self-financed investments. Additionally, it provides a measuring stick for at least some current and future investment decisions simply because the productive achievements of dissimilar industries can be compared according to their capital returns.[6]

Extensive and perhaps wasteful capital utilization would be a temptation to socialist enterprises facing this pricing criterion, so in reform style the GDR introduced an interest charge on capital (*Produktionsfondsabgabe*) to complement the utilization of this price type.

Another problem is that the state of technology in some industries demands labor-intensive production; to the extent that capital-intensive production is overvalued, unprofitable operations are to be expected for these industries. The upshot of such cases would be an inability to generate funds for self-financed investments. Since the resultant unattainable investments would have permitted some degree of modernization and an easing of the heavy labor requirements of that branch of production, the welfare loss to a labor-scarce (e.g., East German) economy would necessarily be great.

The Conception of Pricing Optimality

For some years, economists have held that Soviet-type pricing as discussed above must lead to inefficiency. The venerable propositions of marginal-cost pricing (as recognized by both bourgeois economists and socialists of Lange-Lerner preferences) implied that Soviet pricing, based as it is on average costs and a uniform markup, must lead to distortions in resource allocation.

Thanks to Baumol and Bradford, the socialist debate has taken another step forward. They have shown that the Lange-Lerner rules require modification.[7] The apparent inevitability of enterprise deficits (negative rents) and other public revenue needs in a socialist state will represent a constraint upon the optimal resource allocation sought by market socialists through Lange-Lerner rules.[c] This pathbreaking (if not original) contribution indicates that the existence of deficits will require the imposition of some kind of tax upon the earnings of nationalized industries, causing a departure of prices from marginal costs somewhere in the system.[d,8] The Baumol-Bradford theorem demonstrates, then, that rational (quasi-optimal) prices not only *might* deviate from marginal costs, but that they in fact systematically *must* do so. Planners can hope at best to achieve only "quasi-optimality"—Pareto optimality in the presence of an absolute profit or revenues constraint—or in other words, an optimal departure from marginal-cost pricing.

The very question of achieving "more optimal" performance in socialist planning seems to run counter to the logic of the theory of the second best. In treating the economies of the socialist world, however, it seems justifiable to ignore the proposition that nothing short of Pareto optimality can be evaluated in efficiency terms. The author does not accept the position that because we cannot order second-best states, "groping toward optimality" becomes a meaningless proposition. Whether or not a top-level optimum can be achieved, it has been shown that there is some point in attempting through incremental planning measures to achieve more satisfactory performance, especially when irrationality and inefficiency are gross. Under certain conditions, a more efficient operation can be accomplished by optimizing in certain sectors, even though a top-level optimum is not possible.[9]

It is not difficult to show precisely how prices based on average costs must be associated with a particular profit markup to assure a quasi-optimal outcome. Quasi-optimality can be achieved only if the needed revenues are obtained (assuming, for simplicity, that cross elasticities of demand are zero) by setting each price so that a particular commodity's percentage

---

[c] Deficits will arise in enterprises that fail to cover costs, not only because decreasing costs are encountered, but also because the revenue requirements of the state may exceed the profits of nationalized firms, though the latter may be in compliance with the Lange-Lerner rules and experience diminishing returns.

[d] Excise taxes represent a decision to cause product prices to depart from marginal costs; income taxes force the price of labor to do so. Even with capital collectively owned and investment centrally controlled, Baumol and Bradford deny the practicability of imposing lump-sum taxation, the magnitude of which would be independent of the decisions of those taxed.

deviation from marginal cost is inversely proportional to its price elasticity of demand. According to the Baumol-Bradford theorem, prices might deviate from marginal costs considerably where demand is very inelastic, but the divergence would have to be slight in the case of very elastic demand.

The theorem can be expressed in several ways. For this discussion a simple one will suffice:

$$\frac{p - MC}{p} = k\left(\frac{1}{\varepsilon_d}\right) \tag{4.3}$$

The notation is traditional, so that p = price, MC = marginal cost, and k is defined as $(1 + \lambda)/\lambda$, where λ is a Lagrange multiplier. ε_d represents, as usual, price elasticity of demand.

It can be shown that the Baumol-Bradford quasi-optimality requirement is satisfied, given the correct profit markup, in traditional socialist pricing. Where m again represents Marxian "surplus value" or profit markup, quasi-optimality is achieved when

$$m = MC\left\{1 + \left(k \cdot \frac{1}{\varepsilon_d} \cdot \frac{p}{MC}\right) - \left[\frac{1}{1 + (1/\varepsilon_s)}\right]\right\} \tag{4.4}$$

where ε_s = elasticity of supply. This expression demonstrates the considerations affecting the appropriate, quasi-optimal surplus value, but it is more complex than would be required for purposes of illustration. The quasi-optimality conditions can be expressed in a simple and operational form.

We saw earlier that the socialist pricing rule is given by $p = c + v + m$. For simplicity, let us begin by assuming that pure competition prevails and that there is but one factor of production, labor (variable capital v).

The average cost of labor $(AC = v)$ becomes the average cost of the product, which is also equal to marginal cost:

$$p = AC + m$$
$$= MC + m \tag{4.5}$$
$$p - MC = m$$

Permit m now to take its simplest form

$$m = k\left(\frac{1}{\varepsilon_d}\right)p$$

and substitute it into (4.5), so that the Baumol-Bradford theorem as given in (4.3) is achieved.

In the general, noncompetitive case, characterized by the inequality of average and marginal costs, the theorem as given by (4.3) is satisfied by

$$m = k\left(\frac{p}{\varepsilon_d}\right) + MC - AC \tag{4.6}$$

This expression, a simplified version of (4.4), merely tells us that when the price elasticity of demand is low, the revenue-providing profit markup (surplus value) will be much higher than in those cases where demand is elastic. To attain a given level of required revenues from the production system, the planners must find the "correct" markup of price over average cost [as given by (4.6)] for each industry. That quasi-optimal markup will have prices diverge in a systematic and predictable way from marginal costs.

To the extent that the markup chosen deviates from the Baumol-Bradford markup, it must inevitably share the flaws of average-cost pricing and the distorting effects of taxation for revenues. To the extent that Pareto efficiency is desired, the Baumol-Bradford markup clearly recommends itself to socialist planners.

Incorporating Quality and Technology Considerations and Finding the Equilibrium Price

Perhaps the most notable aspect of the economic reforms is the attempt to provide greater incentive to the enterprise or industrial association to operate efficiently by rewarding profitable performance. When profitability becomes the index of success, some of the notorious outcomes resulting from the utilization of gross output targets (e.g., poor quality, insufficient spare parts, inadequate product variety) can be avoided. A notable East German experiment goes beyond the introduction of profitability as a success criterion. If the quality of a given commodity is judged to be superior, a price surcharge (*zuschlag*) may be added to the normal price. A reduction-in-charge (*abschlag*) will reduce the price of an inferior-quality good. *Preiszuschläge* and *Preisabschläge* are also rewarded or imposed for short or excessively long delivery times, as well as for especially small- or large-quantity orders. Likewise, a surcharge may be awarded for producing special-order goods, the specifications of which deviate from normal standards or which require special production processes.

The introduction of a new product calls for an initially higher rate of return than normally expected, for which a temporarily higher price is also the mechanism.[10] In the course of the product's technological life (admittedly difficult to estimate), the peripheral decision-making unit has the "own responsibility" of reducing the price so that the centrally decreed maximal limit of acceptable profitability will not be exceeded.[11] A reduction-in-charge will be imposed upon technologically obsolete products at the discretion of the center.

In a system that dictates a sharing of surplus by the enterprise and the state, it would be simple to incorporate rewards for product quality Q or technological modernity A. The sum of enterprise surplus s_e and public surplus s_p is the total surplus value, s. Enterprise surplus would be some portion of the total, as expressed by

$$s_e = m\left(\frac{s_p}{A + Q}\right) \tag{4.7}$$

where m is some constant. If pricing were Pareto optimal, the enterprise share of the Baumol-Bradford markup would be greater for the enterprise (or industrial association) producing a high-quality, technologically advanced commodity. This outcome would be guaranteed by the following formula for a constant cost industry:

$$s_p + n\left(\frac{s_p}{A + Q}\right) = k\left(\frac{P_i}{\varepsilon_d}\right) \tag{4.8}$$

Such an industry's supply schedule would therefore guarantee Pareto optimality and reward special production performance if

$$P_s = c + v + k\left(\frac{P_i}{\varepsilon_d}\right) \tag{4.9}$$

Some point on this schedule coincides with a point on the unknown demand curve. This quantity demanded could likely be estimated with reasonable precision by using some index developed for the industry in question. One similar to the following might be appropriate:

$$\frac{\sum[(p_i q_i) + (p^* q^*) + (i p \cdot m)]}{\sum(q_i + q^* + m)} \tag{4.10}$$

where p^* and q^* represent the managers' preferences from the price and quantity solutions they deem feasible, ip represents the price prevailing in international markets, and m denotes imports.

The equilibrium solution, therefore, is given by

$$p_s = c + v + k\left(\frac{p}{\varepsilon_d}\right) = \frac{\sum[(p_i q_i) + (p^* q^*) + (ip \cdot m)]}{\sum(q_i + q^* + m)}$$

$$= q_d \tag{4.11}$$

As was emphasized earlier, if the actual demand exceeds or falls short of that anticipated, the outcome will be queues or an inventory buildup.

Modest price adjustment should eliminate imbalances, though, as has been stressed, other types of adjustment are conceivable.

Conclusions

It is nearly inconceivable that socialist planners will not continue gradually to push on in their pursuit of rationality in resource allocation. It has often been observed that, in spite of traditional bureaucratic inertia (and in many cases outright opposition), inroads have been made on tradition, and progress toward the adoption of marginalist pricing techniques has been more than negligible.[12] So long as totally comprehensive general equilibrium economic planning remains impracticable, decentralization of pricing decisions to peripheral authority must remain an attractive policy solution to socialist planners (a condition guaranteed by the growing complexity of industrial economies and the inflexibility of unwieldy bureaucracies).

Baumol-Bradford optimality will not be achieved overnight, for ideological orthodoxy as a substitute for economic rationality has far from vanished in the socialist states. Still, much more liberal experimentation in price planning represents a subtle but historically important attack on Marxian dogma; though repulsed on some fronts, a patient, persistent, and low-keyed approach may lead ultimately to the triumph of a more liberal socialism.

Notes

1. That the word "revision" is more appropriate than "reform" in socialist pricing can be seen from the Soviet and East German examples. See Morris Bornstein, "Soviet Price Theory and Policy," in United States Congress, Joint Economic Committee, *New Directions in the Soviet Economy* (Washington, D.C.: U.S. Government Printing Office, 1966), Part I; and Hans Böhme, "East German Price Formation Under the New Economic System," *Soviet Studies,* vol. 49, no. 3 (January 1968), pp. 340-356.

2. Contradictory signs appear in the literature now and then, of course. One reads, for example, of experimentations with market research in some of East Germany's industrial associations. See Erika Maier, et al., *Zur Preisplanung in VVB und Betrieben* (East Berlin: Verlag die Wirtschaft, 1968), pp. 86-90. It is difficult to take such indications too seriously, though they may have significance from a very long-term standpoint.

3. It is not necessary here to elaborate on the queuing/inventory

problem. The reader might be referred, however, to J. A. Mirrlees' statement that if economies of scale be disregarded, "prices should probably be adjusted upward when purchases (or orders) are greater than desired production—or, in the case of labor, for example, when the number offering themselves for a particular kind of employment are less than the number of jobs available. But prices should also be adjusted upward if inventories are too small, queues too long, or spare capacity insufficient. The actual price change will have to be related both to the difference between production and sales, and so forth, and to the differences between actual and desired levels of inventories, and the like."

He also makes reference to the complexity of the actual price adjustment process, given the difficulty of rapid collection of good data on production, sales, inventories, queues, etc. See his "The Price Mechanism in a Planned Economy," in *Planning and Markets: Modern Trends in Various Economic Systems,* John T. Dunlop and Nikolay P. Federenko, eds. (New York: McGraw-Hill, 1969), pp. 180-181.

4. See Bornstein, *New Directions,* op. cit. His "traditional school" is pupilled by entrenched bureaucrats and perhaps a minority of "old school" economists, who linger from Stalin's time. The "opportunity cost school" is doubtlessly the wave of the future, with young economists (especially, for example, in Poland and Czechoslovakia) and most of the mathematical economists subscribing. This movement has not as yet gained complete legitimacy throughout the bloc, however, and views of adherents certainly are not descriptive of concepts that best describe the current economic practices of Soviet-type planners.

5. To relate Marxian price theory to Baumol-Bradford quasi-optimal pricing, only a brief review of contemporary socialist pricing and profit markup practices will be necessary. The interested can find in Manfred Melzer, "Preispolitik und Preisbildungsprobleme in der DDR," *Vierteljahreshefte zur Wirtschaftsforschung,* No. 3 (1969), pp. 313-353; and in Bornstein, *New Directions,* op. cit., a more detailed discussion of the nature and advantages of the various price types to be discussed in this section.

6. The East Germans hoped to make the transition to capital-related prices throughout the economy by 1975, if inflation could be avoided in the process. See Deutsches Institut für Wirtschaftsforschung, *DDR-Wirtschaft: eine Bestandsaufnahme* (Frankfurt am Main: Fischer Bücherei, 1971), p. 72.

7. William J. Baumol and David F. Bradford, "Optimal Departures from Marginal Cost Pricing," *American Economic Review,* vol. 60, no. 3 (June 1970), pp. 265-283. Qualifying the Lange-Lerner rules scarcely represents a new pastime. The modification motivating this research must take its place along with other substantive ones treated by Benjamin Ward. See

his *The Socialist Economy: A Study of Organizational Alternatives* (New York: Random House, 1967), pp. 30-40.

8. Baumol and Bradford take pains to show that their theorem has been the object of discussion in several areas of economic literature, but it is worth pointing out, as Joseph Walka kindly did to me, that one of their particular formulations has been around for some time under the guise of the "Lerner Index" of monopoly power. See Abba P. Lerner, "The Concept of Monopoly and the Measurement of Monopoly Power," *Review of Economic Studies* (June 1934). Reprinted in A. P. Lerner, *Essays in Economic Analysis,* London (1953).

9. For a thorough treatment of the problem, see E. J. Mishan, "Second Thoughts on Second Best," *Oxford Economic Papers,* N.S. 14 (October 1962), pp. 205-217.

10. See Fred Matho, *Wie Werden Preise Gemacht?* (East Berlin, 1967), p. 17 and Maier, *Zur Preisplanung,* op. cit., p. 46 for discussions of surcharges and reductions in charge for quality and product technological age considerations.

11. When a response to excess profit is to arise from the "own responsibility" of the enterprise, one may feel justified in skepticism. Supervision is not totally lacking, however, for the local branches of the Price Office, the Industrial Ministries, and the "community price control" on the enterprise level are to assure that the mechanism functions properly. See *Fünfter Tätigkeitsbericht 1965/1969,* Forschungsbeirat, Bundesministerium fur Gesamtdeutsche Fragen, Bonn und Berlin, 1969, p. 109.

12. This is not merely in the socialist mathematical school. See Alfred Zauberman, "The Soviet Debate on the Law of Value and Price Formation," in *Value and Plan,* Gregory Grossman, ed. (Berkeley: University of California Press, 1960), pp. 17-35.

5

Pricing II: Socialist Price Planning in Practice

As was observed in the previous chapter, western economic literature has long held that pricing practice in the Soviet-type economy is unavoidably irrational. Several factors have seemed to justify this position: (a) bureaucratically regulating millions of prices has been an impossibly difficult task resulting in excessive rigidity of the price structure; (b) the evolution of production techniques and consumer preferences over time has prevented inflexibly administered prices from reflecting scarcity values; (c) raw and basic materials have been chronically underpriced throughout the bloc countries, so that the domestic prices of these goods have often been less than those prevailing in international markets; (d) rationality has only been pursued recently in the pricing of capital goods, since the introduction in Eastern Europe of a capital charge came only in the reform decade of the sixties; and (e) Soviet-type systems as a whole seem to have been an uncoordinated patchwork of pricing techniques, with agricultural and foreign trade pricing practices diverging significantly from those prevailing in industrial pricing.

However, these difficulties arise from the institutional and ideological peculiarities inherent in socialist economies, and they certainly do not defy correction and reform. Two more basic systemic considerations, however, have been of transcendent importance in our evaluation of traditional Soviet-type pricing as irrational: (a) socialist prices have been determined almost exclusively by supply factors and (b) pricing has been on an average-rather than marginal-cost basis.[1]

It is the purpose of this chapter to show that the generally accepted view of the inevitable irrationality of pricing in command systems may require modification. Because of the nature of its renewed interest in questions of demand, and because of the almost coincidental way it began to modify its average-cost pricing practices, East European planning appeared, in the reform period, to be groping at times toward a "quasi-optimal" pricing solution. This insight has become possible simply because the Baumol-Bradford theorem tells us that optimality in a world requiring revenues for social purposes *necessitates* departures from marginal-cost pricing.

This chapter will attempt to indicate whither some of the socialist economies are tending with respect to the pricing problem. The case of the

---

See the title footnote to Chapter 4.

GDR (German Democratic Republic or East Germany) will be treated and the developments of the reform period in which the East Germans appeared to be initiating a *tâtonnement* toward pricing optimality will be reviewed. Documentation on the decline of this fortuitous process, as well as the pricing implications of the abandonment of economic reform in East Germany will be presented.

East European Pricing Developments in the Reform Period

This section will merely provide the reader with the flavor of developments in socialist pricing since the beginning of the reform period. A brief sampling of typical and noteworthy events will hopefully set the stage for the more thorough case study that follows.

Yugoslavia

To find the origins of the Eastern European search for more rational pricing techniques, one must go back to 1950. At that time, there was no free market for industrial goods in Yugoslavia, planning was carried on strictly in physical terms, but serious questioning of the traditional command allocation of resources had begun. New views began to appear as to the proper economic mechanism for the establishment of prices.[2]

Many commodities were permitted to seek "real" prices dictated by the market, and the market was seen as an integral part of the planning framework. The prices of those goods over which central authority felt compelled to retain significant control, however, remained centrally planned. Ultimately, two types of price control were instituted in Yugoslavia for industrial commodities. For most important materials and intermediate manufacturing goods, the Federal Executive Council established price ceilings. For the principal consumer commodities and certain other materials, the authorities reserved the right to be informed of the intention of enterprises to increase prices. Approximately 70 percent of manufactured commodities are subject either to price ceilings or to price ratification by the Federal Price Control Office.

Some sectors of the Yugoslavian economy are subject, of course, to no price controls whatsoever. In fact, minimum prices are established for the most crucial agricultural products. Fixed rates have been established by the authorities for dwelling rentals, as well as for the services of the communications and transportation industries. However, in the service industries, price controls vary in extensiveness.

Pricing practices have by no means stabilized under Yugoslavian planning, and discussion regarding potentially better techniques continues. Measures have been initiated in order to facilitate the operation of the price mechanism in domestic and external trade.

Some contemporary socialist economists of "revisionist" bent see price policies as a means by which the plan and the market may be coordinated. Price planners in Yugoslavia, however, have considered price planning as the means of obtaining the planned development of the economy, with the market viewed as a constraint in the planning framework. So in practice, price policies in Yugoslavia have not been in marked contrast to those of other Soviet-type economies. In an attempt to promote accumulation, relatively low prices have been established for capital goods. Complementarily, prices for farm products have been set at a low level, so that rural savings might be utilized for the accumulation of industrial capital and so that the development of agriculture might be kept "under planned control." Finally, as in other Eastern European states, a long discussion has been carried on regarding the normatively "best" concept for socialist pricing.

Hungary

The improvement of the price mechanism has been the basic element of the Hungarian reform debate, and the amelioration of pricing institutions is a matter of high priority in Hungary.[3] Economists there speak of "value prices" and "production prices." When the costs of production of a given product are supplemented by a uniform normative profit markup based upon the cost of labor in the price calculation, traditional "value pricing" is utilized. Since 1964, however, the Hungarians have favored "production prices." These supplement the prime costs of the products with a profit or surplus value markup based upon the cost of total assets (fixed and working capital). The attempt has been to adopt "production pricing" as the basic technique of industrial price planning. By 1970, roughly one-third of industries' social net income in Hungary conformed to the value of assets. The goal of Hungarian planners is to regulate profits so that ultimately two-thirds of net income will conform to the value of assets, while only one-third will conform to wage costs.

Such prices have likewise demonstrated considerable inflexibility; once established, they have remained in force over periods of six to eight years. Though Hungarian economists speak favorably of flexible price mechanisms and of free price formation, they are anxious to avoid upward pressures on the price level and, therefore, deem it necessary to maintain state price regulation. Price flexibility has been sought through the introduction of some interesting techniques: (a) permitting an industry to establish prices freely below a given ceiling; (b) setting a maximum price for one of the leading products within a given product group, hoping that this "socialist price leader" will stablize the price level for the entire group; (c) specifying the principles of price formation that will prevail in a given industry by indicating specific cost and profit normatives; and (d) permitting contracted prices to be arranged between producers and consumers, i.e., permitting market price relations to prevail in given industries.

Czechoslovakia

In Czechoslovakia, price reform has also led to the adoption of "value-based prices" (for which the markup is based upon labor costs in accord with Marxian labor theory) and "production prices" (for which the profit markup is based upon the total capital used by the enterprise in production). Most economists have favored the latter.[4]

The surplus value markup, however calculated, accounts for the divergence of price from "value," and modern Marxist ideology views the maintenance of such a divergence in pricing practice as perfectly acceptable. The price may exceed the "value" of the product, for it permits the accumulation of revenues for both the enterprise and the state. However, preinvasion economic thought in Czechoslovakia advanced a rationale for an additional necessary cause for the divergence of the price and value, i.e., consumer demand for the product in question.

Differing use-values and the varying degrees of substitutability of goods were seen as the determinates of the extent and structure of commodity demands. Czechoslovakian reform economists argued for the necessity of allowing wholesale prices for short periods to deviate from their value base (their cost-of-production price) to assure market equilibrium. The celebrated and once influential Ota Šik contributed much to the preinvasion Czechoslovakian belief that a rational and just allocation of resources requires effective functioning of both plan and market. In Šik's view, even a liberal socialist economy constructed along Lange-Lerner lines cannot guarantee efficient economic performance. Central authority may simply fail to recognize the price equilibrium of each individual commodity. Moreover, conflicts of interest will inevitably arise when rules are set by central institutions for the enterprise. Pareto optimal equilibrium prices can be achieved "only by a direct clash of interests of producers and consumers in the market."[5]

Although some bloc economists are convinced that mathematical techniques allied with the use of computers will soon enable price calculations to be made for all important products produced by the socialist economy, Czechoslovakian economists seem to harbor strong doubts. Their skepticism is based not only on the fact that the mathematical theory of optimum processes has not yet been perfected, but also because the statistical information required for price calculations is imperfect and does not reach the center quickly enough to generate calculated prices that would be appropriate for the momentary state of the economy.[6] Thus, the basic, preinvasion Czechoslovakian posture on price planning seems to have been that the utilization of mathematical techniques and computers would not guarantee the possibility of eliminating the market mechanism. On the contrary, the utilization of such techniques presupposes the existence of an operative market.

Foundations of East German Price Revision and Reform

In order to achieve greater depth in the investigation of pricing practice in a reform and postreform milieu, the East German case will be investigated more thoroughly. This will also present the opportunity to achieve a more detailed understanding of the interaction of theory and practice in socialist pricing.[a]

Like other bloc countries, East Germany initiated an attempt, in the 1960s, to modernize its command allocation processes. The price revisions and reforms instigated were designed to alleviate undesirable economic outcomes generated by prices that had been unresponsive to changing economic conditions for nearly twenty years. Better performance became a possibility only with the advent of the New Economic System, for in East Germany, as in other socialist countries, economic organization and pricing practices had encouraged irrational allocation. Surplus values, for example, were rather arbitrarily determined (though in the light of government revenue needs), and the capital charges that would have provided helpful pricing norms were conspicuously absent. In fact, all of the sources of irrationality inherent in command pricing described earlier could be found in East German pricing.

Once the door was opened to reform discussion, the quest for rational pricing induced some to attempt the creation of an entirely new price analysis. Though few were prepared to cease paying ideological homage to traditional Marxian analysis, the jargon used in the literature could not disguise the use of "bourgeois" economics. Mathematical programming and input-output techniques are still of limited use in actual planning, but

---

[a] My selection of the East German case for special treatment can also be explained by greater familiarity with the language and with East German planning. By now, it should be apparent, however, that the pricing practices of bloc countries parallel one another, and pricing theory and practices in East Germany reflect similar institutions in the Soviet Union and also give insight into types of price theory and practice common to other Socialist countries.

they became the *sine qua non* of the socialist theoretician.

East German price theory and pricing experience is best understood as an organic part of the attempt to establish general economic reform in the command system. It is intended that the price coefficient serve as the principal "economic lever" and, as such, be interrelated with the officially designated index of "profitability" as the new criterion for the adequacy of enterprise performance. Naturally, pricing techniques must be closely related to the attempt to permit the firm to finance a part of its own investment and bonuses for workers and managers through earned revenues. In the endeavor to utilize mathematical economic models and electronic computers in the processes of planning and plan implementation, pricing techniques are clearly of single importance.

With the belated recognition that prices serve both as coefficients of accounting and as mechanisms for resource allocation, it was finally acknowledged that prices must respond much more flexibly to dynamic change in the economic environment. Even Walter Ulbricht declared himself a strong advocate of flexibility in pricing, contending that a "correct" relationship between price and (labor) value can be maintained only through a continual process of review and revision. For this reason, he enjoined price officials to be more responsive to changing economic conditions.[7]

Once the East Germans decided that a massive price revision would be essential, the undertaking had to be preceded by a project of great magnitude in itself. In order to calculate the profit markup properly, it was necessary to reassess enterprise capital values and recalculate depreciation write-offs.[8]

The actual process of price revision occurred in three stages. On April 1, 1964, price revisions were effected for raw materials. On July 1, 1964, they were extended to intermediate goods, and, after difficulties and postponements, the prices of consumer goods were revised on January 1, 1967. By its own admission, the GDR's price revision was made at the cost of a staggering bureaucratic effort, even though the agricultural sector was excluded. Three hundred fifty work collectives participated in the development of the new prices and 6000 specialists were required in the recalculation of the capital values of enterprises.

Planners were determined that these revisions should, in no case, lead to price increases for consumer goods. None of the varieties of goods formerly available was to disappear from the market, nor was the quality of available consumer goods to deteriorate. These were held to be of such importance that they were firmly grounded in law.[9]

With an average cost increase of some 75 percent for raw materials, it would be difficult to believe that the system could maintain price stability. In order to make it possible for enterprises to resist the great upward pressure on consumer prices, the extensive subsidies paid to basic materials producers over the long period when their prices had been held artificially low would have had to be transferred to the producers of consumer goods.[10]

Soon after the revisions were completed, it became apparent that no such subsidies would be forthcoming and that the upward pressure would indeed be irresistible. Press reports began to indicate an increasing number of excessive price increases contrary to the letter and the spirit of the law. Socialist enterprises were censured for attempting to achieve higher profits without unduly exerting themselves.

In other cases, more innovative managers developed ingenious ways to veil price increases; trivial product changes were used as a justification for increased prices, or quality changes difficult to perceive were introduced. Naturally, the effects of such behavior were the same as price increases would have been.

At the 11th Plenary Meeting of the Central Committee of the Socialist Unity Party in December 1965, Walter Ulbricht revealed that prices established in the revision's first and second stages were being reworked for commodities whose costs of production were not covered by revision prices.[11]

The announcement that the inadequacies of the first two stages had necessitated revision of the final (consumer goods prices) stage was of particular importance, for it opened the way for an extensive discussion on the matter of an improved socialist price analysis. Though the ameliorated price structure sought by GDR economists had to some extent escaped them, the benefits of rethinking apparently would not.

The primary thrust of the GRD's price reform was referred to as "complex price planning." Rational pricing practices were sought through mathematical techniques similar to those being developed in the Soviet Union. These mathematical pricing models (*Preisverflechtungsbilanzen*) have been of interest to western economists because they contain elements of established western economic theory.[12] Perhaps most significant is the fact that such attempts represented a search for a general equilibrium price planning strategy.

The GDR's Price Office (in collaboration with the National Planning Commission and the Ministry of Finance) undertook an "industrial perspective price plan." In the plan's first phase, participating enterprises were directed to submit, by the end of June 1969 (in prices prevailing at the first of that year), estimates on costs, inventories, materials in process, and so on for the period from 1971 to 1975. These estimates were used in the construction of an input-output table of 1150 aggregated product groups. The model was designed to assist in (a) forecasting the development of international trade relations, (b) maintaining particular price relations between substitutable materials, and (c) providing information requisite to determining and achieving desirable structural changes in the economy. German planners expect much from the input-output technique, for other ambitious goals have also been given expression in announced expectations of plan achievement. Thus, pricing developments in the resource-furnishing industries are also to be subject to forecasting, as are developments in the level and structure of wages in the industrial sector.

The coefficients generated by the input-output analysis were intended for utilization in the second phase of the development of the perspective price plan. Dynamic pricing techniques were to permit the price office, in collaboration with the ministries, the industrial associations, and some enterprises, to generate "price change coefficients." These would provide norms for upper and lower limits of profitability associated with the outcomes of the price plan.[13]

It is significant that the input-output coefficients (as well as the price coefficients generated from them) are intended for utilization by planners only as "orientation values," rather than as rigid prescriptive data from which deviation cannot be permitted. East German economists emphasized that essential flexibility should be pursued through pragmatic deviation from plan values according to economic necessity.[14]

Because of the limited flow of (often imprecise) information in the system and the highly aggregated linear programming and input-output techniques employed, plan outcomes are not those of a "mathematically programmed economy." The contemporary Soviet-type resource allocation system is best described as the traditional material balance approach supplemented and modified by sophisticated quantitative techniques. The mathematical and statistical tools employed may represent the "wave of the future," but the tide will likely not come in for some time yet.[15]

The East Germans hoped that the introduction of new pricing techniques would permit the price parameter (a) to promote greater efficiency by playing a greater role in resource allocation, (b) to express more faithfully "socially necessary labor costs," and (c) to influence more extensively the economy's consumption patterns.

Though pricing remained basically average-cost pricing with a surplus value (profit) markup, other factors proved to be more fortuitous in the quest for greater efficiency. As has been indicated, prices came to be viewed by German planners as "economic levers," the function of which was to put downward pressure on the prime costs of the producing enterprise. Prices were also to provide whatever impetus might be necessary to force obsolete production methods out of use and stimulate the adoption of new techniques. In short, it was hoped that pricing could represent a substitute for the competitive pressure of normally functioning markets. To the extent that that goal was achieved, of course, greater efficiency would be the outcome.

East German prices were no longer merely to be surrogates of the physical quantities of planning, for it was officially declared that future price planning was to be an organic part of the overall planning process, i.e., a directive force in the process of allocation.

More extensive decentralization of pricing responsibilities within the planning hierarchy was also a part of the pursuit of greater efficiency. Industrial associations were made responsible within certain limits for their own pricing decisions (for all but "structurally determining" commodities such as steel and power). Supply *and* demand factors were to be taken into consideration by the industrial associations, and here, too, prices were to assume more than a purely passive "measuring-rod function."[16] Operating as "economic levers," they were to generate profits for productive economic endeavor just as market prices are able to do.[b]

It should be observed here that East German economists and officials, unlike those in Czechoslovakia, do not view a linkage of the market mechanism and the national plan as a panacea for resource allocation problems. In the GDR, the actual pursuit of dynamics in modified command pricing has taken the form of an authorization by the center of periodic price readjustments by industrial associations or enterprises according to needs that arise from shifts in production functions, consumer preferences, or other such parameters.

Profit-maximizing prices set at industrial and enterprise levels remained, of course, the ideal rather than the general practice. Nevertheless, for a time, planning trends appeared favorable for the achievement of a substantially greater degree of decentralization; after all, some fairly extensive experimentation had begun with less centralized pricing institutions. This was of particular interest in the case of "arranged" prices *(Vereinbarungspreise)*, which were to be established freely between buyer and seller (according to approved methods of calculation but without central supervision). It is noteworthy that these were to permit either higher or lower calculated profit markups than were generally specified.[c] Other enterprises were to be permitted to establish prices freely, so long as they were set below specified maximum limits.[17]

The second objective of reformed pricing—eliminating the difference

---

[b] Profits, as spoken of here, are similar to those we think of in mixed economies which can be used for the private purposes of the firm. Usually, "profits" have meant surplus value for socialist writers—revenues in excess of costs confiscated by the state from the state-owned enterprise for the purposes of the planners. There is still a healthy element of the social surplus value notion when socialist writers speak of "profitability."

[c] These are being applied in several areas including special machinery, new products, and products with unusual and prearranged specifications.

between "socially necessary labor costs" of production and prevailing prices—would make it possible to eliminate the extensive system of subsidies designed to offset the negative rents incurred in the operation of firms producing traditionally underpriced goods. For some new materials, the proportion of these subsidies to total costs had been remarkably high.[18]

The final objective—greater reliance on the price mechanism to control consumption patterns—required giving more attention to the problem of demand and utilizing the turnover tax more extensively. This form of taxation was the chief source of state revenues even before the reforms, and its increasing use would have been guaranteed even without its consumption-regulating function, for the enterprise deficits discussed above represent only one of the elements of an avowed need for increased public revenues.[19]

East German economists were quite willing in certain instances for prices to deviate from "values" (in the long-run cost of production sense), as they must when turnover taxes are imposed. Three of several such instances are listworthy: first, when the planned stock of consumption goods (*Warenfonds*) must be coordinated with the stock of consumer purchasing power *(Kauffonds)*; second, when the deviation of capital goods prices from their "values" can stimulate the substitution of some of the items generally representing bottlenecks in the production process for goods and materials in adequate supply; and, finally, when private firms are called upon temporarily to help cover specific demands that exceed the capacity of nationalized socialist industries, higher product prices may be necessary to cover the temporarily higher production costs.[20]

Willingness to attach a substantial turnover tax to production cost is but one of the evidences that the trend in East German planning was to consider Marxist pricing formulae merely as general guidelines to pricing policy. Deviations of the proper sort had long been countenanced and numerous considerations justified them. Indeed, a whole structure of price-determining considerations had been generated to provide price setters at various levels of the planning hierarchy (e.g., in the industrial associations) with guidelines for "correct pricing" applicable to their unique situations.

It is, perhaps, also worth a reminder that, by the advent of the decade of reforms, socialist planners and economists had come to recognize that price formulation must account for the costs of capital used in production. Ideologically speaking, of course, capital now merely receives a (shadow price) return only because it "aids labor in production," but the effect is the same. Likewise, it has been shown that socially necessary labor *and* demand considerations are now to be taken into account when prices are established. Prices cannot be equated, therefore, with Marxian value, so that (ideological literature notwithstanding), for all practical purposes, socialists in the reform period appeared to be quietly discarding the labor theory of value. Subtly dropping the old doctrine that capital could not be productive (since only labor is) and could therefore not represent a cost constitutes the same kind of Marxian heresy—one which can be afforded in the competitive economic struggle against capitalism.

The Reform *Tâtonnement* Toward Optimality

The most important deviation of price from Marxian "value" had its origin in the reform decision to give ideological approbation to the role of demand in price determination. (Quite clearly, this decision had great bearing on the proposition of controlling consumption patterns via the price mechanism.) At the time, even Walter Ulbricht conceded that past preoccupation with the role of socially necessary labor resulted in inadequate emphasis on supply-demand relationships. He promised that prices would be permitted to find their own equilibrium level (although this was to occur within a given range established by the planners).[21] "Market research" is now being conducted in some of the industrial associations with the intent to reveal the nature of demand, supply, and price relationships in particular markets.

The attempts to modernize price planning relied primarily upon mathematical techniques similar to those being discussed in the literature of other bloc states. In these pricing models *(Preisverflechtungsbilanzen)*, demand conditions are always investigated. It is of little significance, from a long-run point of view, that these techniques are still in a rather uncertain stage of development and experimentation;[22] the important thing is that preoccupation with the structure and elasticity of demand in Soviet-type economies became far greater than it had been a relatively short time before.[23] In terms of achieving Baumol-Bradford optimality, this interest in questions of demand represented the most favorable development for the GDR's reformed economy.

Since one of the express objectives of the New Economic System was to permit prices to have greater influence on directing consumption patterns, greater use was to be expected of the turnover tax for the purpose of constraining strong demand (where commodity supplies are limited, for example, and must be made to suffice).

East German economists also came to recognize that the profit-turnover tax markup must be related to demand elasticity, since demand can be constrained with facility only when it is elastic.[24] By way of illustration, a typical passage from the pricing literature seems unwittingly to recognize the implications of the Baumol-Bradford theorem by denying that production and demand can be brought into equality through an exorbitantly high price.[25] It holds that demand cannot be "tightened down" to the level of supply, because "the elasticity of demand for individual product groups is quite variable.'' It can be constrained only to a limited extent in some cases and not at all in others.

Zuaberman observed some years ago that price discussion in the Soviet Union might lead to increased use of the turnover tax to take care of price and income elasticities of demand for individual goods.[26] Experience with that practice in East Germany could not help but reinforce a natural inclination to derive needed revenues by attaching higher prices to goods whose demand was relatively inelastic than to those of goods characterized by very elastic demand.

At the height of the reform era, planning trends could be viewed with optimism. It seemed that the combined tendencies (a) to pay more attention to considerations of demand elasticity, (b) to seek greater social revenues for public purposes through turnover taxes (applied with an eye to price elasticity of demand), and (d) to use the price mechanism to direct consumption patterns could justifiably be construed as a groping toward pricing practices in harmony with Baumol-Bradford quasi-optimality considerations.

The Eclipse of the Reforms

By 1970, the East Germans began to despair of their system of economic reforms. Insufficiently developed conceptually, and incompletely and inconsistently implemented, reform measures could provide only disappointing outcomes. Numerous difficulties had become apparent at the turn of the decade. Without attempting comprehensiveness, one might refer to some of the most serious ones: there was no clear, systematic set of relationships among the various ''economic levers'' (incentive-providing institutional arrangements); a sharp contradiction had developed between the industrial structure actually developing and the structural development preferred by the planners.

Perhaps one of the most important single causes of the growth difficulties of the late sixties and, consequently, of the shutting down of the reforms in East Germany arises from this last point. Rewarding profitability financially by permitting firms to share in their own earnings, i.e., permitting firms to use their share for bonuses *and* for financing some of their investment choices *(Eigenerwirtschaftung der Mittel)*, resulted in increased competition for investment goods, a market shortage of (and, consequently, inflationary tendencies for) such goods, and a developing industrial structure that did not correspond to planners' preferences.[27]

For the purposes of this investigation, however, it is of great importance to note that the price structure then prevailing in East Germany also played a causal role in the failure of the GDR reform experiment.[28]

In the first place, even though the state was not negligent about confiscating the rental earnings from enterprises involved, retaining relatively high prices for consumer goods resulted in relatively high profitability for producers of consumer goods. They were, thus, in a position to finance investments of types out of harmony with the preferences of planners, thus threatening the development of industrial structures favored by the latter.

Additionally, price adjustments made in the final phase of the revision process were based on costs pertaining in 1967, but these were outdated rather soon. Indeed, cost structures were affected by the reform itself, and this possibility had not been accounted for by planners. As a result, the revisions could have had their greatest effect only if a continual process of price revision had been undertaken.

To some extent this did occur in practice, viz., with the introduction of capital-related prices. The transition to the new price type, however, turned out to be very difficult: barely 30 percent of industrial production was based on capital-related prices when the process ceased in 1971.

The increasing degree of price distortion in East Germany during this period led to an increase in the (originally reduced) state subsidies to producers of nonprofitable commodities and, perhaps more interestingly, to a rise in the price level. Under a state-controlled price system, of course, inflation can occur only indirectly. This happened in East Germany through a changing structure of available consumer goods—some cheaper goods simply were no longer produced and the prices of many "improved" products were increased more than planners considered justifiable.[29]

The official response was firm: ceasing production of current commodities was outlawed and price increases were forbidden uniformly for consumers and producers goods for the remainder of the five-year plan (i.e., until 1975).[30] Exceptions were to be permitted only by the Council of Ministers.

From that point (November 1971), the process of conversion to capital-related pricing came to a halt. Likewise, the System of Industrial Pricing Rules *(Industriepreisregelsystem)*, which had permitted some degree of discretion in price setting for economic agents toward the bottom of the planning hierarchy, was dropped.[31] The intent was, doubtless, that discretion be fully restored to the Office of Pricing of the Ministerial Council. At the same time, the possibility of capturing incentive returns for the introduction of newly developed (and higher priced) products via agreements between suppliers and purchasers was also eliminated. Prices for such products are now subject to the approval of the price office.[32]

It appears, at this point, that the implementation of more effective pricing practices, dependent as this process is upon the willingness to countenance meaningful reform measures, has ceased for the time being. Under a firm price freeze and in a planning milieu characterized by a reemphasis of centralism and traditional planning methodology, at least for the near future, prices seem destined to play a rather passive role in the resource allocation processes of socialist Germany.

Since pricing methodology implemented in the planning bureaucracy always lags several steps behind theoretical developments anyway, one might hope that theorists, at least, would continue working on the problem of the role of demand and elasticities in pricing. In this case, socialist economic theory could at least continue its *tâtonnement* toward optimal pricing. Unfortunately, however, even this aspect of the reform movement seems moribund.

It seems likely that price theoreticians either feel that further efforts in this particular direction momentarily are ideologically inappropriate or simply that such efforts are pointless. In any case, there has for some time been no significant discussion of pricing theory or price planning problems in East German economic literature.[33]

Reform phraseology has not totally disappeared from the GDR economist's vocabulary, of course, and from a long-term perspective the need for economic reforms seems no less apparent for the administrative economy today than it did in the 1960s. However, a near-future adoption of the optimum reform is scarcely an historical inevitablity, and it cannot be foreseen when a meaningful price discussion might be resumed in East Germany.

Notes

1. The most limited reference to the literature would logically include Abram Bergson, Hans Böhme, and Morris Bornstein. See Bergson, "The Soviet Debate on the Law of Value and Price Formation: Comment," in *Value and Plan*, Gregory Grossman, ed. (Berkeley: University of California Press, 1960), pp. 36-40. His question for command pricing is "not merely how to fix rational prices but whether such prices can be fixed at all" (p.38). See also Hans Böhme, "East German Price Formation Under the New Economic System," *Soviet Studies* (January 1968), pp. 340-358, and "Gebrauschwert und Preispolitik im sozialistischen Wirtschaftssystem: Untersucht am Beispiel der DDR," *Weltwirtschaftliches Archiv*, no. 1, Band 106 (1971), pp. 78-125. Morris Bornstein discusses the viewpoints of some soviet economists who also favor marginal-cost pricing. See his "Soviet Price Theory and Policy," in the United States Congress, Joint Economic Committee, *New Directions in the Soviet Economy*. (Washington, D.C.: U.S. Government Printing Office, 1966), I, pp. 65-98.

2. For a good survey of developments in Yugoslavian price theory and policy, see I. Maksimovic and Z. Pjanic, "Price Problems in Yugoslav

Theory and Practice," in *Economic Development for Eastern Europe*, by Michael Kaser, ed., (New York: St. Martin's, 1968), pp. 185-195.

3. Bela Szikszai, "Changes in the Price System and in the Price Mechanism in Hungary," in *Planning and Markets: Modern Trends in Various Economic Systems*, John T. Dunlop and Nikolay P. Federenko, eds. (New York: McGraw-Hill, 1969), pp. 254-266.

4. Ota Šik, "Prices in the New Economic System of Management in a Socialist Economy," in Dunlop and Federenko, *Planning and Markets*, op. cit., pp. 217-228.

5. *Ibid.*, p. 222.

6. O. Kyn, B. Sekerka, and L. Hejl, "A Model for the Planning of Prices," in *Socialism, Capitalism, and Economic Growth: Essays Presented to Maurice Dobb*, C.H. Feinstein, ed. (London: Cambridge University Press, 1967), p. 102. This article takes the position that market forces must supplement price planning. Price calculation is important because it can yield information on the manner in which fundamental macroeconomic price relations should be developing, "in other words, how the relations between aggregate price levels of individual industries should develop." Information generated in this fashion can be of assistance to planners attempting to influence economic processes indirectly so that "current prices," established by market forces, come as close as possible to "planned prices." It is desirable, of course, that the planned price "be an equilibrium market price, with current market price moving according to monetary supply and demand." (See pp. 102-103.)

7. Walter Ulbricht, *Zum Neuen Ökonomischen System* (East Berlin: Dietz Verlag, 1967), pp. 180-181. Ulbricht's attitude is reflected in the often expressed sentiment that price reform in the German Democratic Republic would, in the future, no longer be an event but an ongoing process.

8. Capital values were adjusted upward by more than 50 percent on the average, with the aggregate value rising from 56 to 85 billion marks. Depreciation write-offs in nationalized industries were adjusted downward from 4.2 to 3.6 percent, which represents an increase in the expected productive life of capital equipment from the former 24 to the current 28 years. See Gert Leptin, "Das 'Neue Ökonomische System' Mitteldeutschlands," in *Wirtschaftsreformen in Osteuropa*, Karl C. Thalheim and Hans-Hermann Höhmann, eds. (Köln: Verlag Wissenschaft und Politik, 1968), p. 120.

9. See Karl Thalheim, *Die Wirtschaft der Sowjetzone in Krise und Umbau*. (Berlin: Duncker & Humblot, 1964), p. 102.

10. Helmut Mann reports that prices of bituminous coal, lignite, iron, scrap metal, wood, furs, and many other basic products did not cover costs. Likewise the bulk of raw materials imports were unprofitable, since

domestic prices were significantly lower in these goods than world-market prices. See his "Notwendige Veränderungen des Preissystems der DDR," *Wirtschaftswissenschaft*, Vol. 10, Heft 11 (November 1962).

11. See Ulbricht, *Zum Neuen*, op. cit., p. 184.

12. Böhme, "East German Price Formation," op. cit., p. 355.

13. See Manfred Melzer, "Preispolitik und Preisbildungsprobleme in der DDR," *Vierteljahreshefte zur Wirtshaftsforschung*, Heft 3 (1969), pp. 347-348.

14. See E. Maier, et al., *Zur Preisplanung in VVB und Betrieben* (East Berlin: Verlag die Wirtschaft, 1968), p. 23, 29.

15. Price planners still rightfully complain that their art is rendered very difficult by the interactions between the development of prices and all other material and financial processes (such as costs, profitability, commodity flows, investment, etc.). Changing a price sets off a chain reaction of other changed values, whereby the whole set of requirements of technical and economic development are altered. See *Zur Preisplanung* op. cit., p. 16. The fact that the price plan is worked out *after* completion of the perspective plan, rather than simultaneously with it, must represent some sort of indication of the unperfected state of Soviet-type (pregeneral equilibrium) planning. See p. 36.

16. Fred Matho, *Wie Werden Preise Gemacht?* (East Berlin: Deitz Verlag, 1967), observes that supply-demand relationships should be utilized not "mechanically" but only to provide "orientation," since profitability considerations and state participation in the pricing process will inevitably continue to be important. Böhme, "Gebrauchswert und Preispolitik," op. cit., provides an extensive discussion of the role of demand in East German pricing at the height of the reform endeavor.

17. For more detailed treatment of these three fundamental price types, see Hulmut Mann, *Grundfragen zur Industriepreisbildung* (East Berlin: Verlag die Wirtschaft, 1968), pp. 16-17. See also *Gesetzblatt,* vol. 2, no. 122 (1968), pp. 973-976.

18. See Melzer, *"Preispolitik,"* op. cit., p. 315. Such subsidies came to 55 percent of total costs for metallurgical products and machine building; 50 percent for wool, cotton, and timber; 45 percent for paper, pasteboard, and transport tariffs.

19. See Maier, *Zur Preisplanung*, op. cit., for the citation of an address by Walter Ulbricht, who says that "even in the case of declining prime costs product prices will not sink proportionately, for the enterprises simply must have increasing profits to accomplish the great social tasks confronting them."

20. See Edda Köhne, *Die Preisbildung in der Sowjetischen Besatzungszone Deutschlands* (Bonn: Deutscher Bundesverlag, 1966), p. 9.

21. Ulbricht, *Zum Neuen*, op. cit., pp. 186-187.

22. Ota Šik, "Prices in the New Economic System," op. cit., p. 226, makes this apparent when he confesses that "the use of mathematical methods in calculating the elasticity of demand for different incomes and prices does not yet make possible a reliable forecasting of detailed changes in the structure of demand. It would seem that even in the future these methods will be more suitable for making prognoses of consumption in certain aggregate groups of consumer goods, and not specifically for the currently produced or new products."

23. Bornstein, *New Directions*, op. cit., p. 90, refers to the discussion, in the Soviet Union, on demand problems. Surpluses there have been due not only to overpricing, but also to poor demand estimates. Only in recent years have demand studies been given serious attention. The early studies suffered from hyperaggregation of demand estimates. Excessively broad categories of goods, very large geographic areas, and an inadequate breakdown of demands from different income groups were all negative characteristics of Soviet attempts to deal with the problems of forecasting.

24. The turnover tax can be viewed simply as an additional markup and in the analytical framework utilized in Chapter 4 it merely becomes part of the surplus value markup m which is constrained by the elasticity of demand.

25. See Matho, *Wie Werden*, op. cit., p. 34.

26. See Alfred Zauberman, "The Soviet Debate on the Law of Value and Price Formation," in *Value and Plan*, by Gregory Grossman, ed. (Berkeley: University of California Press, 1960), pp. 29-30. Although he found a declining role for the turnover tax as a mechanism by which the aggregates of monetary purchasing power could be equated with marketplace prices (seen in East Germany as equating *Warenfonds* and *Kauffonds*), he foresaw a strengthening of the tendency of the turnover tax to account for elasticity of demand.

27. For a detailed description of these investment difficulties, see Buck Hannsjorg, "Umkehr zur administrativen Befehlwirtschaft als Folge nicht behobener Steuerungsdefekte der Wirtschaftsreformkonzeption," in *Das Ökonomische System der DDR nach dem Anfang der siebziger Jahre*, Bruno Gleitze et al., eds. (Berlin: Duncker & Humblot, 1971), pp. 77-108.

28. I am indebted to an excellent unpublished manuscript by Gert Leptin (1972) and to him personally for discussions bearing on price theory and planning in the GDR in recent years.

29. Deutsches Institut fur Wirtschaftsforschung, *DDR-Wirtschaft: eine Bestandsaufnahme* (Frankfurt am Main: Fischer Bucherei, 1971), p. 200.

30. "Beschluß Über Maßnahmen auf dem Gabiet der Leitung, Planung

und Entwicklung der Industriepreise vom 17. *Gesetzblatt der DDR*, teil 2, nr. 77 (November 1971), p. 669.

31. This system called for upper and lower limits of permissable profit earnings for each product group. If the upper limit were exceeded in a given year, at the beginning of the following year price reductions were to be undertaken. These were to permit only the predetermined minimal profit yield. Such price reductions would not be undertaken if they would stimulate demand in excess of productive capacity, distort relative prices so as to create adverse substitute relationships among goods, or otherwise prove disadvantageous. See Deutsches Institut für Wirtschaftsforschung, *DDR-Wirtschaft*, op. cit., p. 73.

32. With hindsight, incidentally, it may be suspected that the "arranged prices" mentioned in an earlier section were never really intended for general (or even broad) application. These free arrangements between producers purchasing inputs and their suppliers were restricted to particular and limited productive outputs. See Friedrich Haffner, "Reformen der Preissysteme," in *Die Wirtschaftsordnungen Osteuropas in Wandel: Ergebnisse und Probleme der Wirtschaftsreformen*, Band II, Michael C. Kaser and Karl C. Thalheim, eds. (Freiburg: Verlag Rombach, 1972), p. 92.

33. An article by Kurt Ambrée and Helmut Mann, "Die Vervollkommnung der planmaßigen Preisbildung zur Sicherung der Einheit von materieller und finanzieller Planung," *Wirtschaftswissenschaft*, vol. 20, no. 11 (November 1972), pp. 1642-1657, represents, in this respect, an unimportant exception. In treating the question of use value, they submit that its inclusion in the problem of price determination remains "an open problem." Their own position seems to be that use value is irrelevant for the determination of a commodity's *value*, though supply *and* demand questions are relevant in establishing the appropriate *price*. Once again, price may deviate from value for purposes of social expedience.

6 Investment I: Centralist Investment and Economic Control

The degree to which economic control, especially investment processes, should be maintained by central authority in the socialist countries remains a matter of debate. In recent years, however, the exigencies of contemporary ideology have dampened the enthusiasm of the discussion in socialist literature, and there is no reason to expect any substantial decontrol of investments in the near future. The Yugoslavian proclivity for market processes remains generally unacceptable to planning bureaucrats throughout the remainder of the more orthodox socialist world.

Central planners subscribe to the notion that effective economic control excludes any extensive decentralization of investment planning, and it is difficult to conceive a clearcut refutation to that proposition. According to traditional values, control of both the level and the structure of investments is essential for the achievement of the desired long-term performance.[1]

The level of investment can be seen only as a function of variables that do not readily yield themselves up to analytical precision. Though hypotheses can be developed regarding the preferences of planners within the constraints of productive and social possibilities, the matter remains largely one of political economy. The allocation of investment resources must occur in competition with resource demands for regional and international development efforts, for defense and public goods, as well as for consumer goods. Finding the particular balance between investment and consumption has long been of central importance for economic planning. The question seems inherent to the socialist dilemma: "What is more advantageous for achieving increased consumption and its continuity, a rapid rate of growth of national income or a sinking rate of productive accumulation (investment outlays)?"[2]

The advantages of a lower rate of accumulation (defined by socialists as the difference between national income and consumption[3]) are seen to be lost when, after a short period of time, the rate of economic growth begins to decline, unless the reduced investment outlays happen to be characterized by a greater degree of effectiveness.[4]

The other macro question, of course, bears on the industrial structure of investments and future output mixes.[5] Perhaps we should not find the socialists' lack of more substantive analytical progress with "structural" investment problems surprising, for they are difficult indeed. But some progress has been made; socialist economics has for some time been quite willing to countenance the bourgeois, cost-benefit approach to analysis, and the East European mathematical school has kept the socialist technology at a level that can be compared in concept if not in detail with theory in Western countries. This is not to say that cost-benefit analysis can provide an ideal, peremptory solution to the investment problem; even Western technicians point out that quantification is difficult and at best approximate. Many costs are not measurable, and, even after the attempt has been made, the final choice is often a compromise between technical economic and broad political considerations.[6]

The question as to the effect of reforms, in the 1960s, upon investment planning also begs to be addressed. The coming of age of shadow pricing at the theoretical level, as well as the adoption of the Liberman mandate ("let the enterprise find profit in that which benefits the society"), might have some impact on investment planning and practices designed to achieve greater effectiveness at the micro level.

Although the problem has been solved for the ideologist, economists in eastern Europe still have to evaluate the possibility of market-type solutions in the pursuit of efficiency. For many years, under a basic, bread-and-butter, autarkic industrialization program, questions of structure could be ignored and continued socialist growth required little more than high levels of savings and investment. The share of national income devoted to investment usually amounted to from 20 to 30 percent.[7] In the past decade, however, socialist economists began to face the problem of declining efficiency: the output-capital ratio was reduced, the ratio of national income to productive funds diminished, new capital construction was less effective than anticipated, long gestation periods were experienced, a large volume of poor quality or uncompleted construction accumulated, estimated capital construction costs were often exceeded, projects were developed without any real necessity, and the planning of investments was generally based on inadequate analysis, or even none at all.[8]

These problems arose in part because some of the projects selected violated even the primitive selection criteria that were available. The Soviet case is probably not exceptional, and writers there complained that some of the selected projects were outmoded before they were even completed and had unacceptably high costs and long recoupment periods. Bad information, poor documentation for project proposals, and planning errors and misspecifications came to be ubiquitous in Soviet invest planning.[9]

The hope that many of these difficulties could be overcome by implementing "economic levers" (incentives to make rational economic behavior rewarding to the economic agent as well as to society) was certainly not inappropriate. However, reforms had to achieve more than a correction of institutional shortcomings. As Robinson has observed, the socialists had approached the problem of project selection on the basis of how much an addition to investment could save in future labor costs. But new criteria became necessary, since little more was to be achieved by continually "deepening" the capital structure. The problem became one of finding methods more conducive to fostering technical progress, i.e., finding production techniques that save present investment costs as well as future labor costs.[10]

At the height of the reform movement and before the demise of the Czechoslovakian experiment, it was not difficult for some to be optimistic about the trend toward market-type solutions to allocation difficulties. It appeared, at that time, that possibilities were ripe for the extension of decentralization in some moderate degree even to the sphere of investment policy, though the typical assessment was that "planning will continue to play an important part, especially in the field of investment policy."[11]

On other than ideological grounds, markets are not unacceptable per se. They are institutionally traditional for socialist countries where consumers' goods have almost always been distributed by such means to the public. Not all socialist economists refuse to recognize that some economic processes are simply too complex for computation, even in the age of large-capacity computers.[12]

Nevertheless, even Oskar Lange, once a foremost advocate of non-bureaucratic, market-type processes, is inclined, in the face of contemporary computational capacity, to believe that the greater potential for speedy economic adjustment recommends computer allocation over market allocation.[13] The market is not only slower, but, even after time-lags and oscillations, its cumbersome iteration process may fail to converge at all. In traditional socialist style, Lange finds the existence of cobweb cycles, inventory cycles, and reinvestment and general business cycles adequate to demonstrate this point.

However, particularly in the area of investment planning, Lange accuses the market of failing to provide the right foundation for adequate growth and structural development. Long-term investments are simply not to be left to the whims of the market, for they are the means and the substance of economic development policy. Investments based on current prices and market conditions reflect only present data. In both capitalism and socialism, investment processes *change* data. This is done by "creating new incomes, new technical conditions of production, and frequently also by creating new wants."[14] The creation of a *new* industry creates new demands, not vice versa.

Benefits of Centralization in Investment Planning

To the extent that peripheral decision-making units in the economy, and in particular the enterprise, are given more discretion in investment decision making, decentralization *and marketization* are the result. If for no other reason, this is true because enterprises, as potential investors, compete for the scarce resources available for investment projects, and the result is a market process. That benefits and costs are associated with this phenomenon was implied above. At this point, it will be helpful to deal with the problem of costs and benefits of investment (de)centralization more directly and somewhat more extensively. Economic control can be seen as the most persuasive general rationale for centralization of investment decision making, and the attempt here will be to enlarge on the particulars.

Stability has to be rated high on the benefit list. Because investment projects are planned for years ahead and because structural direction of the development of the economy is a top priority of central planners, investment cycles and instability can allegedly be avoided through planning.

As was already indicated, maintaining control over current performance and future development is a primary benefit of centralization from the socialist standpoint. Reforms adopted in the East European states threatened to diminish this control. In the abortive Czechoslovakian experiment, for example, it was of central concern to some that individual enterprises could undertake projects of their own choosing. They could simply reinvest profits, avoiding loans from banks and the associated investment regulations. Eastern and Western economists alike believed this could well lead to an experience such as Yugoslavia's, where state control over the overall rate of capital accumulation and growth had been lost. No wonder the Yugoslavs had experienced inflation, regional imbalances in the development effort, and general "loss of control by the planning authorities over the direction of development of the economy."[15]

At a conference in Berlin, East German and Soviet economists investigated the subject of "intensifying production processes and socialist accumulation."[16] A central theme of this conference was that the way to economic efficiency had to be found through a careful structuring of the social production process as a whole, so that the necessary proportionality between the various industrial sectors could be achieved. Only in this way could stable and continual development be assured. Because planners have perspective over the economic structure, they can achieve the proportional development that eludes producers acting without the benefit of central direction.[17]

For countries that have begun in recent years to overcome the taste for autarkic behavior, central investment direction holds particular appeal in structuring the "international socialist division of labor." Not only can an economy be subject to central direction, but in the currently orthodox socialist view, the entire socialist world can develop in a planned and coordinated manner. Moreover, through combining means, higher levels of economic concentration can be pursued in the areas of research and development, as well as in production. Marketing the specialized output is achieved on the basis of "stable delivery and purchasing relationships" that are made possible by coordination of investment plans.[18]

Finally, control over investment processes gives the state direct and immediate influence over various external economies that do not enter into the private calculations of investors in nonsocialist economies. Improvements in planning techniques also tend to increase the probability that this influence will be beneficial. By this is meant that interindustrial relationships and structural development problems can be better understood, for example, through dynamic input-output analysis. Socialist economists have recognized that additional "nonmaterial" production variables interact with each other and also with material processes of production. Cost-benefit analysis offers the opportunity to include more than real variables, for it can also deal with such growth factors as science and education.[19]

Beyond these social considerations, investment control provides greater possibility to influence industrial processes that threaten the environment: air, water, esthetics, and so on.[20]

Costs of Centralization in Investment Planning

A discussion of the costs of extensive centralization logically complements the treatment of benefits; to treat centralization costs is also indirectly to discuss the benefits of decentralization. The avoidance of the costs of centralized control (the pursuit of the benefits of decentralization) represents the motivation behind the proposal and implementation of economic reforms in the sixties. If a discussion of reform measures is to be profitable, an appreciation of their necessity is essential.

One of the most obvious disadvantages of the centralized investment planning experience is its inevitable bureaucratic nature. It is traditional that the Central Planning Bureau (within the framework of the grand development design laid down by the party, of course,) establishes specific objectives of investment policy. This might be, for example, that specific outputs will be maximized while a given employment level is also assured.

The CPB also establishes requirements regarding the desired production methods (such as securing a smaller share of total inputs from capitalist countries, substituting one source of power for another, etc.). These objectives are transmitted to "project bureaus" or "project institutes" (in the Soviet Union) as investment coefficients and efficiency mandates.[21]

Project proposals, whether originating from enterprises or project institutes, should be in correspondence with CPB guidelines. They are subject to approval by a "large number of different agencies."[22]

Regulations laid down in 1964 require that Gosplan examine and approve all project proposals (a) exceeding a cost of one million rubles,

(b) requiring imported technical equipment, or (c) receiving the designation "especially important projects."[23] Only then can such projects be submitted to annual investment planning as a request for funds. That processing investment proposals can take so long (often from five to seven years) and that so many people and agencies can be involved can fail to surprise only the uninitiated.[24]

The Bulgarian economist, Mateev, has proposed a decentralization of the preliminary economic evaluation of individual investment proposals. Given the access of the enterprise to relevant information at that level, and knowing production coefficients, one need merely determine the relative effectiveness for individual production designs. Then, the conditions would be at hand for the necessary preliminary screening of technical information at the periphery. The most effective among the proposals of the enterprises could then be selected until the volume chosen for an individual sector had been reached.[25]

Perhaps a more subtle cost of permitting the center to preempt peripheral decision-making authority is the implied loss of consumer sovereignty. To the extent that one accepts the liberal tradition that maintains the belief in consumer sovereignty, this cost can be more significant than the cost of bureaucracy. That central authority has determined the mix of outputs produced by East European industry is reflected by consumption patterns prevailing in those countries.

Since production has been designed to satisfy the needs of the average wage earner, individuals with higher than average incomes have been forced (in the absence of any ability to exert effective sovereignty) to purchase bundles of goods and services that do not likely represent their first choice.[26]

The third cost is a variation on a theme played above to the tune of bureaucracy. The loss of information (both before messages are formulated and after they are transmitted) involved in making decisions at the center can reduce efficiency considerably, and this deserves special empahsis. Optimal technical variants can be selected successfully for each of the multitude of basic production processes only if they are backed by sufficient and correct information. Mateev holds that this can be done only from "below"—where the basic productive processes are carried out and decision makers have sufficient and accurate information.[27]

Another of the dangers of planning is that planners find it difficult not to fully use the economic powers at their disposal; to the extent that this power is wielded incompetently, it can become anticontrol.[a] In the history of socialist economic planning, the overambitious pursuit of growth has to some degree meant that this has been the lot of the socialist economy.

---

[a] The phraseology used attempts to avoid argumentation along conservative (Hayekian) lines, viz., that such power *must* be wielded incompetently and it *must*, therefore, be anticontrol.

When growth targets are overambitious, the system becomes taut, i.e., inventory levels are held excessively low and resource supplies are overstrained. As the limits of raw materials and energy supplies are approached, limited import capacity proves incapable of opening bottlenecks. Over time, massive investments become essential for these capital-intensive industries. In the pursuit of generating these, the development of consumer and agricultural industries has to be neglected, even if planners intended in good faith to steer the economy toward greater output levels in these sectors.

Unavoidably, incentives for work and greater productivity of labor are reduced. For a period of time, the system may shift attention to the neglected consumer goods and agricultural industries, and difficulties abate to some extent. But a low-pressure status quo merely serves to stimulate planners to reestablish high growth goals, return to performance standards that ensure tautness throughout the system, and begin the cycle again.[28]

The overambitious development scenario is not the only potential cost of centralized investment planning, for other scenarios can be drawn that likewise have historical precedents. Inflexibility of development may be among the most important of these other alternatives. Once decisions regarding structural development have been made, investments have implicitly been predetermined for a period of several years. It then becomes difficult to maintain an economy's investment commitments at a level that does not rob the system of elasticity.[29] This problem is particularly crucial in technologically dynamic environments.

Finally, investment controls require other controls. This cost of centralization is of particular pertinence in a reform era. In such a period, one is sometimes tempted to assume that central authority could relinquish almost, if not all, controls *except for* those over investment (structural development). Unfortunately, this view is utopian and ignores the general equilibrium nature of economic planning.

Even if one were to assume that socialists would accept any kind of structural development so long as a continued minimum growth rate were assured, it is doubtful that this could be achieved merely by attempting to control the *level* of investments. To control the aggregate level of investment is to control the level of consumption. A volume of consumer goods below that desired by the populace could generate inflationary pressures and lead to balance of payments problems. The latter would arise when individuals attempted to import the consumer goods sacrificed to the domestic growth effort, competing for the foreign exchange required by investors for capital goods imports. State authorities would probably be unable to overcome the temptation to attempt to eliminate the instability inherent in that situation, even if they ignored the inclination to assure that scarce foreign exchange be used for the high-priority investments.

In an economy like that of the Soviet Union, these considerations are not without importance. In the smaller, more trade-dependent nations of Eastern Europe, they can be absolutely crucial. Under the much more realistic assumption that planners retain their interest in influencing both the level *and* structure of investments, one cannot simply ignore the vital interactions of interindustrial forces in the economic milieu.

To emphasize certain desirable ("structurally determining") industries is to provide the means for their expansion. This cannot be achieved simply by providing investment funds. Other resources, particularly labor, must be attracted, and it, therefore, becomes appropriate to influence the structure of wages. However, influencing the demands for labor is just the beginning of planning requirements in this respect. Either the resource-furnishing industries would have to be developed, or arrangements for purchasing resources from beyond national boundaries would have to be made.[30]

Supplying labor in selected industries with greater stocks of capital often comes about only after various kinds of research and development problems have been solved. The pursuit of growth may likewise bring into being the need for particular kinds of training for labor. The development of any kind of growth factor, the socialists have observed, requires and, at the same time, furthers the concomitant development of all other growth factors.[31]

As an illustration of the fact that investment controls alone are not sufficient to achieve the aims of central planners, the East German case recommends itself. Since the end of 1970, a large number of planning changes have served rather drastically to modify the reform movement that began in the early sixties. In large part, this was due to the inability of the system to meet plan targets in spite of investments for the period 1966-1970 that exceeded those of the previous plan period by 52 percent.[32]

A good share of the growth difficulties that the East Germans were experiencing at the turn of the decade can be traced back to investment problems. Low factor productivity, insufficient reserves and inventories, and a neglected technical infrastructure rendered the economy susceptible to difficulties (such as the energy supply problems that occurred during difficult winters in 1969 and 1970). Excessive concentration of investments in structurally determining sectors also had negative effects, as it became difficult to utilize these new capacities when deliveries from neglected resource-furnishing industries were not forthcoming. New investments often failed to meet projected efficiency levels, and this was "not seldom the result . . . of inadequately schooled and qualified personnel."[33] These difficulties were interpreted, apparently, by East German authorities as being caused by decreasing the degree of central control through reform measures.

One intent of the reforms was that firms be permitted to generate their own investment funds (as a part of net earnings), and within approved limits determine the utilization of such funds. Now firms are more dependent upon banks for investment credits, and central authority has firm control over how these are used. From 1971 on, investments were again determined almost strictly by the central plan.[34]

The Reforms and Beyond

An exhaustive survey of reform developments will not be undertaken here, but a brief review of some representative types of development in investment planning in and after the reform age is appropriate.

Because there are no capital markets in orthodox socialism and because the processes of providing and utilizing capital are socialized, the enterprise finds its sources of investment finance generally limited to state budgets, credits from central and specialized state-subservience banks, and its own earned revenues. The primary thrust of the reform movement was to attempt to channel a larger share of these funds through banks and to leave the enterprise greater discretion over a larger share of earned revenues. To the extent that these sources replaced the central banking influence, more investment decisions would be made where the quantity and quality of appropriate information are greater.

For several reasons the reforms were expected to guarantee greater efficiency in investment processes. The socialists have sought to reduce widely publicized inefficiencies through improved planning techniques (e.g., greater analytical appreciation of optimality) and tools (especially computers); through greater cooperation within the socialist world (standardizing capital equipment specificiations, exchanging technical information, and participating in mutual projects); through the introduction of capital charges; and through the adoption of the profitability success criterion (so that enterprises no longer secure and hoard equipment from which they cannot benefit).

In the Soviet Union, the progress of theory regarding investment efficiency, as in the socialist states in general, has not been insignificant. Progress in practice has been less observable. Khachaturov observed, in the late sixties, that the proportion of capital investment coming from enterprise funds was small, but promised they would increase substantially.[35] Several years later, however, although the financial flexibility of enterprises had increased to some extent, investment planning remained strongly centralized.[36]

In Hungary, efficiency calculations for investments have been based on "shadow prices" (those which, under particular constraints, are required for the achievement of particular objectives—an "objective function"—in a planning or programming framework). Shadow prices have also been used in cost/benefit calculations. The long-term benefits of a project are reduced to a discounted present value for comparison with its current costs.[37]

In Czechoslovakia, the basic efficiency criterion of Soviet planning was totally abandoned, its substitute being "substantially identical to that of enterprises in the capitalist economies."[38] The use of discounting had previously been limited to the addition of investment expenditures when they occurred at different dates. In Czechoslovakia, this practice was extended to the whole realm of investment decision making with the introduction of discounted cash flow methods. For the first time in socialist countries, the internal rate of return criterion of investment choice was admitted into the realms of planning practice.[39]

The reader should be warned that these innovations described by Nuti could legitimately be published in 1970. They cannot at that date, be expected to reflect the reorganization after the postinvasion return to orthodoxy. Dramatic (and as Nuti indicates) inflationary annual investment increments in 1968 (10.5 percent more than in 1967) and in 1969 (13 percent more) became the object of planning corrections by 1970.[40] One must sense a general process of sclerosis (if not rigor mortis) in the liberalization movement when one reads of the "energetic measures in . . . drawing away of excessive financial investment resources as well as regulation of new investments as far as enterprises are concerned" in the postinvasion consolidation process.[41]

In Poland, although the basic standard methodology (the Khachaturovian recoupment period criterion) retained the field of investment practice, it was modified. The reform spirit generated a methodology whose approach to the problem of varying life spans was more sophisticated.[42] The new technique allows for varying longevities of equipment, and represents a significant improvement over the traditional recoupment period methodology, since one of the strongest standard criticisms of the recoupment criterion is that it ignores the question of capital longevity.

In the more productive environment of the reform age, analytical progress was more dramatic in most of the socialist countries. Time series analyses with aggregated Cobb-Douglas production functions not only found their way into economic literature, but were used more widely in planning.[43]

Systemic extrapolations were developed to generate central coefficients such as net product, productive or unproductive investments, and consumption, from which conclusions could be drawn regarding the growth of national income, wages, investments, and so on for the planning period.[44]

Theoretical progress has been possible to the extent that the importance of ideology has declined in recent years or at least to the extent that solid analytical improvements could be sufficiently decorated with ideological verbiage. The lagged improvements in the realm of actual investment practice and planning is a result, perhaps of the fact that bureautic forces maintain a more entrenched position in economic planning than ideology does in the minds of socialist economists pursuing efficiency.

Notes

1. See Joan Robinson, "Socialist Affluence," in *Socialism, Capitalism and Economic Growth: Essays Presented to Maurice Dobb,* C.H. Feinstein, ed. (London: Cambridge University Press, 1967), p. 186.

2. A.I. Notkin, "Die Akkumulation und ihre Rolle in der Sozialistischen Reproduktion," *Wirtschaftswissenschaft,* vol. 19, no. 7 (July 1971), p. 1012.

3. Accumulation consists of (a) additions to the stock of fixed assets in material production, as well as such additions in the (b) nonproductive sphere. (The GDR, however, excludes this from the accumulation concept.) In addition, accumulation includes (c) net additions to the stock of circulating assets in the process of production, (d) net additions to reserves, and (e) the foreign-trade balance. Amortization ("depreciation" in bourgeois terms) is subtracted from gross investment, so that net investment only is included in accumulation. See J. Wilczynski, *The Economics of Socialism,* (London: G. Allen, 1970), p. 78. Nonproductive investment is defined as that which is *not* for fixed and variable costs, viz., for such things as durable consumers goods (both private and public), for housing, education, defense, public buildings and equipment, and for social, cultural and sporting facilities.

4. Notkin, loc. cit.

5. The socialist countries desire, no less than others, to make these decisions in the framework of an industrial world of international specialization and labor division. The subject is closely related to the one at hand; it will be treated more thoroughly in Chapter 8.

6. See E.N. Eden, "Investment Criteria in Public Enterprises: A Case Study of an Investment Choice in Electricity Supply," *Acta Oeconomica,* vol. 6, no. 1/2 (1971) p. 85.

7. Since producers goods, however, have not been subject to the turnover tax typically levied on consumers goods, the former are consequently undervalued. As a result, this estimate is undervalued and the share in real terms must be considered larger than twenty to thirty percent. See Wilczynski, *The Economics of Socialism,* op. cit., p. 79.

8. T. Khachaturov, "Economics of Capital Investment," in *Contemporary Soviet Economics,* vol. 1, Murray Yanowitch, ed. (New York: International Arts and Sciences, 1969), p. 153.

9. For a summary of institutional problems see Marvin R. Jackson, "Information and Incentives in Planning Soviet Investment Projects," *Soviet Studies,* vol. 23, no. 1 (July 1971), pp. 16-19, 21.

10. See Robinson, loc. cit.

11. See Kurt W. Rothschild, "Socialism, Planning, Economic Growth: Some Untidy Remarks on an Untidy Subject," in Feinstein, *Socialism, Capitalism, and Economic Growth,* op. cit., p. 171. It is interesting that the observer of the socialist scene can make perfectly valid observations that, after even very short periods of time, seem to belong to a totally different era. Rothschild's remark is characteristic in this respect. He says, "At some future date it may appear as a joke of history that socialist countries learned at long last to overcome their prejudices and to dismantle clumsy planning mechanisms in favour of more effective market elements just at a time when the rise of computers and of cybernetics laid the foundation for greater opportunities in comprehensive planning. These two opposing trends will be with us for some time to come. They will necessitate a constant reconsideration of the proper relations between planning and socialism, between growth and other aims."

12. See Oskar Lange, "The Computer and the Market," in Feinstein, *Socialism, Capitalism, and Economic Growth*, op. cit., p. 160.

13. See ibid. Lange observes appropriately: "Were I to rewrite my essay today my task would be much simpler. My answer to Hayek and Robbins would be: so what's the trouble? Let us put simultaneous equations on an electronic computer and we shall obtain the solution in less than a second. The market process with its cumbersome *tâtonnements* appears old-fashioned. Indeed, it may be considered as a computing device of the pre-electronic age," (p. 158). The reader may justifiably feel some surprise at Lange's optimism toward contemporary computer capacity, assuming all the data could even be gathered for the solution of the notorious equations.

14. Ibid., p. 160.

15. Domenica Mario Nuti, "Investment Reforms in Czechoslovakia," *Soviet Studies*, vol. 21, no. 33 (January 1970), p. 370.

16. The Central Institute for Economic Science of the German Academy of Sciences in Berlin and the Institute of Economics of the Soviet Academy of Sciences met from May 21 to May 25, 1972. Papers were reproduced in *Wirtschaftswissenschaft*, vol. 19, nos. 7, 8, and 9 (July-September 1971).

17. Cf. Karl Bichtler and Harry Maier, "Intensivieriung des volks-wirtschaftlichen Reproduktions-prozesses und Sozialistische Akkumula-tion," *Wirtschaftswissenshaft*, vol. 19, no. 7 (July 1971), p. 998; and M.J. Lemeschew, "Das Programmprinzip der Akkumulationsstruktur," ibid., no. 9 (September 1971), p. 1332.

18. See Bichtler and Maier, "Intensivieriung," op. cit., p. 999.

19. Ibid., p. 1008.

20. Probably arising from the lower general level of industrialization and the compulsion to demonstrate that socialism is the "wave of the future" (that the East-West technology lag can be overcome), the lag with which socialist literature demonstrated concern for environmental prob-lems was conspicuous. This is especially so because the near-hysteria level of preoccupation with such problems in nonsocialist literature stood for some time in stark contrast. But notice that concern has reached even the technical literature in the GDR. See the article by Gerd Knobloch and Klaus Steinitz, "Akkumulation und Gestaltung einer effektiven Struktur der Volkswirtschaft," op. cit., p. 1026.

21. J.G. Zielinski, *On the Theory of Socialist Planning,* (Ibadan: Ox-ford University Press, 1968), pp. 33-34.

22. Jackson, "Information and Incentives," op. cit., p. 5.

23. Ibid., p. 6.

24. Ibid., passim. Note especially that, in 1966, "there were 1290 so called 'project and survey' organizations carrying out work for capital construction in the Soviet Union. They employed over half a million engineers and technicians." (p. 4).

25. Mateev recognizes, of course, that "the reservation must be made that, in many cases, it may be possible and necessary to abandon a more effective proposal in favor of a less effective one, provided certain consid-erations of extra-economic nature become involved." See Eugene Mateev, "Mathematics and the National Economy," in *Planning and Markets: Modern Trends in Various Economic Systems,* John T. Dunlop and Nikolay P. Federenko, eds. (New York: McGraw-Hill, 1969), pp. 254-266.

26. Michael Kaser and Janusz Zielinski explain that "households with high incomes buy more food and drink and fewer cars, housing and tourism than they prefer. In the absence of domestic expenditure patterns usable for a high income plan, reliance is placed upon 'scientifically-determined norms', a combination of expert assessments of desirable compositions of diet, housing and leisure use and of consumer research through question-naires, and experience in capitalist market economies." See their *Planning and East Europe* (London: Bodley Head, 1970), pp. 62-63.

27. Mateev, "Mathematics and the National Economy," op. cit., p. 362.

28. Soviet economists are, of course, aware of the general nature of these systemic characteristics. See Notkin, who refers to this cyclical trait (though insisting it does not bear the characteristic of periodicity). In his view, this is strictly a result of an "inappropriately high rate of growth of social production and an inappropriately high rate of productive accumulation." See his "Die Akkumulation," op. cit.

29. Knobloch and Steinitz, "Akkumulation und Gestaltung," op. cit., p. 1023.

30. W.I. Majewski says, "In order to increase capital outlays, one must not only increase capacity in the machine-building and construction industries, but also in the sectors that produce raw materials and inputs essential for the final product." See his "Akkumulationsrate und Verflechtungsbeziehungen," *Wirtschaftswissenschaft,* vol. 19, no. 8 (August 1971), p. 1172.

31. Sigrid Maier and Martliese Mehnert, "Intensivierung des volkswirtschaftlichen Reproduktionsprozesses und sozialistische Akkumulation," *Wirtschaftswissenschaft*, ibid., p. 1156.

32. Peter Mitzscherling, "Die Wirtschaft der DDR," in *Die Wirtschaft Osteuropas ze Beginn de 7oer Jahre*, Hans-Hermann Höhmann, ed., (Stuttgart: Verlag W. Kohlhammer, 1972), p. 71.

33. Ibid., pp. 80-81.

34. Peter Mitzscherling, et al., *DDR Wirtschaft: Eine Bestandsaufnahme*, Deutsches Institut für Wirtschaftsforschung, Berlin, (Frankfurt am Main: Fischer Bücherei, 1971), p. 79.

35. According to Khachaturov, decentralized investments (coming from various local agencies as well as from enterprises) amounted to no more than 20 percent of total investments. See "Economics of Capital Investment," op. cit., pp. 156-157. Officially, of the 61.4 billion rubles for aggregate investment in 1968, 43.1 billion (70 percent) were made by the central government. In 1971, little change had been made: of 88 billion rubles invested in the aggregate, 61.1 billion (68 percent) was still central government investment. See *Narodnoe Khozyaistvo SSSR: Statisticheski Ezhegogodnik*, 1969 u 1972, (Moskva: Statistika, 1972).

Notice Khachaturov's observation (p. 157) "that long-term, large investments in the founding of new branches of production, etc., will still require a national approach in calculating investment effectiveness."

36. See Höhmann, *Die Wirtschaft*, op. cit., p. 27.

37. Kaser and Zielinski, *Planning and East Europe*, op. cit., p. 78.

38. Nuti, "Investment Reforms," *op. cit.*, p. 367.

39. Ibid.

40. See Franz-Lother Altmann, "Tschechoslowakei," in Höhmann, *Die Wirtschaft*, op. cit., p. 131.

41. Jaroslav Kirasek, "Is the Economic Reform Going On?" *Czechoslovak Economic Papers*, no. 13 (1972), p. 76.

42. See Michal Kalecki, "The Curve of Production and the Evaluation of the Efficiency of Investment in a Socialist Economy," in Feinstein, *Socialism, Capitalism, and Economic Growth*, op. cit., p. 98.

43. Hans Dieter Anders, "Probleme der Modellierung des sozialistischen Akkumulationsprozesses," *Wirtschaftswissenschaft*, vol. 19, no. 9 (September 1971), p. 1351.

44. Ibid., p. 1352.

7

Investment II: Calculation and Economic Efficiency

For many years, under a program of autarkic, basic industrialization, the directors of socialist economies could ignore questions of investment efficiency and development structure. Continued socialist growth required little more than high levels of savings and investment. The share of national income devoted to investment usually amounted to from 20 to 30 percent.[1]

In the past decade, however, socialists began to face the problem of declining efficiency: the output-capital ratio was reduced, the ratio of national income to productive funds diminished, new capital construction was less effective than anticipated, long gestation periods were experienced, a large volume of poor quality or incomplete construction accumulated, estimated construction costs were often exceeded, projects were developed without any real necessity, and the planning of capital investments was generally based on inadequate analysis, or even none at all.[2]

These problems arose in part because some of the projects selected violated even the primitive selection criteria that were available. The Soviet case is probably not exceptional, and writers there complained that some of the selected projects were outmoded before they were even completed and had unacceptably high costs and long recoupment periods. Bad information, poor documentation for project proposals, and planning errors and misspecifications came to be ubiquitous in Soviet investment planning.[3]

Through the sixties, reforms were introduced in the hope that many of these difficulties could be overcome. The adoption of a system of "economic levers" was certainly not inappropriate. The reforms were expected to correct more than just institutional shortcomings. As Robinson has observed, the socialists had approached the problem of project selection on the basis of how much an addition to investment could save in future labor costs. But new efficiency criteria became necessary, for little more was to be achieved by continually "deepening" the capital structure. The problem became one of finding methods more conducive to fostering technical progress, i.e., finding production techniques that would save present investment costs as well as future labor costs.[4]

At the height of the reform movement and before the demise of the Czechoslovakian experiment, it was not difficult for some to be optimistic

The material in this chapter was originally published as "Investment Efficiency in Centrally Planned Economies," *Konjunkturpolitik*, vol. 21, no. 3, pp. 129-147.

about the trend toward market-type solutions to allocation difficulties. It appeared, at that time, that possibilities were ripe for the extension of decentralization in some moderate degree to the sphere of investment planning, though the typical assessment was that "planning will continue to play an important part, especially in the field of investment policy."[5]

That evaluation turned out to be an understatement. The reform effort proved, at least for those who hoped that decentralization and greater efficiency might be achieved, to be a disappointment. Bureaucracies never really relinquished their control grips; reform measures were carried through halfheartedly at best; and, at the first indication of continued difficulty, were often scrapped.

The degree to which economic control should be maintained by central authority in the socialist countries remains a matter of debate. The exigencies of contemporary ideology, however, have in recent years dampened the enthusiasm of the discussion in socialist literature. For the moment, market-type processes have regained their wonted abhorrence and the ideologist and bureaucrat have succeeded in reassociating markets with revisionism.

There is no reason to expect any substantial decontrol of investment processes in the near future. The Yugoslavian proclivity for markets remains generally unacceptable to most of the remainder of the more orthodox socialist world.[a]

To the extent that efficiency must be sought through synthetic planning techniques, it becomes essential that the efficiency criteria used by planners in the socialist system be given more attention, or at least continued attention. The objective here will be to investigate contemporary socialist investment theory and planning practice in its framework of renewed, postreform importance. Efficiency problems and prospects will hopefully be brought into focus.

The Pursuit of Efficiency: The Khachaturovian Tradition

In economic administration of the Soviet type, planners first decide that a given investment project is desirable, then engineers determine investment and operating cost parameters for alternative variants, and economists must, finally, demonstrate which technical variant is most efficient. In 1946, through the pioneering work of Khachaturov, a "standard methodology" was developed for the microeconomic problem of choosing this most efficient available investment project.[6]

As is widely known, the Standard Methodology approach to the selection of project variants is simply that of the recoupment period. The

[a] Hungary and Poland are, of course, somewhat exceptional in this regard.

objective is to answer the question as to which of two different methods of achieving the same outcome represents greater efficiency. If one project has both lower initial capital outlays and operating costs, no analysis is required.[b] If the project with the lower operating costs has a higher initial capital outlay, however, one must determine if the lower operating costs incurred later justify the higher initial capital outlays. The recoupment period is the number of years it takes for the more capital-intensive investment project to recoup the difference via its reduced operating costs (including depreciation). This is defined as

$$T = \frac{I_1 - I_2}{c_2 - c_1}$$

where I_1 and c_1 represent the (larger) initial cost and (lower) annual operating costs, respectively, and I_2, c_2 represent counterpart costs for investment project 2.

In the event that the coefficient T is less than or equal to the normative recoupment period applied by planners, T_n, project 1 will be selected. Its short recoupment period means that the lower operating costs more than justify the larger initial capital expenditure.

The inverse of T, or E, is given as

$$E = \frac{c_2 - c_1}{I_1 - I_2}$$

This form of the coefficient is to be compared with E_n, the "normative net marginal efficiency of capital" or the "normative coefficient of comparative economic efficiency." E_n is in fact a proxy for an interest rate in economic calculation, and it is more popularly used than T_n. "The norm E is also recommended by the Standard Methodology for discounting to comparable terms, different expenditure and income time streams."[7] Dobb tells us that "if E is taken as some standard coefficient of effectiveness, then investments at future dates can be equated to present values for purposes of comparison by multiplying them by $1/(1 + E)^t$."[8] When the efficiency calculation for the investment alternatives yields $E \geq E_n$ project 1 will, of course, be chosen.[9]

Generalizing, for the case in which two investment options are available, it is apparent (by rewriting) that one should choose the first variant if

$$c_1 + I_1 \frac{1}{T_n} \leq c_2 + I_2 \frac{1}{T_n}$$

For more than two options, one chooses the project that minimizes the sum of operating costs and capital charges, $c + I(1/T_n)$ or $c + E_n I$.

---

[b] Capital outlays include costs of buildings, equipment, installation, and improvements to the project site, though not the land itself.

The payback criterion of investment efficiency is very easily applied and can, of course, act as a rough measure in selecting high-profit projects that are very clearly desirable. Likewise, it can reject quickly those projects showing so little promise that they do not merit more sophisticated analysis. In the case of highly progressive technologies, i.e., where the risk of rapid obsolescence is high (or in any case where capital wastage is hard to foretell), the payback method may prove useful. Since it heavily weights earnings early in the project's life, the criterion represents an automatic hedge against the possibility of error in estimating receipts and outlays.[10]

Given the correct outlook and some ambitious searching, one can find virtue in almost everything, of course. Still, in theoretical terms, it is difficult to overlook serious faults in the payback or recoupment criterion. There is no dearth of critical literature on the subject, and the criticisms of the method require only brief summary here: (a) by confining analysis to the project's initial outlays and recoupment period, the crucial question of the life pattern of earnings subsequent to the payback period is neglected; (b) indirect repercussions of the project selection are not included in the analysis—if the project selected required, for example, the construction of a new highway, this additional cost could greatly exceed economies arising from the lower operating costs of the selected variant; (c) treating the productive outputs as given results in neglecting possible returns to scale and their obviously important efficiency implications; and (d) the commodity prices used in the practical application of the recoupment period method in the socialist countries are, in the words of Zauberman, "nonefficiency parameters par excellence."[11]

Since prices in centrally planned economies fail to reflect scarcity values, they cannot give correct answers to questions regarding rationality and efficiency. Where efficiency measures for any proposed investment project are based upon costs of production and potential profitability, poor investment decisions will inevitably result from the use of biased prices in investment calculations. Where the price structure fails to reflect actual costs of production, as was the case for the economies of Eastern Europe in the 1960s, one could hope to achieve reliable estimates of efficiency only after an effective price revision. This was the purpose, at least in part, of price revision endeavors in Eastern Europe during the past decade. Since it was clear that revision processes alone would not suffice to eliminate this difficulty in the long run, Eastern Europeans also discussed at some length various pricing reforms designed to achieve more rational pricing processes and structures.

Unfortunately, in many cases the reforms failed to align prices with actual costs. The very nature of Eastern European pricing methodology guarantees problems of bias. It will be remembered that the profit (surplus value) markup added to average prime costs in Marxian price theory can be based on labor costs, capital costs, or some combination of the two.[12] When it is based, for example, on labor costs, labor intensive commodities will be relatively high priced. This would be expected to distort demand in the direction of capital-intensive production. Incorrect input substitutions and unfortunate investment decisions will be the consequence.

In the East German case, the breakdown of the economic reforms caused the planned introduction of capital-related (*fondsbezogene*) prices (for which surplus value markups are calculated as a percentage of capital costs in production) to cease. This meant that the opportunity of comparing productive achievements of dissimilar industries on the basis of their capital returns was lost to the East German planners. An additional outcome was that since the required capital investment in East German products is not properly accounted for in the price, capital-intensive products are considerably undervalued.[13]

Hopefully, these brief observations on pricing will suffice to alert the reader to the kinds of difficulties that invariably arise when prices cannot perform their normal (market) function of signaling valuable information (e.g., relative scarcities, preferences, costs of production, potential profitability or investment returns, etc.) to investment decision makers. The inadequacies of the payback calculation and of proposals of variations on the socialist Standard Methodology in investment calculation (to be discussed below) will be *in addition* to these problems of biased pricing. Likewise, recommended ameliorative techniques that may be suggested or implied below can promise greater efficiency only if improvements in pricing methodology and processes can be assumed.

Of further critical importance is the fact that the coefficient of investment efficiency represents an attempt to allocate resources in some rational way only *after* central planners have already decided on some investment project that may have much higher costs and lower benefits than many other possible investment projects.

Not only is it appropriate to attempt to determine the theoretical advisability of utilizing the Khachaturovian criterion, it is also of interest to note what recoupment period (or efficiency criterion) is applied in practice. The coefficient used in the investment formula is of importance because it has a direct impact on the degree of capital intensity of selected projects and, thus, indirectly limits the demands for investment funds. If properly applied, the coefficient should constrain these demands to the level of the planned supply of investment funds.

Zielinski tells us that in the Polish case (which is of interest because the other socialist countries have had similar experience), the level of the investment coefficients was *not* established to limit the use of scarce capital or even to achieve some desirable degree of capital intensity appropriate to the level of economic development in Poland. Rather, "it was fixed at the level corresponding to certain macroeconomic relationships, without any effort whatsoever to examine the total effect of such determined coefficients of the choice of methods of production.[14]

Khachaturov points out that the interest-rate proxy, the coefficient of effectiveness, is determined by both the level of available resources (capital and human) and the available investment opportunities (depending in turn on the state and progress of technology). The more capital available, the lower the effectiveness norm can be.[15]

To the extent that productive conditions vary among industries (due to varying supplies and qualities of labor and capital, rates of technological progress, etc.), economic correctives need to be applied, i.e., forces tending to generate desirable economic equilibria must be operative. These include flexible pricing, the capacity for wages to adjust to market needs, and various kinds of subsidies and taxes. The corrective forces necessary to allocate resources effectively among industries could be generated either by properly functioning markets (those capable of generating rational, i.e., scarcity, prices) whose workings are modified by skillful policy implementation or, simply, by the kind of highly efficient (reformed?) planning system not yet found in the socialist countries. Khachaturov is prepared to put a heavy burden of responsibility upon the effectiveness norm. Until planning correctives were ready for implementation or more rational, reformed planning was achievable, Khachaturov holds that these various interindustrial conditions of production "must be reflected in correctives to the normed effectiveness coefficient.[16]

Until just before the 1970s, Khachaturov reasoned that it would be incorrect to apply a uniform capital charge over the whole economy. A higher efficiency norm would permit more capital-intensive (and, of course, less labor-intensive) investment projects.[17] One could hope, therefore, by applying varying coefficients across industries, to develop that industrial structure preferred by the planners (fostering capital intensity in select industries). A uniform coefficient may yield technologically inferior outcomes in those industries characterized by high durability.[18]

As a means of finding ways to achieve given objectives with the lowest cost, the Soviet calculus at that time was of some worth. As a tool for macro decision making, however, a single rate for E would have been much more helpful for efficiency purposes. The single value would permit decision makers to set the objectives and choose the desirable investment projects for which different competing variants could then be compared. On the strength of this consideration, the Poles and the Hungarians adopted a single rate for E, and the mathematical school in the Soviet Union gave "virtually unanimous support" for the application of a single rate.[19]

In 1969, the Soviet Union's Standard Methodology was modified by the adoption of a new Standard Methodology for Determining the Economic Effectiveness of Capital Investments. Although it did not dramatically alter the basic, traditional approach to investment decisions, it did address itself directly to the problem of variable industry normative coefficients of effectiveness (interest rates).

To solve the problem of distributing investment resources to those sectors promising the most favorable returns, a new coefficient of effectiveness (the ratio of incremental net national income to investment, $\Delta NI/I$) was adopted. At the same time, it was hoped that overinvestment in consumer goods could be avoided by the introduction of an intrasectoral criterion for investment distribution that would base the decision on enterprise profitability calculated before the imposition of the turnover tax (a tax markup added to the price at the retail level). Because turnover taxes are used largely to ration scarce consumer goods and because they represent a significant portion of the price of such goods, such calculation reduces substantially the profitability of investments for consumer goods and, likewise, the incentive to undertake such projects.

As a result of the introduction of these new investment considerations, opposition to the application of a single interindustrial efficiency norm has disappeared. With the introduction of the new norms, it is felt that a single interest rate will no longer represent a stimulus for overinvestment in nonpriority sectors. In fact, Khachaturov was the chief author of the new methodology.[20]

The Pursuit of Efficiency: Approaching Modernity

It has already been observed that the original analysis of Khachaturov was adopted in Soviet-type planning as the Standard Methodology for selecting project variants. When analysis is used in practice in Soviet investment planning, this is the best analysis that can be hoped for. Socialist theorists, however, have made substantial advancements in the theory of investment planning. Modern socialist work does not compare poorly with that being done in market countries. At the time of Khachaturov's pioneering work, it was preoccupied with the technical aspects of particular projects. Thereafter, it extended its concern to allow for their immediate economic aspect. It currently investigates projects within the framework of overall optimality in the economy.[21]

It is the intent of this section to show the relationship between the Khachaturovian tradition and modern Soviet and bourgeois analysis. It is hoped that this will reveal the degree of soundness of socialist theoretical foundations on the one hand and the difficulties of current investment planning practice on the other. At the same time, implicit relationships between socialist and bourgeois conceptualizations of investment optimality should come into focus.

For these purposes, the work of Irving Fisher, as representative of western economics, recommends itself.[22] This is because of the similarity of the investment problems that interested both Fisher and Khachaturov. Fisher, like his younger Soviet contemporary, was interested in comparing two investment options. He did not wish in general to deal with the discounting problems of a single project, and, for his analysis, it is appropriate to assume that two projects would be mutually exclusive.[c] He wished to show that the ranking of alternatives according to the criterion of maximum wealth could yield different outcomes depending on the (market) rate of interest. His calculus served to determine all the interest rates at which one project would be preferred to another. Above some particular rate of interest, the ranking would change. Fisher's rate of return over cost can be given as follows:

$$\int_0^t \{[R_1(t) - E_1(t)] - [R_2(t) - E_2(t)]\}e^{-rt}\,dt$$

where $R(t)$ and $E(t)$ represent receipt and outlay streams, respectively, both as functions of time, while e^{-rt} is the discount factor for t. The equation gives the difference in present worths of investment options 1 and 2 when each is discounted at the interest rate r. The particular rate of interest that sets the difference in present worths equal to zero is what Fisher had in mind as the marginal rate of return over cost. If Fisher had assumed, as did Khachaturov, that both variants were to provide the same yield (i.e., that $R_1 = R_2$), we would have

$$\int_0^t \{[R(t) - E_1(t)] - [R(t) - E_2(t)]\}e^{-rt}\,dt$$

Take now the traditional Khachaturovian investment situation where $E_1 = I_1 + c_1$ and $E_2 = I_2 + c_2$, letting $I_i > I_2$ and $c_2 > c_1$. This can be expressed in Fisherian terms as

$$\int_0^t \{(I_1 - I_2) + [c_2(t) - c_1(t)]\}e^{-rt}\,dt$$

As a matter of simplification, if we let $t = 1$, the discounted cost outlays for the two variants can be shown as

$$D_1 = I_1 + \frac{c_1}{r} \qquad D_2 = I_2 + \frac{c_2}{r}$$

Letting $D_1 < D_2$, we get

$$I_1 + \frac{c_1}{r} < I_2 + \frac{c_2}{r}$$

---

[c] And, of course, his practice of simplification, by assuming away uncertainty, is also of importance. It will be followed here.

which is quite apparently in the same form as the standard methodology. We need merely to substitute the norm E_n for the market interest rate r. Rewriting, we then find that

$$c_1 + I_1 \frac{1}{T_n} < c_2 + I_2 \frac{1}{T_n}$$

and we choose, according to the Khachaturov rule, project 1. Generally, we choose the project that minimizes $c + I/T_n$ or, since they are equal by definition, $c + E_n I$.

Apparently, then, the recoupment period criterion can be derived algebraically from a simplified form of the discounting procedure. However, we must not forget that the Standard Methodology, though it attempts to deal with the same data that interested Fisher, is *not* a discounting method and can give wrong answers for (among others) the reasons discussed in the previous section. Moreover, the recoupment period criterion in this form can be shown to give outcomes contradictory to those of the discounted present value method, so that, by relying on the Standard Methodology, irrational choices can be made.[23]

Moreover, as was mentioned above, Fisher's rate of return over cost analysis gives different rankings for two projects when the rate of interest varies.[24]

It is not difficult to find sets of numbers for two projects (assuming equal revenues and different initial capital outlays and operating costs) for which the discounting process, at different interest rates, will give different outcomes. It is interesting to compare these outcomes to the solutions yielded by the Standard Methodology.

In Table 7-1, this is done for two projects A and B, assumed to have identical output (revenue) characteristics, ten-year production lives, and with $T_n = 1.33$, but with varying costs for each of three experiments. High (20 percent) and low (2 percent) interest rates are applied in the discounting procedure. The high discount rate can have an important impact when applied to a project whose operating costs increase over time (such as project A in each experiment in the table).

Symbols for the table are the same as have been previously used. Column (8) gives the project that is selected by the Standard Methodology for each experiment, while in column (5) the project with the least discounted total cost (the one selected by the discounting procedure) is indicated for each interest rate in each experiment by a footnote f.

Note that in experiment 1, a clear-cut case, the Standard Methodology gives the correct answer. In experiment 2, the decision is more difficult. When the high rate of discount is applied to the gradually increasing operating costs of project A, its total costs decline almost to the level of project B with its low initial capital outlay. This is always to be expected. In

Table 7-1
Cost Comparison of Project Variants

I (1)	c (2)	r (3)	$\sum_{n=1}^{10}[c/1+r)^n]$ (4)	(1) + (4) (5)	E (6)	T (7)	SMS[a] (8)
Experiment 1							
A 125[b]	8[c]	2%	6.97	131.97			
B 110	17[d]	2%	15.27	125.67[f]			
					.60	1.66	B
A 125	8[c]	20%	2.50	127.50			
B 110	17[d]	20%	7.05	117.05[f]			
Experiment 2							
A 125	8[c]	2%	6.97	131.97			
B 110	20[e]	2%	17.96	127.96[f]			
					.80	1.25	A
A 125	8[c]	20%	2.50	127.50			
B 110	20[e]	20%	8.30	118.30[f]			
Experiment 3							
A 125	8[c]	2%	6.97	131.97[f]			
B 115	20[e]	2%	17.96	132.96			
					1.20	.83	A
A 125	8[c]	20%	2.50	127.50			
B 115	20[e]	20%	8.30	123.50[f]			

Discounting formula yield $= \sum_{n=1}^{10}[R/(1+r)^n] - I - \sum_{n=1}^{10}[c/(1+r)^n]$.

[a]The Standard Methodology Selection of a project variant.
[b]Since *relative* values are significant this can be hundreds, thousands, millions, or billions in national monetary units.
[c].25 in first period + an additional .25 every other period.
[d]1.7 per period.
[e]2 per period.
[f]Best project under discounting (least discounted costs).

terms of the formula $T = (I_1 - I_2)/(c_2 - c_1)$, the application of a high discount rate reduces the denominator, causing the T value to rise. This naturally reduces the probability that a capital-intensive project will be selected. When no discounting is done, T remains artificially low: the traditional Soviet technique, in other words, assures us of a higher probability that capital-intensive projects will be chosen. This is clearly seen in experiment 3.

In this final experiment, we have the instance in which the application of lower and higher discount rates leads to the Fisherian outcome expectedly common in the real world, viz., a reversal of the project rankings. Here, the Standard Methodology properly selects when the discount rate is low, but after the higher discount rate reverses the rankings, the Standard Methodology aborts.

In such cases, the Standard Methodology would correctly select the capital-intensive solution for high-priority industries where low interest rates would be applied. In the case of the socialist milieu characterized by the application of a relatively high discount rate E_n and with the utilization of the standard methodology to analyze the same choice of variants, one would (just as feared by Khachaturov and the advocates of variable discount rate applications according to sectoral priorities) erroneously adopt some capital-intensive solutions.

If there exists a propitious coincidence of low-return and low-priority phenomena for the industry in question, Soviet planners would probably have established norms assuring less capital-intensive solutions (viz., a short recoupment period T_n). This would assure correct solutions, too. But if, in fact, as suggested in socialist literature, the matter simply comes down to choosing norms that provide capital-intensive solutions for industries that appeal to planners, consistently optimal solutions could hardly have been expected. In the history of socialist planning, priority industries have seemed more often to be ideologically determined than by any sort of cost-benefit notions that might have been concerned with the determination of industrial undertakings to which high returns might accrue.

As Abouchar has observed, the New Standard Methodology recently introduced in the Soviet Union still fails to provide any indication as to an appropriate volume of investment for given individual sectors. Even if the sectors are ranked according to the net incremental national income criterion, planners still have no indication as to how much should be allocated to each industry. Moreover, rankings calculated for a billion-ruble investment allocation wouldn't necessarily correspond to those for a five-billion-ruble allocation. Abouchar appropriately concludes, therefore, that "the amounts actually calculated will be somewhat arbitrary, even if the planners are committed to economic calculation."[25]

It is appropriate to turn now to a discussion of post-reform investment theory in the Soviet Union and in the East European countries. Its intent is the development of methodologies that assure that local calculations conducted on the basis of information available in individual units of the economic system will reflect the full national economic effects resulting from a project. It will be seen that, in spite of substantial improvements and sophistication, most of contemporary theory has not reputed the traditional heritage (or legacies, depending upon one's point of view) of analysis.[26]

Kantorovich, Bogachev, and Makarov develop a scheme for calculating the effects of investment undertakings mathematically, letting processes represent outputs and describing investment activities in terms of combinations of vectors.[27] (They observe that the same principles underlie the analysis of the Standard Methodology.) They give the following as the general formula for calculating a proposed investment project's effect:

$$I^* = \sum_{t=0}^{T+\lambda} (1 + E)^{-t}(TS_t - C_t - K_t + D_t - R_t) + TS_{oct}(1 + E)^{-(t+\lambda)}$$

where
$TS_t = $ the aggregate of marketable product

$C_t = $ the aggregate of operating expenditures measured according to prices describing the economic environment over the relevant period

$K_t = $ total capital outlays for project construction

$D_t = $ "external effects" of the project not reflected in direct earnings (e.g., changed labor conditions, expansion of infrastructure base, etc.)

$R_t = $ the rental component of social cost: national economic costs of utilization (rental payments) or exhaustion (capitalized rent) of nonreproducible natural resources.

$TS_{oct} = $ the residual value of the equipment in the final period $t + \lambda$.

$T = $ the service life of the project.

It can be shown that this expression, though substantially more sophisticated, is basically just an elaboration of the Standard Methodology formula, $C + E_nI$. As above, this can be seen by assuming first that the alternatives will have the same yields, so that

$$I^* = \sum_{t=0}^{T+\lambda} (1 + E)^{-t}(-C_t - K_t - R_t)$$

Let it further be assumed:

a. that proposed variants have infinite service lives ($T = \infty$) and $\lambda = 1$.

b. that alternatives have production costs that remain constant with respect to structure and level over time. The prices applying for all cost components have the same dynamics, i.e., $C_t = C$. (As was emphasized in Part I, appropriate decisions can be expected from the calculations, cereris paribus, only if the prices utilized are rational prices.)

c. that the capital investment is developed in the single year before it is put into operation, i.e., $K_t = K$.

d. and, finally, that no nonreproducible resources (rental components) are involved in the development of variants, i.e., $R_t = 0$.

Under these assumptions, we have

$$I^* = -C \sum_{t=0}^{\infty} (1 + E)^{-T} - K = -\frac{C}{E} - K$$

Maximizing this expression gives us the same result as minimizing discounted costs.

Kantorovich, et al. note that the assumptions involved in applying the Standard Methodology, though often failing to be recognized by planners, are extremely artificial. In practice, the variants from which choices are to be made offer nonidentical volumes and compositions of output.[28]

They also suggest some further investment criteria that follow in the same spirit. Hoping the lack of information and the inadequacy of prices won't prove to be too vitiating, they make concrete suggestions on the utilization of cost-benefit analysis. Were their analysis applied, of course, Soviet-type investment methodology would have come another step toward the triumph of reason over tradition in socialist planning.

Notes

1. Since producers goods, however, have not been subject to the turnover tax typically levied on consumers goods, the former are consequently undervalued. As a result this estimate is low and the share in real terms must be considered larger than 20-30 percent. See J. Wilczynski, *The Economics of Socialism* (London: G. Allen, 1970), p. 79.

2. T. Khachaturov, "Economics of Capital Investment," in *Contemporary Soviet Economics*, vol. 1, Murray Yanowitch, ed. (New York: International Arts and Sciences, 1969), p. 153.

3. For a summary of institutional problems see Marvin R. Jackson, "Information and Incentives in Planning Soviet Investment Projects," *Soviet Studies*, vol. 23, no. 1 (July 1971), pp. 16-19, 21.

4. See Joan Robinson, "Socialist Affluence," in *Socialism, Capitalism and Economic Growth: Essays Presented to Maurice Dobb*, C. H. Feinstein, ed. (London: Cambridge University Press, 1967), p. 186.

5. See Kurt W. Rothschild, "Socialism, Planning Economic Growth: Some Untidy Remarks on an Untidy Subject," in Feinstein, *Socialism, Capitalism, and Economic Growth*, op. cit., p. 171.

6. For other traditional discussions of the methodology, see Mateev, "Mathematics and the National Economy," in *Planning and Markets: Modern Trends in Various Economic Systems*, ed. by John T. Dunlop and Nikolay P. Federenko, eds. (New York: McGraw-Hill, 1969), pp. 254-266; Alfred Zauberman, *Aspects of Planometrics* (New Haven: Yale University Press, 1967), pp. 139-153; and Maurice Dobb, *An Essay on Economic*

Growth and Planning (London: Routledge and Kegan Paul, 1960), pp. 15-28.

7. See L.V. Kantorovich, V.N. Bogachev and V.L. Makarov, "Ob Otzenka effektivnosti kapitalnich Zatrat," *Ekonomika i Matematicheskyi Metody*, vol. 6, no. 6 (1970), p. 812.

8. Those economists for whom the light first dawned in the Soviet Union had a long struggle with ideological forces before the concept of an interest rate began to acquire some limited degree of acceptability. For a brief history of the struggle, see Gregory Grossman, "Scarce Capital and Soviet Doctrine," *Quarterly Journal of Economics*, (August 1953), pp. 311-343. It is very common now, however, to encounter in Socialist literature observations based on interest-rate concepts and discounting procedures. See Khachaturov, "Economics of Capital Investment, op. cit.

9. The recoupment period (or the coefficient of effectiveness) is not the only criterion used, of course. Zauberman informs that a number of other standards are applied. These are largely indicators in physical terms intended for parallel use. See his *Aspects of Planometrics*, op. cit., pp. 151-152.

10. These benefits, as well as some of the costs to be mentioned here are discussed by Joel Dean, "Measuring the productivity of Capital," in *The Management of Corporate Capital*, Ezra Solomon, ed. (New York: Free Press, 1959), p. 26.

11. See Zauberman, *Aspects of Planometrics* op. cit., p. 150.

12. For a good, detailed discussion of what can only be briefly sketched here, see Manfred Melzer, "Preispolitik und Preisbildungsprobleme in der DDR," *Vierteljahreshefte zur Wirtschaftsforschung*, no. 3 (1969), pp. 313-353. See also the discussion on price types given in Chapter 4.

13. Deutsches Institut fur Wirtschaftsforschung, *DDR-Wirtschaft: Eine Bestandsaufnahme* (Frankfurt am Main: Fischer, 1974), p. 107.

14. J.G. Zielinski, *On the Theory of Socialist Planning* (Ibadan: Oxford University Press, 1968), p. 46.

15. Khachaturov, "Economics of Capital Investment," op. cit., p. 158.

16. Ibid., p. 163.

17. A rigorous proof of this is given in Michal Kalecki, "The Curve of Production and the Evaluation of the Efficiency of Investment in a Socialist Economy," in Feinstein, *Socialism, Capitalism, and Economic Growth*, op. cit., pp. 87-100.

18. Gregory Grossman, "Scarce Capital," op. cit., cites Khachaturov to this effect as of 1953.

19. Zauberman, *Aspects of Planometrics*, op cit., p. 151. The status quo has prevailed thus far because most Soviet economists and practition-

ers feel that the efficiency calculus is designed "to discover ways of achieving objectives with the lowest cost, and not to set the objectives themselves. Indeed, it is contended that a single rate would inhibit the conscious structuring of investments according to the planner's hierarchy of aims" (p. 150).

20. It should be mentioned, however, that "exceptions are permitted to stimulate technical progress and to take account of industry or regional wage variations." See Alan Abouchar, "The New Soviet Standard Methodology for Investment Allocation," *Soviet Studies*, vol. 24, no. 3 (January 1973), p. 405. This article gives a terse and effective evaluation of the new Standard Methodology for Investment Allocation.

21. Zauberman, *Aspects of Planometrics*, op. cit., p. 153. For the flavor of contemporary work on efficient capital formation, see also Zauberman's chapter 14 on that subject. Western economists should be careful not to condemn Soviet theory on the basis of Soviet planning practices. Alec Nove made a helpful statement in this regard in (note the date) 1970: "Economists insist on comparing Soviet irrationalities not with the real troubles of a real western economy, but with the textbook model. I have seen lengthy criticisms of Soviet investment criteria, for instance. Yet a western manager facing a major investment decision, say concerning a factory requiring four years to complete, must make a guess at the following: wage rates in 1973, the prices of his inputs and outputs in 1973, the behavior of competitors, the rate of exchange, the rate of import duty at home or in foreign markets, the future rate of interest, and a few other unknowns." See his "Management and Control in Eastern European Economies," in *The Managed Economy*, Alec Cairncross, ed. (Oxford: Blackwell, 1970), p. 56.

22. For the purposes of this investigation, it is sufficient to refer the reader to Armen A. Alchian, "The Rate of Interest, Fisher's Rate of Return over Costs and Keynes' Internal Rate of Return," in Solomon, *The Management of Corporate Capital*, op. cit., pp. 67-71.

23. Pierre Massé gives a proof formulated by M. Boiteux, and cites the latter's "Comment calculer l'Amortissement?" *Revue d'Économie Politique* (January/February 1956). See Massé's *Le Choix des Investissements, Critères et méthodes* (Paris: Dunod, 1964), chap. 1.

24. See Alchian, "The Rate of Interest," op. cit., p. 68. Alchian gives an example in which (directly opposite to the Khachaturov case) both projects are assumed to have the same costs, but different revenue streams. Above a 6 percent for r, one project has a higher present value. Below 6 percent for r, the other project is favorable. The 6 percent r which sets the present value difference equal to zero is, of course, Fisher's marginal rate of return over cost.

25. Abouchar, "The New Soviet Methodology," op. cit., p. 407.

26. Admittedly, the problems of socialist investment theory are not as complex as those facing economists concerned with investment in market countries, largely because of the substantially greater significance of uncertainty in the capitalist environment. The integration of uncertainty into the theory and econometrics of investment has been described as "the most important open question." See Dale W. Jorgenson, "Econometric Studies of Investment Behavior," *Journal of Economic Literature*, vol. 9, no. 4 (December 1971), p. 1142.

27. It is my view that Kantorovich, Bogachev, and Makarov, "Ob Otzenka," op. cit., represent important socialist work on investment. No claim is made, of course, that this alone represents the forefront of socialist progress in analysis.

28. Ibid., p. 819. They bemoan the fact that the "'mass consumer' of the 'Standard Methodology' scarcely realizes that they (such formulae) are justified only under assumptions (a)-(d), which are usually not fulfilled in the actual economy."

**Part II
The International Socialist
Economy**

8 International Economics: Trade, Decentralization, and Growth for the Domestic Economy

Experts on trade relations among command economies have long maintained that traditions and institutions prevailing in Eastern Europe have produced international economic behavior that can only be described as irrational.[1] Recently, however, Johnson and Montias have expressed a preference for treating protectionism and discrimination in trade as behavior that is designed to reach specific political objectives rather than as behavior that is simply "irrational."[2] The performance of the Council for Mutual Economic Assistance (CMEA) would be seen in this contest as the outcome of central planners' pursuit of optimal policy decisions.

Though clearly difficult to establish, the notion that command planners attempt to behave in an optimal fashion is a compelling one, and the objective of this chapter is to develop an analysis of constrained planners' choice in questions of international trade as conducted by the reformed command economy.[3] The model to be developed will account for the contemporary socialist view of the importance of trade decisions in directive planning and will permit an exploration of the implications of current planning doctrine in East Europe. Rather than focus on Johnson's nationalism-internationalism trade-off, however, planning choices will be subsumed in more fundamental policy alternatives confronting planners: economic efficiency and growth vs. effective economic control.[a]

The model will incorporate aspects of the trade reforms of the sixties. It will illuminate some of the effects of decentralization, industrial concentration, composition and level of imports, the foreign exchange constraint, and the growth rate.

The analysis of planners' choice regarding the target level of economic growth and the degree of decentralization of planning decisions is of particular interest because it gives some indications as to why the trade reforms of the 1960s were doomed to failure. It will also show why we may expect more thoroughgoing reform endeavors later on.

The material in this chapter was originally published as "Socialist International Economics: An East European Model of Trade, Decentralization and Growth," *Weltwirtschaftliches Archiv,* vol. 111, no. 1 (1975), pp. 138-158.

[a] In Johnson's view, the alternatives facing central decision makers are nationalism (implying protection achieved through central planning practices) vs. internationalism (implying discrimination against exchanges with the West and the pursuit of integration with other bloc countries).

The Environment

In discussing socialist trade problems, it is important to keep in mind the unique institutional characteristics that apply. As we have seen, nonmarket price planning cannot generate scarcity prices reflecting actual costs and consumer preferences. For foreign trade, therefore, it becomes necessary to maintain a separate (usually world-market-oriented) price system. Since domestic prices do not reflect opportunity costs, other (more crude) indicators are used to determine comparative advantages in intrabloc trade.[4]

Bilateral trade compounds pricing difficulties, though it offers planners stability and certainty, as well as an improved bargaining position when the exports they have to offer are not highly competitive.

Other characteristics of centralized trade control include overvalued currencies and inconvertibility;[5] extremely buoyant import demand; limited foreign exchange reserves; "taut" trade planning;[6] and, possibly as a result of these difficulties, "trade aversion."[7] Currency inconvertibility has its real counterpart in the phenomenon of commodity inconvertibility. Nonresidents find it nearly impossible to purchase goods from East Europe because the planned flow of commodities permits only those goods to be exported that are specifically designated in the plan for export. Consequently, most transactions must be negotiated in advance directly with the state foreign-trade monopoly.

Needless to say, these things have constrained the expansion of foreign trade that the small, trade-oriented economies of the socialist world would favor. By the early sixties, some decentralization seemed essential in both domestic and international spheres. Through the 1960s, the centrally planned economies began, with varying degrees of enthusiasm, to introduce economic reforms. It appeared to most observers that some substantial degree of planning decentralization was actually in process or at least could be anticipated. Industrial associations, or in some cases, even individual enterprises, played greater decision-making roles in establishing foreign-trade plans, in conducting operations in capitalist countries, and even in establishing direct dealing with Western enterprises. Price revisions and reforms were also undertaken, and material incentives were adopted to achieve greater efficiency (e.g., in a limited number of export enterprises foreign exchange earnings above target values could be utilized for unplanned purchases of equipment and materials in world markets). Greater flexibility was also encouraged through CMEA's provisions for multilateral trade. Though these have to this point been ineffective, the socialist mentality, nevertheless, came closer to perceiving that country-by-country balances are not essential in international trade. Quantitative trade planning (linear programming) invaded the socialist economic literature, and, in some instances, became an object of experimentation.

The Model

The hypotheses to be developed in this section have for the most part been conceptualized by socialist economists and planners. Most of the principal postulates are clearly expressed in the bloc's economic literature. The production and financial sectors of the model account additionally for some important conceptions left implicit both in the bloc's economic literature and in the behavior of its economic directors. This will illuminate some implications of the trade reforms that seemed to elude socialist planners.

The Production Organization Sector: Principal Variables

Concentration as Growth Inducement. A key ingredient in the socialist recipe for reform is "scale superstitution"—the belief that concentration of industry automatically implies benefits of large-scale production and more dynamic technological performance. A strong but typical expression of this belief is that vertical and horizontal cooperation between enterprises is necessary and that other such arrangements "providing for industrial concentration represent an objective requirement of the law of concentration."[8] This belief was strong enough to overrule the reformist desire to encourage competition. It was, in part, responsible for the establishment of industrial associations and the integration of state-owned enterprises throughout East Europe in spite of the classical Marxist hatred of the renowned "exploitative and imperialistic tendencies of monopoly."[9] The danger of socialist monopoly is that the source of its profits may lie not merely in its greater ability to reduce costs and detect demand developments early. It is not clear how "illegitimate" or exploitative monopoly profits could be extricated from the desirable sources mentioned. Therefore, socialist planners have elected to rely on an alternative method of public control of monopoly power.

International Trade as Competitive Control. Competition has always been seen as an ameliorant to the undesirable effects of monopoly, and where a country is so small that optimally scaled economic structures preclude internal competition, it must be imported. Though the Hungarians (and before 1968, the Czechoslovakians) have expressed the greatest interest in effecting policy based on the principle, the solution of foreign competition has appealed to almost all of the socialist states.[10] Since, for both historical and technical reasons, the scale of plant in those countries has been large while the home market has been of comparatively diminutive proportions, associations, and even large enterprises, have been granted monopoly positions. The admission of competitive foreign goods, or at least the continued threat of admission, has been used in the attempt to maintain a more satisfactory degree of competitiveness and innovative dynamism than would otherwise be achieved.[11]

It is the hope of socialist planners that opening their markets to foreign competition will provide greater incentive for domestic enterprises to upgrade their innovative performance and to produce higher quality products with considerably greater cost consciousness.

Above all, as Neuberger has pointed out, if trade can serve as a countervailing power to the negative effects of industrial concentration, a modicum of automatic social control of industry is introduced, so that the benefits of decentralization need not be lost.[12]

Decentralization as an Efficiency Experiment. It has already been observed that some decentralization of allocative decision-making powers from the center to the industrial association or sometimes even to the large enterprise has been practiced in the quest for domestic and international economic efficiency. The difficulties of communication and control have, at times, been great enough to motivate planners to relinquish at least some of their directive authority.

Naturally, the appeal of decentralization as a means to more effective trade performance is much greater to the trade-dependent, small socialist countries than to the Soviet Union. But since threatened incursions into the realm of the trade monopoly's powers are viewed always with suspicion and sometimes with hostility by CMEA's leading power, the desire to decentralize has materialized in little actual progress.[13] Wilczynski indicates that, though some progress has been made in liberalizing exports, foreign exchange scarcity keeps importation subject to "extreme centralization."[14]

The tortuous process of decontrol of imports (which in the pilot case of Yugoslavia was measured not in years but in decades) is doubtlessly due to the problem of foreign-exchange scarcity, for which the potential importers of capital goods and consumers goods provide enthusiastic competition.

Capital Imports as a Second Growth Inducement. Planners feel it is imperative that they conserve scarce foreign exchange for their own purposes, especially for the importation of capital equipment that can assist in reducing the severity of the "technology gap" between East and West Europe.[15]

Since capital goods imports from the West give the command economies access to sophisticated Western technology, they have been of considerable importance in the socialist drive to accelerate industrialization processes. Importing growth through advanced Western machinery and equipment is clearly preferable to undergoing the slow and wasteful process of developing it domestically.[16]

Production Sector: The Model

This section will analytically incorporate the relationships treated in the above discussion. Economic growth G is seen by the socialists as a function of the degree of concentration of industry C, capital imports KM, and domestic investment I: $G = f(C, I, KM)$ where each is measured in some standard unit.

In the graphical analysis of this growth relationship, a diagrammatic shorthand technique is utilized that can best be understood with reference to Figure 8-1. In quadrant I, where $G = f(KM)$, higher rates of growth can be achieved with a given level of capital imports by moving up vertically on the family of potential investment curves. Likewise, a given constant rate of growth could be maintained while permitting a diminution in the rate of domestic capital investment as the level of capital imports is permitted to rise (seen diagrammatically as moving out horizontally to lower investment curves). In quadrant II, $G = f(C)$.

At any given growth rate, the first investment value on a given investment curve (I_0', I_1', or I_2') represents the level of domestic investment associated with the greater degree of concentration given by $G' = f(C)$. The second investment value (I_1, I_2, or I_3, respectively) represents the investment level associated with $G = f(C)$. The third value (I_2, I_3, or I_4) represents required investment in a situation characterized by no concentration at all (pure competition).

A given percentage rate of growth G_1, for example, will require some specified quantity of capital imports KM_1 when combined with the level of domestic investment I_2. A greater degree of concentration C_2, given by the function $G' = f(C)$, would require the same volume of capital imports only if a lower level of domestic investment I_1' is applied. Put differently, a shift from G to G' at a constant level of capital imports (KM_1, here), results in an upward shift of the family of investment curves. Likewise, if the degree of concentration were reduced to zero, the growth rate G_1 could be maintained by KM_1 only if domestic investment of I_3 were achieved: a shift to a lower concentration function causes a downward shift of the family of investment curves. The investment curves need not shift downward, of course, if, with pure competition and investment of I_2 the importation of capital equipment were increased to KM_2.

Figure 8-1 is incorporated in the production-organization sector of the model, shown in Figure 8-2, and will be recognized there as Part b and quadrant II of Part a. In quadrant III of Figure 8-2, consumer imports CM are given as a proxy for foreign competition FC, and CM is a direct function of the degree of concentration, for the planners' decision to regulate monopolistic and oligopolistic market power by exposing domestic markets to foreign competition is a decision to permit a greater volume of imports.

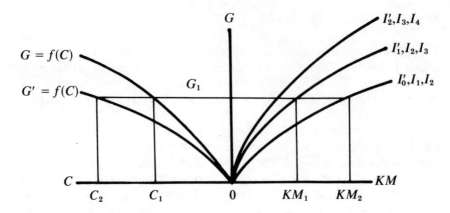

Figure 8-1. Growth as a Function of C, I, and KM

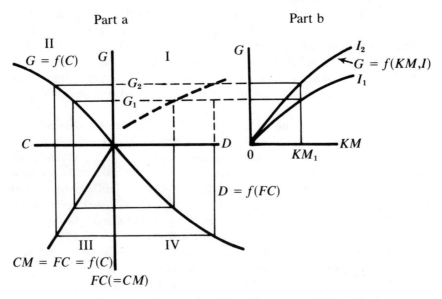

Figure 8-2. Production-Organization Sector of the Model

Quadrant IV demonstrates another policy decision, viz., that the benefits of decentralization can be enjoyed, so long as foreign competition can be relied upon to offset the potentially damaging effects of monopolistic power in domestic markets. Here, decentralization D is represented as a function of foreign competition FC; over some range it can increase pari passu with the growth of consumer imports.[b]

[b] I am grateful to J.M. Montias for the apt observation that there is no a priori reason to believe

The production-organization sector of the model shows that with the given feasible level of domestic investment, a particular level of concentration and a specific degree of decentralization will require, for purposes of adequate social control of industry, some companion level of foreign competition. Two illustrative sets of growth rates, G_1 and G_2, and their accompanying organization conditions are given in Figure 8-2. From varying conditions and growth rates, a smooth function can be derived in quadrant I, showing that more rapid rates of growth are associated with higher degrees of decentralization of decision making in planned economies. Since concern here is primarily with the foreign trade sector of the economy and with the growth and enlarged capacity associated with increasing concentration, decentralization, and so on, it would seem appropriate to label this function "export capacity."

Note that the shapes of the functions in quadrants II and IV indicate that the relevant dependent variables respond only over a certain range of potential change in the independent variables. They are assumed to be continuous and integrable. The export capacity XC function will, therefore, increase at a decreasing rate, taking the general form $G = a_1 + b_1 \log D$.

The International Financial Sector: Principal Variables

Foreign Exchange as a Constraint on Capital Imports. Because the socialist demands for capital and consumers goods from the West are great, the means of procuring them are often found wanting. The effects of the scarcity of foreign exchange have been widely discussed.[17] Briefly, they are that, in spite of the general thrust of the command economies toward greater East-East trade, where markets and sources of materials are assured and would be difficult to replace, there is also a sense of urgency about developing more extensive trade relations with the hard-currency trading nations of the West, even if trade must sometimes be conducted in a fashion that is discriminatory to other socialist countries.[18]

Once earned, foreign exchange will generally be spent by the recipient bloc country without delay in Western markets, in spite of provisions for joint use of Western currency through CMEA's International Bank for Economic Co-operation.[19] If socialist export receipts in Western markets were to increase, increased purchases could likewise be expected. On the other hand, obstructions to Eastern imports in Western countries must lead directly to diminished Eastern purchases in the West.

Decentralization as a Complement to Greater Foreign Competition. Hopes that monopoly power can be rendered socially responsible as it is exposed

that the decentralization function is necessarily continuous. Assuming that it is so, however, will keep the model simpler than it would otherwise become.

to the rigors of international competition must be based on the availability of foreign exchange. Unfortunately, the threat to import will generally be as abortive as the actual attempt, since these countries are constantly threatened with heavy balance-of-payments deficits vis-a-vis the convertible currency countries with which they seek to trade.[20]

To the extent that foreign exchange is available and decentralization is pursued, however, less foreign exchange will be available for importing the capital goods requisite to rapid growth and technological improvement. For this reason, command economies can be expected to keep tight control of their foreign-exchange system. Neuberger tells us that dismantling the centralized Yugoslavian foreign-exchange system was one of the "more difficult tasks of the transition period (from classical Stalinist to market socialism)." Economic reforms in 1952, 1961, and 1965 have failed to eliminate some of the strong elements of central control over foreign exchange that exist to the present.[21]

Decentralization, however, may constrain growth (by permitting low-priority use of scarce foreign exchange) only in the short run. In the long run, positive benefits may accrue to decentralized decision making. Where foreign-trade corporations or enterprises are permitted to spend some portion of their convertible exchange revenues where they wish (as reform measures sometimes permitted without recourse to the trade monopoly in East Germany, Czechoslovakia, Hungary, Poland, the U.S.S.R., and Yugoslavia), they may opt for capital imports that will stimulate growth. In addition, this practice could result in greater multilateral flexibility.[22]

International Financial Sector: The Model

The financial sector of the model, shown diagrammatically in Figure 8-3, utilizes some of the functions developed previously in the production sector and Figure 8-2. Growth, given in quadrant II this time, is once again a function of capital imports and domestic investment. This relationship is shown again in Figure 8-3, since it can now be seen in juxtaposition to the foreign exchange constraint in quadrant III. The foreign-exchange level pertaining (FE_1 or FE_2 for example) must be taken in the short run as a given. Each FE function shows the total of capital imports possible if foreign exchange were exhausted on the purchase of such goods exclusively, the total of consumer goods imports given exclusive purchases of that type, or the combinations of both capital and consumer goods imports that are feasible. FE_2 permits greater purchases of both types of imports, of course, than does the smaller foreign-exchange endowment FE_1. Whatever the endowment, it will yield some level of total imports M that is the sum of capital KM and consumer goods imports CM.

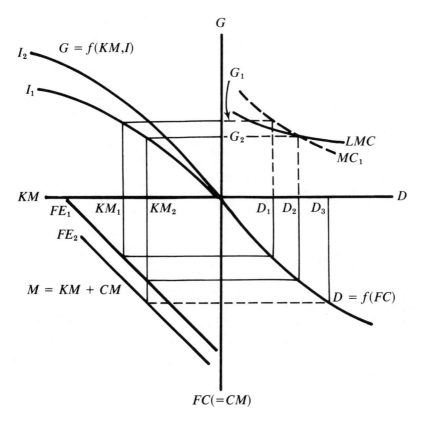

Figure 8-3. The Financial Sector of the Model

When planners choose some level of desired concentration in their pursuit of economic growth, a complementary degree of decentralization will be necessary as well. Sufficient control will be achieved by the introduction of foreign competition, i.e., imported consumer goods. If the foreign-exchange endowment is FE_1, the level of such imports is implied in the degree of decision-making decentralization chosen (D_1, say, in Figure 8-3). The remainder of the available convertible currency will be exhausted in purchasing capital imports KM_1, that will be necessary to sustain the rate of growth sought G_1. Note that the greater degree of decentralization D_2, will require a greater share of the limited foreign-exchange endowment, requiring a reduction of capital imports and some growth potential. The effect of this linkage is seen once again in quadrant I, where higher growth rates are associated with lesser degrees of decentralization and their respectively enhanced possibilities to control the use of foreign exchange for the growth priorities of the planners. The function derived in quadrant I might appropriately be labeled the import efficiency ME function. The inverse relationship between the growth rate and the degree of decentralization will decrease at a decreasing rate and take the general form $G = a_2 - b_2 \log D$.

The import capacity function will be flatter in the long run, as can be seen by the LMC curve in Figure 8-3. At least this will follow if decentralization leads to greater efficiency and flexibility (because, for example, exporting enterprises can now import their own capital equipment). Note, too, that a greater foreign-exchange endowment will permit more extensive foreign competition without drastically curtailing capital imports. In a later period, with FE_2 pertaining, a greater degree of decentralization D_3 can be achieved without reducing growth.

The Sectors Combined

The export capacity XC function and the import efficiency ME function are taken from the first quadrant of the production and financial sectors, respectively, and combined in Figure 8-4. Together, these functions constrain the possibilities of growth and decentralization; the shaded area shows the feasible combinations that can be chosen by planners. It is given mathematically by

$$\int_0^{D_a} a_1 + b_1 \log D + \int_{D_a}^{K} a_2 - b_2 \log D$$

Should planners attempt to achieve the desired growth rate G_d with the degree of decentralization D_1, they would find they had sufficient control over foreign-exchange resources to do so, but that a lower actual growth rate G_a was the best that could be achieved. Here, growth would be constrained by the XC function, i.e., overcentralization, insufficient and inept provision of motivation to the enterprise manager, inadequate exploitation of scale economies, and so on.

Were a much greater degree of decentralization pursued (D_2, let us say), the desired growth rate G_d would still remain unattainable. In this instance, however, growth would be constrained by the ME function, i.e., exhaustion of scarce exchange for nonpriority consumers' purchases at the cost of essential, technologically-charged capital imports.

The actual growth-decentralization combination selected will be either at the point of intersection of the XC and ME functions, or on the XC function to the left of the intersection. Naturally, this does not follow because market forces work to that end. Rather, the solution actually achieved will be the result of conscious choice on the part of the planners.

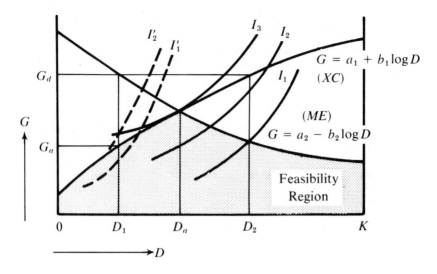

Figure 8-4. Growth and Control Possibilities

Their tastes are reflected in the indifference functions I_1, I_2, and I_3. If K represents the maximum possible degree of decentralization, it also represents, by definition, complete lack of economic control for the planners. That planners derive positive utility from their ability to exercise control is no secret. Hence, a movement from K toward the origin in Figure 8-4 provides a positive increase in satisfaction to the directors of the command system. A movement upward vertically from K or 0 likewise provides utility. The indifference function then shows the willingness of planners to substitute growth for control and vice versa.

If the tastes of East European directors are as shown here, the level of decentralization actually chosen will be D_a. If the marginal rate of substitution of control for growth is substantially greater than depicted in Figure 8-4, the solution will be given by a point of tangency between an indifference curve and the XC function to the left of the intersection of XC and ME (as does I_2 the preference function of the bureaucrat with a fetish for control).

The very phenomenon of the reform movement, however, seemed to indicate a preference function unwilling to make inordinate growth sacrifices to maintain an extremely high degree of economic control, so a short time ago an equilibrium at or near the intersection would have seemed probable. At present, it is quite evident that the preference for extensive control has far from vanished in the socialist states, so outcomes to the left of D_a seem inevitable for some time to come.

In any case, the actual preference can be expressed in general form as a Cobb-Douglas preference function $U = G^\beta(K - D)^\alpha$, where the exponents α and β sum to less than unity (thus assuring diminishing utility).

Permitting utility to be constrained by the XC and ME functions it is possible to write the Lagrangian expression:

$$U = G^\beta(K - D)^\alpha + \lambda_1(G - a_2 + b_2 \log D) + \lambda_2(G - a_1 - b_1 \log D)$$

Because the unique growth-decentralization solution can be found only at the ME and XC intersection (given normal reform preferences) or along the XC function to the left of the intersection (given the control fetish), the Kuhn-Tucker conditions become relevant. They are

$$\frac{\partial U}{\partial G} = \beta G^{\beta-1}(K - D)^\alpha + \lambda_1 + \lambda_2 \leq 0$$

$$\frac{\partial U}{\partial D} = -G^\beta \alpha(K - D)^{\alpha-1} + \lambda_1 \frac{b_2}{D} + \lambda_2 \frac{-b_1}{D} \leq 0$$

$$\frac{\partial U}{\partial \lambda_1} = G - a_2 + b_2 \log D \geq 0$$

$$\frac{\partial U}{\partial \lambda_2} = G - a_1 - b_1 \log D \geq 0$$

$$G\left[\beta G^{\beta-1}(K - D)^\alpha + \lambda_1 + \lambda_2\right] + D\left[-G^\beta \alpha(K - D)^{\alpha-1} + \lambda_1 \frac{b_2}{D} - \lambda_2 \frac{b_1}{D}\right] = 0$$

$$\lambda_1[G - a_2 - b_2 \log D] + \lambda_2[G - a_1 - b_1 \log D] = 0$$

where $\quad G \geq 0, D \geq 0, \lambda_1 \geq 0,$ and $\lambda_2 \geq 0.$

Solving these expressions simultaneously for G, D, λ_1, and λ_2 yields a unique solution of the kind found above in the diagrammatic treatment.

Implications of the Model

If one accepts the assumptions of the substantial part of East European planning literature that underlies the model developed in the previous section (i.e., that externally introduced competition can serve as social control of socialist industry, that concentration of industry does generate technological progress and growth, that a substantial degree of state control over foreign exchange is essential, etc.), then one might expect that the introduction of a greater degree of economic decentralization was designed to, and should have, achieved a renewal of success in the pursuit of growth.

There are, however, both theoretical and practical reasons to indicate that the reforms were bound to prove inadequate and that reorganizational measures would be found necessary.[c] It is the intent of this section to specify those factors that would prevent the planning mechanisms of reformed socialism from representing a stable equilibrium situation.[23]

Let us begin with the thesis that the reforms don't go far enough.[24] The basic (irrational) elements of central planning have not been eliminated from command trade: for the most part, exports and imports are still centrally planned; Western markets to a significant extent remain markets of last resort—unexpected surpluses can be unloaded there and unexpected shortages (due to planning errors or other unforseen difficulties) can be eased there; a separate international trade pricing system remains necessary; and, above all, the basic pattern of inconvertibility and bilateral trade remain the fundamental eyesore on the socialist landscape.

It may be doubted that material incentives (associated with making profitability of enterprise management the principal success criterion) will prove strong enough to generate the radical improvements in production that would be required to render most socialist products competitive in Western markets. The easier course for the enterprise manager would be to continue to produce for the less demanding, far less satiated sellers' markets still available in the bloc countries.[25]

The issue of convertibility remains one of the most difficult. The essential requirement of any authentically multilateral system is that the clearing of imbalances occurs automatically. In CMEA, the transferable ruble is really convertible only when balances remaining at the end of a period are converted to claims on socialist countries' goods through a tedious (in any case, far from automatic) process of negotiations.[26]

One interesting suggestion aimed at resolving the inconvertibility problem has been made by Berliner.[27] Since the utilization of Western prices has helped substantially in facilitating bloc international trade, why not resort as well to the utilization of Western foreign exchange? The difficulties inherent to the bloc reliance upon bilateralism and inconvertibility would be largely removed if the socialist states were to build up a stock of convertible valuta by running a balance-of-payments surplus for a few years and, thereafter, conducting all trade in convertible currencies.

Berliner is not unaware that there are obvious reasons why the socialist countries would likely find this unappealing. Building up such a stock of

---

[c] In fairness, it should be observed that, because reforms were poorly conceived and incompletely and inconsistently implemented, less centralization (i.e., the scrapping or marked deemphasis of reform measures) was perceived by socialist planners as the path to better growth performance. From a short-term perspective (and given the inadequacy of the actual reform attempted), the socialists were probably right.

From a long-term perspective, the preference in the Soviet bureaucracy, and even in the orthodox ranks of the bloc countries, for control may be expected to be a more or less permanent part of the planning landscape. Nevertheless, the reform movement came into being in spite of the influence of bureaucrats, and as younger faces in East Europe's growing technical elite gradually replace older party functionaries, forces representing the kind of tastes reflected in indifference functions I_1' and I_2' may ultimately become defunct.

convertible currencies would, in essence, be like granting a long-term loan to leading Western currency countries, though interest would be earned on holdings of dollars, sterling, and so on. Dependency upon foreign currencies would doubtlessly be politically repugnant to the socialists, too. It might be observed, however, that they have borne well under the ignominy of using world-market prices to conduct trade, and the advantages of convertibility might more than offset these costs.

Whether the process of replacing command with market allocation mechanisms in foreign trade should be considered a redirection or merely a drastic extension of the reform movement, it is difficult to say. In any case, some analysts seem to take the position that in spite of setbacks, reliance upon market-type mechanisms, at least in some of the important sectors of the economy, will ultimately come to characterize socialist economics.[28]

Such an assumption clearly seems to be adopted by Spulber when he discusses the overhauling of bloc foreign-trade practices and the attempt to let these systems "be guided by market and price considerations." This tendency, he believes, may even result in the ultimate adoption of "the traditional array of tariffs, export taxes, subsidies, and exchange rate manipulations to control, up to a point, the level and composition of their trade, as the market-directed economies do."[29]

The viewpoint taken here is that the movement toward market practices will not be a direct one. Rather, it was to be expected, even before the disappointing outcome of the reform endeavors of the 1960s, that "the notorious pendulum between centralization and decentralization to which Communist planning has been subject" could be expected to take at least one more swing toward recentralization before socialist international economics reached a stable equilibrium liberalization.[30]

Recentralization could have been expected if one accepted the basic analysis of the production-organization sector of the model, as developed in Figures 8-1 and 8-2, but rejected the socialist assumption that concentration of industry necessarily represents a positive growth input.

Socialist economic literature seems to show that growth performance depends upon concentration because it (a) permits economies of scale and (b) is the chief characteristic and requisite of effective research and development performance. Great emphasis is given the second point, which seems to have been elevated to the level of official ideology.[d] If this belief can appropriately be referred to as "scale superstition," the East European hope that industrial concentration is the solution to rising capital/output ratios is bound to be frustrated.[31] In terms of the model, capital imports and domestic investment levels (quadrant I of Figure 8-1) are the significant determinants of growth because concentration (quadrant II of Figure 8-1) contributes nothing to economic growth. If the rate of growth is determined

[d]This holds at least in the East German and Soviet literature.

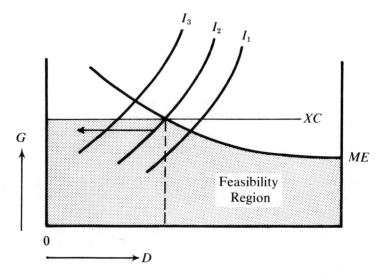

Figure 8-5. Growth and Control without Concentration

entirely in Part b of Figure 8-2, $G \neq f(C)$ in quadrant II of Part a. Exogenously determined, it can be shown as a horizontal line in Figure 8-2, Part a's second quadrant. As can be seen in Figure 8-5, this modifies the model quite dramatically by making the export capacity function unresponsive to decentralization, i.e., a horizontal line.[e]

The planner's ultimate awakening to the folly of scale superstition would logically lead to dramatic recentralization of economic control. Decentralization, a positive disutility to the socialist bureaucracy and an essential complement to the policy of concentration, is rendered less attractive once concentration proves to have been a vain hope. Higher indifference levels can be reached as the socialist directors move along the *XC* constraint line toward the origin.

In actual fact, another more simple model would seem more appropriate. It would necessarily de-emphasize concentration as a growth variable and select instead a direct functional relationship between growth and decentralization, focusing on its control and communication benefits. As before, capital imports and domestic investment levels would also be growth variables. Decentralization would be achieved in the domestic arena by standard reform principles (replacing gross output targets and "petty tutelage" with the profitability criterion of success) and, in the

[e] Put less strongly, if concentration does in fact have some minor positive effect on growth due to scale advantages alone, the export capacity function will have a very slight positive slope. This will also result in recentralization just as the horizontal *XC* function does, though recentralization need not be complete in the less extreme case.

international arena, by permitting foreign competition (consumer imports) and the gradual demise of the state trade monopoly, bilateralism, and inconvertibility. Limited foreign exchange would be divided between capital imports and consumer imports. As growth proceeded and industrial capacity, in general, and export capacity, in particular, expanded, the foreign-exchange endowment would increase. This would in turn permit greater decentralization, capital imports, and consumer goods imports.

This model is presented diagrammatically in Figure 8-6. With a given foreign-exchange endowment (quadrant IV) FE_2 and the prevailing level of decentralization D_1, the rate of growth and the volume of capital and consumer goods imports are determined as G_1, KM_1, and FC_1. In the next period, with an expanded capacity to produce not only more domestic goods but also a greater volume of exports, FE_3 allows KM_2, G_2, and FC_2. Moreover, if decentralization proceeds to the level D_2 with its corresponding changes in both domestic and international spheres, these beneficial results can be expected with an even lower level of domestic investment than I_3, which was assumed to prevail in the first period.

As before, this model permits an analysis of constrained planners' preference. Diagrammatically, the ME function would be derived as in Figure 8-4, but the XC function is merely the relevant growth function taken directly from quadrant II of Figure 8-6. When the planners' indifference curves are superimposed on the XC and ME functions, the solution values of growth and decentralization are readily determined.

At best, however, such a model must be considered the "wave of the future" for socialist countries. The degree of decentralization and the extent of the reforms as applied to international economic relations fell short of permitting the degree of rationality that would stimulate these economies to more dynamic performance. And since socialist expectations of stimulation through industrial concentration are likely to be proved barren, a resurgence of the forces favoring recentralization would have been forthcoming even had the reforms proved ineffective for other reasons.[f] After a period of greater authoritarianism in resource allocation, that policy may once again be found counterproductive, so that ultimately, a more peremptory decentralization of the socialist economic mechanism may be achieved. It would necessarily go much further than the token measures and experimentation that characterized trade reforms in the 1960s.

Bloc economists are already discussing planning options for the future, and many hope for an abandonment of bilateralism and nonconvertibility as

[f] No claim is made, of course, that trade problems alone can be held responsible for the general cessation of the reform movement of the 1960s. In a paper representing an earlier version of this chapter, before I was convinced that the reform movement had nearly lost its inertia (failing to foresee the extent of planning difficulties that had been developing in other spheres), I simply predicted an end to the reform for trade reasons on the basis of the model's logic.

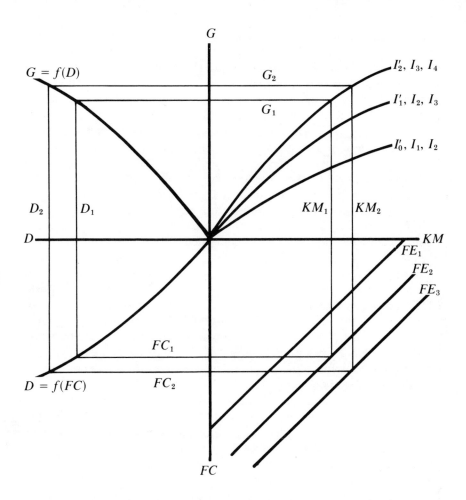

Figure 8-6. Growth as a Direct Function of Decentralization

soon as possible. Soviet, Polish, and East German economists appear to have a preference for general optimization (programming) models and the calculation of dual prices for domestic and trade purposes. Though such models imply the formulation of parameters to be supplied to individual enterprises as guidelines for decentralized economic calculation, they also seem to betray a poorly veiled traditional penchant of Soviet planners to hope to improve performance through yet more, rather than less, extensive central planning.

Many of the economists of other bloc countries (in preinvasion Czechoslovakia and Hungary, in particular) have found the "mega-models" unrealistic and too centralized. Their view is that the Foreign Trade Plan must merely be semiglobal and indicative. The state trade monopoly should be dismantled, and individual enterprises should make their own import and export decisions. They would, of course, operate in a framework reflecting planners' priorities and utilizing incentives, financial controls, and, if necessary, even quantitative restrictions.[32]

The latter group is particularly in favor of convertibility, believing that it would merely be expressive of world economic interdependence and would facilitate more reasonable levels of East-West trade.[33]

Vajda, one of the most eloquent spokesmen of this group, called for the creation of a new international socialist system over the next decade or so, achieving a greater degree of integration of world markets. A greater East-West division of labor seems to be particularly desirable, since it would extend the possibilities of continued growth for both East and West.[34]

In any case, it is doubtful to all observers that an extension of the "socialist division of labor" through a rejuvenated or more powerful CMEA could prove to be the savior of bloc international economic difficulties. The hope that trade mega-models could be developed and administered by CMEA for the bloc as a whole has repeatedly been grounded on the shoals of bloc power politics. The 1968 Polish drive for greater CMEA integration was no more successful than numerous others have been over the past near decade.[35]

It seems almost inconceivable that CMEA, in its present form, could survive indefinitely. The expansion of East-West trade, earnestly sought for reasons spelled out in detail above, would alone militate against its preservation.[36] The drive to adopt truly reformed trade-planning institutions in order to achieve a state of international economic viability (rather than to achieve the state of isolation from "the vagaries of world markets" formerly pursued) will eventually signal the rise of a new international economic order in Eastern Europe.

Notes

1. See Joseph S. Berliner, "Discussion," in *International Trade and Central Planning,* by Alan A. Brown and Egon Neuberger, eds. (Berkeley: University of California Press, 1968), pp. 306 sqq.; A.A. Brown, "Towards a Theory of Centrally Planned Foreign Trade," in ibid., pp. 57 sqq.; Harry G. Johnson, "Notes on Some Theoretical Problems Posed by the Foreign Trade of Centrally Planned Economies," in ibid., pp. 393 sqq. See also other papers presented to a conference on central planning and interna-

tional trade held at the University of Southern California in Los Angeles between December 30, 1966 and January 1, 1967. Most of the participants agreed that the governments of the command economies "are consistently economically irrational." (Johnson, op. cit., p. 396.)

2. Johnson, ibid.; Michael Montias, "Comments on the Papers on East-West Trade: 3," in *International Economic Relations, Proceedings of the Third Congress of the International Economic Association*, Paul A. Samuelson, ed. (New York: St. Martin's, 1969), pp. 142 sqq.

3. Little work has been done on the impact of the reforms on bloc trade. Publishing as late as 1969, Wiles prudently chose not to anticipate some of the as yet unrealized effects of decentralization, especially since these have had little application in international economics. Peter J.D. Wiles, *Communist International Economics* (New York: Praeger, 1969). Refusing to speculate "upon what may shortly be" (p. 38) proved to be wisdom in light of the then imminent bogging down of reform implementation.

4. The plethora of indices developed by the command economies to establish "real costs" and comparative advantages are treated in some detail in Heinz Köhler, *Economic Integration in the Soviet Bloc, with an East German Case Study* (New York: Praeger, 1965). Also in Jozef Wilczynski, *The Economics and Politics of East-West Trade* (New York: Praeger, 1969).

5. The issues arising from the inconvertibility of bloc countries are best illucidated by Franklyn D. Holzman, "Foreign Trade Behavior of Centrally Planned Economies," in *Industrialization in Two Systems, Essays in Honor of Alexander Gerschenkron*, Henry Rosovsky, ed. (New York: Wiley, 1966), pp. 237 sqq., though the fundamental problems described some time ago in Donald A. Wells, "Impediments to ECE Clearing Operations," *The Southern Economic Journal*, vol. 25 (1959), pp. 447 sqq., remain largely unchanged.

6. See Brown's description, "Towards a Theory," op. cit., p. 64. "Taut" planning in foreign trade is characterized by the acceptance of export price estimates that are unrealistically high and estimates of import prices and required foreign-exchange reserves that are unrealistically low.

7. The term is also Brown's, ibid.

8. Karl Morgenstern, "Erfordernisse und Wege zur Weiterentwicklung der sozialistischen internationalen Spezialisierung und Kooperation," *Wirtschaftswissenschaft*, vol. 18 (1970), pp. 669 sqq. Morgenstern calls for participation of national enterprises in international investment projects, the establishment of international socialist enterprises (*gemeinsame Betriebe*), and cooperation in R & D as well as in general production

undertakings. He refers to the 23rd Meeting of CMEA and the call made there for international socialist cooperation in the construction of research institutes, multinational enterprises, etc. Ibid., p. 684.

9. See Ljuko Sirc, *Economic Devolution in Eastern Europe* (New York: Praeger, 1969), pp. 69 sqq.

10. See Sirc, ibid., p. 72.

11. For a more detailed treatment of the evolving use of trade as a substitute for domestic competition in particular bloc countries, see Michael Kaser and Janusz G. Zielinski, *Planning in East Europe: Industrial Management by the State, A Background Book* (London: Bodley Head, 1970).

12. Egon Neuberger, "Central Planning and Its Legacies: Implications for Foreign Trade," in *International Trade and Central Planning*, op. cit., p. 355.

13. An interesting citation in A. Nove, "East-West Trade," in: *International Economic Relations*, op. cit., pp. 113 sqq., brings this point home. Baibkov, Gosplan's chairman says, "The proposal to give industrial associations the right to trade in foreign markets is objectively directed towards the weakening of planning and the loss of the advantages which accrue from the centralization of export-import operations."

14. Wilczynski, *The Economics and Politics*, op. cit., p. 392.

15. Much of the work done on the technology question, insofar as it relates to East-West trade, can be conveniently found in one volume. See *East-West Trade and the Technology Gap*, Stanislaw Wasowski, ed. (New York: Praeger, 1970).

16. See Wilczynski, *The Economics and Politics*, op. cit., pp. 41, 264, 360, and passim; Andrzej Korbonski, "Theory and Practice of Regional Integration: The Case of Comecon," *International Organization*, vol. 24 (1970), p. 959. This trend is by no means confined to an earlier period of socialist development. Whereas the bloc countries imported twice as much machinery from the West than they exported to it in the mid-1950s, they now import four times as much.

17. See, for example, Rudolf Nötel, "Future Development of East-West Trade," *Economia Internazionale*, vol. 23, 1970, pp. 212 sqq.; and Nove, "East-West Trade," op. cit.

18. Nove, ibid., p. 108, refers to the practice of nearly all of the bloc countries of reserving the better tourist accommodations for Westerners bearing convertible valuta, and of exporting better quality and better packed goods to western markets.

19. Ibid.

20. The Bulgarian Communist Party has faced this issue by searching for a different means of providing competitive control over the monopoly

power inherent in product-defined associations. They have discussed a more appropriate use of the market mechanism and greater economic competition between socialist enterprises as possible answers. See Kaser and Zielinski, *Planning in East Europe,* op. cit., p. 99.

21. Egon Neuberger, "Central Planning," op. cit., p. 362.

22. See Wilczynski, *The Economics and Politics,* op. cit., p. 213.

23. Many of the reasons given by Neuberger, "Central Planning," op. cit., for his expected decline of centrally planned economies as currently known, naturally have a bearing here too. As he puts it, "Just as Marx has argued that the capitalist system digs its own grave—both by its successes, which make it less necessary, and by its failures, which make it less desirable— . . . the Soviet system does likewise." Interestingly, the trade issue is seen as a central one in the decline: "the probable life of the system will be shorter in a small, less potentially self-sufficient country, where foreign economic relations play a much more crucial role, such as Yugoslavia or Hungary." Again, "in a small country the problems faced in the field of foreign trade are the crucial ones in forcing changes in the system."

24. A list of adherents to this viewpoint would be formidable. At a bare minimum can be given: J. Benard, "Comments on the Papers on East-West Trade: 1," in *International Economic Relations,* op. cit., pp. 134 sqq.; Berliner, "Discussion," op. cit.; Neuberger, "Central Planning," op. cit.; Nicolas Spulber, "East-West Trade and the Paradoxes of the Strategic Embargo," in *International Trade and Central Planning,* op. cit.; Imre Vajda, "Wirtschaftswachstum und internationale Arbeitsteilung," *Kyklos,* vol. 19 (1966), pp. 670 sqq.

25. See Wilczynski, *The Economics and Politics,* op. cit., p. 217, which informs us that "recent experience in some of these countries, such as Czechoslovakia, has demonstrated that the (partial) freedom extended to enterprises to fix their own prices largely removes the economic pressure from producers to adapt their production to the needs of foreign markets."

26. Ibid., p. 210.

27. Berliner, "Discussion," op. cit., p. 309.

28. Together with the present author, at least Benard, "Comments on the Papers," op. cit.; Spulber, "East-West Trade," op. cit.; and Imre Vajda, "The Problems of East-West Trade," in *International Economic Relations,* op cit., pp. 121 sqq. seem to qualify here.

29. Spulber, "East-West Trade," op. cit., p. 123.

30. The quotation is from Wiles *Communist International Economics,* op. cit., p. 294, who says, "first, we centralize, and pile up an excessive bureaucracy, inhibit initiative, etc. So, secondly, we decentralize, and find we are paying too heavy a penalty in irrationality. That irrationality is, indeed, the second pole of the pendulum has not been enough appreciated.

138

Naturally, total decentralization would have very different effects, but that is, of course, ruled out by the institutions and ideology—and perhaps also by its effect on goals other than rational resource allocation."

31. The evidence indicating that this belief is erroneous is formidable. The reader will be interested in Edwin Mansfield, *The Economics of Technological Change* (New York: Norton, 1968), chapter 5. See also John Jewkes, David Sawers, and Richard Stillerman, *The Sources of Invention,* Second ed. (New York: Norton, 1969).

32. For more detail on these opposing positions, see the account in Benard, "Comments on the Papers," op. cit.

33. Particularly strong on this point is Vajda, "The Problems of East-West Trade," op. cit., p. 131.

34. See Vajda, "Wirtschaftswachstum," op. cit., pp. 686-688. According to Vajda, "the final goal should be the formulation of a conception (of trade) that strives to go beyond the phase of regional integration schemes to one that incorporates a global division of labor, extending into the sphere of the entire world market."

35. The interesting history of such attempts is summarized in rather rich detail in Herta W. Heiss, "The Council for Mutual Economic Assistance—Developments Since the Mid-1960's," in: *Economic Developments in Countries of Eastern Europe,* Subcommittee on Foreign Economic Policy of the Joint Economic Committee, Congress of the U.S., 91st Congress, 2nd Sess. (Washington, D.C., 1970) pp. 528 sqq., which draws the conclusion that "developments since the beginning of 1969 suggest that the idea of endowing CMEA with planning and other supranational authority will once more fall by the wayside. At the same time, the crisis may have provided the necessary push for a more determined exploration of other approaches to closer economic integration which would combine a closer mutual tuning of members' major economic policies with allowance of some scope for market forces in other spheres."

36. Korbonski, "Theory and Practice," op. cit., p. 966, says this expansion "may mean the kiss of death for the chances of integration in the East." This outcome is almost assured because even the most entrenched bureaucrats now perceive the implications of the East-West "technology gap" and the consequent need to import capital from beyond regional borders. Korbonski also holds that, to an ever greater extent, CMEA has "seemed to act primarily as a clearing house for ideas and suggestions, providing an institutional umbrella for bilateral and occasionally multilateral agreements; serving as a forum for the exchange of economic and technical information; conducting research; and acting as an arbiter in cases of disagreement on non-fulfillment of contracts. However important and useful, all these functions could be seen as a terminal rather than an initial stage in the East European integration process."

9

Socialist Integration I: Economic Constraints and Prospects

Although economic integration is sometimes seen as a mechanism for the ultimate achievement of political unification, it is viewed in eastern Europe primarily as an end in itself. Whatever integrative progress the socialists are able to achieve is, of course, dependent upon how successfully centripetal or disintegrative forces can be overcome. These forces seem, in spite of the presence of centrifugal forces and Soviet diligence, to be growing with the passage of time.

In eastern Europe, the Stalinist-autarkic conception of national economic development had largely proved inappropriate for the traditionally trade-dependent, small European socialist states within a single decade of its adoption. Once it has taken root, however, Stalinist planning cannot easily be eradicated; after it has become intellectually moribund, one must continue to reckon with its legacies.[1]

After a quasi-awakening to the unquestionable benefits of Ricardian trade wisdom that had been achieved by the end of the 1950s, the socialist states had first to pursue increased economic cooperation through a decade of economic reforms.[2]

By 1970, the reform movement had become bogged down, and the eastern Europeans were prepared to search for another means to achieve better economic performance and a more substantial specialization and division of socialist labor.[3] This time, the means was a new drive for economic integration utilizing, in fact, little more than an intensification of old planning techniques. National planners, however, were to begin to work in coordination rather than in isolation. Such is the conception of the Complex Program, or (officially) the Comprehensive Program for the Further Deepening and Improvement of Cooperation and the Development of Socialist Economic Integration of the Member Countries of CMEA,'' passed in 1971.

Rather than to pursue economic integration on a market or financial basis, the aim in Eastern Europe is to achieve an integration of production processes. This should permit, so it is believed, a maturing of the productive potential of cooperative effort. It should bring about the development of institutions and (centrifugal) forces enhancing integration in the region. These forces are generally well known: (a) the common ideology and goals;

The material in this and the following chapter, co-authored with Erich Klinkmüller, was originally published as "Eastern European Integration: Constraints and Prospects," *Survey*, vol. 21, no. 1/2 (Winter-Spring 1975), pp. 101-127.

(b) the geographic proximity of the socialist states and the progress already made in establishing trade relationships within the "socialist world market;" (c) the relative reliability and stability inherent in the economic interaction of planned economies; and, above all, (d) the universal desire to increase foreign trade as a means of increasing general welfare (increasing the political acceptability of the socialist regimes).

In socialist literature, glowing phrases are used to describe integration achievements, especially in the area of new bilateral and multilateral cooperative projects. Coordination of national plans for the period 1976-1980, it is affirmed, is well under way. The development of joint forecasts, the drawing up of joint planning contracts, and specialization and cooperation in productive efforts are described as commonplace.[4] Economic structures, it is claimed, are "developing increasingly in the context of the socialist division of labor," reflecting an increasingly "close, multifaceted interaction of reciprocal effects between the production processes of these economies."[5]

On the other hand, the real proof of integration is the coordination of investments that will bring about the desired structural changes in the economy. A more critical (Hungarian) view of integration progress reminds us that the coordination of investments for the 1966-1970 period did not represent significant progress. The CMEA countries most advanced in the important field of engineering industries submitted investment projects that represented but a small percentage of planned total investments in engineering industries. They thought, in other words, "that the rest could not be made dependable on international coordination."[6]

A reliable Western assessment, which is most probably representative of a consensus of judgment on the progress of attempts to develop common integrative projects in Comecon, expresses in short, apt terms that such projects up to this point represent "*peu de choses*".[7]

The centrifugal forces that tend to act as a brake on expanding trade within CMEA are numerous and complex and require more extensive treatment. That is the aim of this and the next chapter, since an understanding of these forces gives an insight into the possibilities for future East European economic and political development.

Centripetal political and economic forces are encountered by the East Europeans at two levels: national and international. Though the problems encountered at both levels have reciprocal, interacting effects, they can be treated (for the sake of simplicity) separately.

At the national level, planners must decide (a) to what degree they wish to discard economic nationalism, i.e., to participate in trade and integrative endeavors and (b) to what extent external trade should be given a Western, rather than an Eastern emphasis.

The centripetal forces present at the international or community level will be discussed in an order that largely reflects the authors' views on the relative importance of the issues. The most fundamental stumbling block facing East European integration is an economic one. If integration is to proceed satisfactorily, the socialists must ultimately come to grips with some well-entrenched problems: (a) agreeing on some balance of planning and market elements that can best serve the long-term domestic interests of the socialist state; (b) establishing some system of pricing and financial arrangements in the international economic sphere (where market elements have always been of necessarily greater importance for the CMEA countries) that can best oil integration machinery;[8] and (c) undertaking policies to alleviate the problems of technological backwardness and the scarcity of capital and raw materials.

It is apparent that the resolution of these difficult economic problems is to be sought in the complex domestic and international political relationships prevailing in the socialist bloc. Political questions are of such significance that the following chapter will be devoted exclusively to their treatment.

The various political and economic problems of integration are interrelated to an extent that makes it difficult to treat them separately. The degree to which the East Europeans interact with each other or with the West is therefore a matter not only of optimal economics, but also of political sovereignty. Indeed, when almost any CMEA problem is discussed, the sovereignty issue soon arises. Likewise, when one treats the problem of scarcity of capital, the closely related (political) issue of levels of economic development cannot be ignored. For purposes of organizational clarity, devoting separate chapters to economic and political issues seems to recommend itself, but at the same time the discussion will unavoidably combine elements from both spheres.

Integration Constraints at the National Level

National Action in the International Sphere

Economic nationalism is currently (and is for some time likely to continue to act as) a brake on the socialist integration process. It is easy to make the initial general decision to pursue cooperative economic ventures and increased trade as a matter of welfare policy. It is a different matter, however, for planners to specify the first domestic industry they wish to shut down, so that the relevant product can, henceforth, be imported more cheaply. This issue is not merely one of avoiding problems of unemployment in the period of transition, when productive capacities are being altered to express the logic of specialization rather than the instinct of autarky.[a]

Traditionally, export enterprises attempting to maximize planning rewards produced planned export goods with an eye only to gross output targets or offered for export those goods that were simply easiest to produce. Often, they would ignore potential exports that were actually in greater demand, even though usually these would probably command a significantly better price. The result has generally been that socialist countries must reckon with a frequently unsatisfactory level of import quality. It is quite natural, therefore, for CMEA members to fear that specialization may not only imply an employment problem; it may also assure that future imports will be of lower quality than the displaced domestic output. While some have felt that the matter of supplying other socialist countries with high-quality products demands self-commitment and self-responsibility on the part of the socialist state,[9] others have called for a new set of legal relationships and contract laws to provide security for those willing to abandon autarky.[10]

Though contributors to socialist integration literature have often called for the elimination of certain inefficient branches of production,[11] actually eliminating them might mean that some export possibilities and foreign currency sources in third markets would be endangered.[12]

It is most difficult to persuade a country to abandon an activity in which it has been engaged. The standing commissions of CMEA can recommend all sorts of possible specializations requiring structural adjustments, but few such recommendations are well received. In the final analysis, there simply exists no mechanism to compensate for losses (subsidies, for example, to support a decision to pursue a specialization project) or to cover whatever risks may be encountered in the integration process.[13]

Balancing Western and Eastern Economic Ties

Once national economic directors recognize the positive welfare effects of participating in an international division of labor, it must be determined to what extent external economic endeavor should bear an eastern emphasis. This problem amounts to finding a balance between cooperation and competition with other socialist states, at least to the extent that such policy maneuverability is possible and the requisite foreign currency is available.

---

[a]The wording here is deliberate. The authors are aware that deliberately eschewing economic interdependence remains a national policy option (for primarily noneconomic reasons, of course). But the force of Ricardian trade logic and, perhaps even more germane to the noneconomist, the thrust of recent international trade history seem all too apparent. Even in the few instances where it might be feasible, the cost of economic isolationism is so high as to render the policy, for all practical purposes, imprudent.

It is clear that one must proceed with political prudence, but intensified Western economic connections have, for some time, been quite acceptable.[14]

Intrabloc trade remains in many respects highly beneficial for the socialist countries. The stability of long-established trade relationships reduces planning uncertainty to a minimum, trade relationships do not imply the necessity of generating markedly scarce foreign exchange, and the less saturated consumer merkets do not place such difficult quality demands on export products. Certain goods, however, are simply not available in Eastern markets. When it comes, for example, to modern Western machinery, technical and engineering equipment, and computers, their potential role in helping to "master the challenges of the scientific-technological revolution" has long since been recognized and emphasized by both technicians and politicians throughout the CMEA region. The foreign exchange required for the purchase of such goods in Western markets can be obtained only through an expansion of exports to the West.[b]

The trade behavior of the East European states is itself the best evidence that East Europeans are anxious to earn the hard currencies that will permit expanded imports of sophisticated Western industrial goods. It is the generally accepted practice for the bloc countries to practice trade discrimination by reserving, for example, better tourist accommodations for Westerners bearing convertible valuta and by exporting higher-quality, better-packed goods to the more demanding western markets.[15]

Economic Constraints on CMEA Integration

Many of the questions facing individual socialist countries assume new dimensions when they are encountered by the eastern European nations acting in concert. Tools for solving the problems of economic integration are different at the international or community level, and constraints placed on the group differ from those relevant to individuals.

Rejecting Market Forces in Resource Allocation Processes

The root of socialist economic difficulties lies in the unfaltering allegiance of socialist decision makers to economic planning and their mistaken perception of market-type allocation processes as antiplanning. This chapter takes the following position: even if it could be assumed that the

---

[b] This is not excluding, of course, outrageous hotel prices and required minimum exchanges of currency for western visitors.

integration process were characterized by a complete lack of disintegrative forces, total integration along the lines of development proposed by the "complex program" is not technically feasible.

The entrenched bureaucracies of Soviet and other socialist states still dream of the day when the process of integration will lead "to the establishment of a unified economic organism," i.e., the "unified, common plan ordering the economy of all nations under the leadership of the proletariat," prophesied by Lenin. Socialist planners admit, of course, that "this process will doubtless develop over a long time period with several stages."[16]

However, how can everything for the CMEA states be completely planned in Moscow, when Moscow is not currently in a position to overcome the tremendous challenge of putting together an efficient and promptly completed annual economic plan for the Soviet Union alone?

Naturally, the response of orthodox socialism to such objections makes reference to activity analysis and the computerization of the world. However, even in the history of the development of corporate planning in the United States, with much smaller planning units, decentralization ultimately became unavoidable.[17] Additionally, it should not be forgotten that computers are a product of the *pre*reform era and that socialist specialists themselves have, in large numbers, rejected the notion that computers of any vintage would ever be endowed with the capacity to treat data describing every preference and production function in the socialist world, even if enough information gatherers could be located to collect such data.[18]

Regardless of how much central planning persists or expands to accomodate CMEA integration, economic theory demonstrates that the bureaucratic costs of international command planning (i.e., the costs of coordinating and administrating CMEA's "production integration" and the costs of gathering and processing the required planning information) do not merely make planning more tedious. These costs must be balanced against the higher returns accruing to the production integration process, the latter arising largely from the reduced unit costs of production associated with the larger scale operations undertaken by more specialized integration participants. According to the fundamental logic of economics, because the costs are higher in socialism, the degree of economic integration achieved (when the most favorable balance is struck between the costs of and returns to integration) will be lower for socialist than for market countries.

In more precise terms, the marginal returns to integrative specialization must be equated to the marginal costs of coordinating the process. Expressed simply, the total returns to integration *TRI* are given as the difference between total costs of autarkic production and the total costs of production after specialization. This difference is, of course, a function of

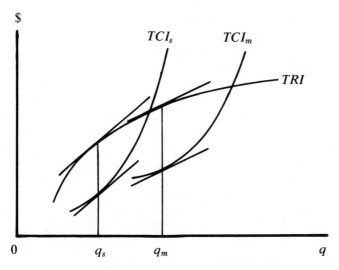

Figure 9-1. Socialist vs. Market Economic Integration

the level of output, so that $TRI = f(q)$, and can be assumed to increase at a decreasing rate with greater volumes of output produced for integration (as the most promising opportunities for specialization are exhausted).

The total costs of integration TCI are the sum of the costs of coordination C, administration A, information I, and transportation T. They are likewise a function of output, increasing at a constant or increasing rate as the level of integrative output rises.

The profitability of integration πI is the difference between total returns to and total costs of integration, $\pi I = TRI - TCI$, which can be maximized by equating its first derivitive to zero, so that

$$d\pi I/dq = dTRI/dq - dTCI/dq = 0 \quad \text{or} \quad dTRI/dq = dTCI/dq$$

This last expression is a mathematical statement that can also be presented, as was done above, in prose.

The integrative costs are greater under socialism than in the market economies, since $C_s + A_s + I_s > C_m + A_m + I_m$ (where the s and m subscripts represent socialist and market economies respectively), so $TCI_s > TCI_m$. As can, perhaps, best be seen graphically in Figure 9-1, this higher cost level (which, for convenience, could be measured in dollars) guarantees that the optimum output of socialist integration q_s is lower than that associated with market integration q_m.

The claim cannot be made, of course, that socialists uniformly fail to observe the efficiency implications of imperative, physical planning. Relatively progressive forces in Hungary, sometimes in Poland, and in preinvasion Czechoslovakia have favored an approach referred to as the "planned market economy." To maintain symmetry, the approach of the Soviet Union and East Germany to national and international economic problems might be expressed as the *"planned* planned economy."

At the height of the reform endeavor in the late sixties, it appeared that the Hungarian approach had a great possibility of assuming the position of an alternative variant to the classical and Yugoslavian models of socialism. In the area of foreign economics, as domestically, the Hungarian model applied a significant degree of decentralization of decision making.[19]

With the demise, or at least downgrading of the reform movement, one might question the utility of discussing the integrative implications of the Hungarian model. It is our view that the Soviet-type planning apparatus has not yet reached a final stable equilibrium and that the need for reform has not disappeared. Moreover, if further reforms are undertaken at a later date, the only other available option would be a more genuine, thoroughgoing decentralization than that achieved (or attempted) in the 1960s. Though it may be some time in coming, it would probably have to appear at least more like the Hungarian or Yugoslavian model than the still prevalent Soviet system.

In any event, as long as the Leninist "single plan" remains a distant, eschatological concept, community economic relationships will be characterized by a substantially greater set of financial problems than those encountered at the national planning level.

Domestically, of course, financial planning and monetary values are of subsidiary importance to physical planning, through which resources can be allocated by direct central commands. At the international level, value and money problems become much more significant. The presence of national values immediately creates, for example, balance of payments considerations that necessarily constrain international resource flows.

The attempts to achieve integration through more extensive decentralization would imply the achievement of transferability and ultimately of convertibility of East European currencies as well as the development of multilateral, rather than bilateral, economic relationships within the bloc. This has long been seen by the Hungarians as the *sine qua non* for the development of the East European economic area. This Hungarian goal was seen as requiring a stage of regional development in which the Soviet "clearing ruble" would serve as a reserve currency or real money regionally (rather than as a mere accounting unit).[20] Trade restrictions should be reduced to a minimum, and the reserve currency must be convertible into gold or some capitalist convertible currency, at least under certain conditions. Naturally, numerous structural tensions may be expected to persist, especially in the initial period. Vajda believed these could be overcome only by assuring economic connections with the convertible currency markets.[21] It should be observed that, even in the reform milieu, Vajda conceded these thoughts to be politically unrealistic (graciously attributing this to be the "currency crisis" of the capitalist countries).

Tibor Kiss, another Hungarian, expressed the view that CMEA integration would have to proceed "along two parallel lines, notably that of coroordinating national economic plans and that of market integration.[22] It is in the framework of the latter that the convertibility of socialist currencies, multilaterality in regional trade, and CMEA customs union should be achieved."

Today, optimism is much less prevalent in Hungary. Though many feel that a genuine economic integration would be impossible without the triumvirate of liberalization, multilateralism, and convertibility, they have apparently accepted in recent years a disassociation of these elements and resigned themselves to the hope that they might be achieved in the distant future.[23]

It has already been seen that the Soviet mentality would favor the implementation of mega-planning and ultimately a single plan for the socialist world. The emphasis here is on an integration of production through physical balancing techniques rather than through decentralization and financial refinements. The East Germans likewise tend (at least officially) to be suspicious of anything resembling market-type economic arrangements. Integration is dutifully described in East German literature as a process requiring greater interdependence of economic structures. It is to be achieved through mutually determined research exercises, joint investment projects, and greater industrial concentration. These are seen as the means also to avoid developing anti-import production. Investment efficiency would be pursued through extending work on effectiveness criteria and indices of economic efficiency.[24]

The Soviet view is that planning inadequacies of the past are in no way attributable to the "hypertrophy of centralism." Rather, problems have strictly been the result of inadequate coordination in CMEA. Decentralization is consequently not required; rather, the development of common planning activities, comprehending all economic processes in the framework of an integrated community is needed.[25] In other words, *everything* should be centrally planned.

The problem extends beyond mere overambitiousness, however. Also very disadvantageous is the apparent failure of the Soviet planning apparatus to comprehend the implications of general equilibrium in an economic system, viz., that everything to a greater or lesser degree, directly, or indirectly, affects, and is affected by, almost everything else. Patchwork planning changes affect not only the areas under direct consideration, but have numerous, sometimes very significant, indirect effects in other areas of the economic system. A careful reading of socialist planning literature reveals complaints that imply recognition of this shortcoming.[26] Ironically, the tendency reflected in the literature of Soviet persuasion is to seek to solve all problems by bringing more economic activity under the influence of planners.[27] Even where writers express dissatisfaction with past outcomes, the demand for improvement never insists on less planning or even the implication that more planning would not be desirable, but only that planning should be better and that multinational coordination should be improved (likewise an enlargement of the labor burden of planning officials).[c] In sum, the Soviets view computer and programming possibilities with tremendous optimism, expect the old techniques somehow to suffice, or wish to retain tight control regardless of the efficiency costs.

Soviet writers are willing to admit that multilateralism and convertibility will someday be achieved in CMEA trade relations. The welfare losses of bilateralism may be greater than socialists generally realize, but there is no question that the benefits of multilateralism have gradually become apparent in Eastern Europe.[28] The degree of recognition seems to be inversely related to the geographical size (and, therefore, directly related to the degree of trade dependence) of the country represented by the recognizer. Van Brabant reminds us of why this is so, pointing out that "the cost of bilateralism is in proportion much larger for the smaller countries than for the larger one, simply because the latter has profited less from free trade. The greater the divergence in available resources, the smaller is welfare foregone due to bilateralism."[29]

Attempts to multilateralize trade through the establishment of the International Bank for Economic Cooperation[30] reflects their awareness, even if "commodity inconvertibility," insufficient capital, and other traditional trade difficulties have kept CMEA's international bank from having any substantial impact on traditional, bilateral trade patterns.[31]

Finally, whereas the Hungarians have tended to view multilateralism as the means to assure improvements in the structure and volume of trade activity, the Soviets seem to have a different view of cause-effect relationships in this respect. Senin expects the bilateral relationships of CMEA "unavoidably and objectively" to be transformed into multilateral relationships. "The first cause of this," he believes, "is the existence and the intensification of the international division of labor and cooperation."[32]

This seems to be yet another form of the Russian planning maxim: "do more of what we're already doing, and do it better, then everything will turn out right."

---

[c]The difficulty planners have in imagining the world other than as it currently is can also be encountered, of course, outside the CMEA region. Experience with governmental control over West German dwelling-unit construction and agricultural planning and EEC agricultural planning are not the only examples that come to mind in this regard.

CMEA Pricing Problems

The unusual pricing methodology of socialism is one of the main sources of behavior impeding the development of increased regional cooperation in CMEA.[33] Because each socialist country practices centralized price fixing, individual pricing systems yield no common, internationally acceptable values for worldwide markets.

Because prices remain inflexible over long periods and do not adequately express real economic conditions (supply costs are distorted through structural anomalies that reflect planners' preferences, and hardly any attempt is made even to consider consumer preferences and other demand factors), prices applying in a given planned economy are quite arbitrary from the point of view of any nonnational economic agent.

Since prices do not reflect economic reality, it becomes impossible to determine, at the community level, just who can produce what commodities most cheaply. Only in cases where extremely obvious comparative cost advantages exist can specialties be perceived. Since no precise and accurate pricing comparisons can be made, the degree of integration CMEA can achieve will be more modest than is possible where markets are at least minimally free to function in a normal way.

Because the socialists mutually agree not to accept their domestic prices for purposes of international trade, a separate socialist international price system has been developed. It is alleged that the foreign-exchange prices applying to their trade are negotiated on the basis of world-market prices, though cleansed from monopolistic distortions prevailing there.[34]

In each socialist country, foreign-trade enterprises receive domestic prices for their outputs, but these are sold by the state foreign-trade monopoly for a completely separate set of international prices. The foreign-trade enterprises do not receive actual foreign-exchange earnings (or suffer foreign-exchange losses incurred). This "price equalization system" (*Preisausgleichsystem*) requires, of course, that the foreign-trade monopoly within the framework of the two separate (foreign and domestic) price systems balance the aggregate of the economy's foreign-trade transactions with an eye towards avoiding balance of payments deficits.[d]

When a socialist country trades on the world market, a second (nonsocialist) international price system is encountered. The existence of two international sets of prices logically has to be a hindrance to the development of intensified CMEA cooperation. So long as individual socialist countries can deal independently of CMEA on the world market, the difference in CMEA and world-market price levels tempt the socialist

---

[d]It is not easy to determine to what extent a given socialist country will succeed in this endeavor in a given year, since these countries publish no balance of payments accounts. It is clear, however, that foreign exchange is always in short supply.

countries to behave rationally, importing from the cheaper market and exporting to the one with higher earnings potential.

Beginning from either a world-market price or a price prevailing in the domestic market of an East European country, a particular commodity's actual price is negotiated for CMEA trade. Assume that it is lower than would be given by a competitive market outcome. With an artificially low price, the producing country will not be able to meet demand and cover costs. Although this may be impossible to calculate and difficult to notice, it will become evident that foreign-exchange earnings aren't going very far. Economic pressure to give up the production of the commodity or adjust the price will increase. An upward adjustment of the price may be perceived as an ambarrassing admission that the producing country really has no comparative advantage. The danger exists that political pressure (not to mention bureaucratic inertia) will militate against the recognition or, at least, the admission of this disadvantageous economic outcome.

Assume now the opposite case, viz., that the established price is artificially high. Economic pressure builds in this case for buyers to look westward to find better bargains. In the case of long-term contracts for the purchase of overpriced goods, the socialist buyer would tend to work within the CMEA political arena for more open individual and community relations with the West, or at least to become a hard bargainer in future trade negotiations. Another possibility is, of course, that an artificially high price will ultimately indicate, in the planning coefficients of the purchasing country, that the relevant commodity could more reasonably be produced domestically. In short, if an East European partner's price is too high, one eithr goes shopping in the West or opts for the "do-it-yourself" (autarkic) solution. Either outcome acts as a brake on CMEA integration.

The problems of two international markets do not end here. It would be logical for the socialist countries at least to divide up the capitalist markets among themselves in some jointly profitable manner. The Hungarians complain, however, that data show sales prices to be "highly uncoordinated." Because CMEA countries even underbid each other in their desire to earn hard currency, they incur substantial price losses. Moreover, it sometimes even becomes impossible for some Eastern sales to be made in Western markets.[35]

Likewise, when it comes to the matter of purchasing licenses from capitalist countries, the socialists have failed to achieve a sufficient degree of cooperation. Apparently, the individual CMEA countries are willing to wage their own individual competition in capitalist world markets.[36]

A final, crucial problem of CMEA pricing is particularly intriguing. The trade institutions discussed above have resulted, in recent years, in an unusual economic quasi-exploitation of the Soviet Union by the satellite states. The Soviet Union has, of course, nobody else to blame for the universal East European adoption of Stalinist-style development of heavy industry. But this phenomenon, combined with the use of world-market-based prices, has resulted in high prices on relatively plentiful heavy industrial outputs and lower prices on increasingly scarce raw materials and fuels.[37]

As is well known, the Soviet Union has committed itself, through long-term trade agreements, to exporting raw materials to the East Europeans (at prices that in recent years, have been very low) in exchange for heavy industrial equipment (of poorer quality and of less attractive technological characteristics than could be obtained in the West). These highly disadvantageous terms of trade are doubtlessly part of the motivation behind Brezhnev's *Westpolitik* and cannot help but have negative implications for future block cohesion.

Capital Scarcity, Technological Backwardness, and The Raw Materials Crisis: Searching for Options

As a Polish economist has observed, the necessity for balance of payments equilibrium and the absence of a free flow of labor and investment among cooperating countries meant that national industrialization drives and the leveling-up of the productivity of social labor between countries occur "primarily on the basis of each country's internal resources."[38] Traditionally, more rapid and sophisticated development of industry had been pursued by planning extremely high levels of investment, which were in turn achieved by techniques of forced savings. Even so, capital has remained in short supply. Since the Complex Program has specified the leveling of economic development of member countries as a primary objective of CMEA integration, one would anticipate a community attempt to achieve some international mobility of capital, mutual investment projects, capital assistance, and so on. Since capital is scarce, however, any given bloc country can export it only to the detriment of domestic development goals and at the cost of a lower growth rate.[39]

Investment requirements for the bloc are likely to remain (or become even increasingly) burdensome. This is a result of the need for extensive capital investments to exploit large deposits of raw materials on the territory of the U.S.S.R. for export to the other bloc countries. Not only the Russians recognize that other investment projects currently appear more attractive to the Soviet Union. Covering the requirements for raw materials of brother socialist countries implies not only heavy capital outlays, but future commitment of raw material deliveries to a region that yields substantially lower returns (especailly since the energy crisis) than could be enjoyed by rechanneling this trade to Western countries. Even loyal non-

Russians recognize that the resolution of this problem will require the labor, capital, and financial participation of other East European countries in the further development of raw materials industries in the U.S.S.R, receiving future deliveries of the required materials in return.[40]

Without being sure of some control over the production and utilization of raw materials outputs, of course, it is difficult to imagine that the East European states will be anxious to participate in such capital investments. That the Soviet Union would grant such control seems no less difficult to imagine. In any case, East European planners are most assuredly weighing up what other sources of raw-materials supply might be pursued and from whence the foreign currency might come to finance them.

Given these conditions, it is of importance that CMEA's international financial institutions are not in a position to contribute significantly to the resolution of the capital scarcity problem. The International Investment Bank (IIB) cannot be relied upon to supply more than "two or three percent of overall net investment activity" in any given period.[41] After all, the IIB is limited to resources generated internally in the CMEA region.

It had been hoped, with the creation of the International Bank for Economic Cooperation (IBEC), that long-term credits for common investment projects could be financed from the bank's own funds. Not surprisingly, the bank turned out to be playing merely an intermediary role, allocating resources contributed by member countries over and above their prescribed quotas.[42]

One pleasant outcome had not been anticipated, however, viz., that the bank might (though in a modest way) demonstrate the possibility of tapping Western investment capital. This possible source of capital is particularly important, because reliance upon forced savings as the impetus to industrial development has come to be an increasingly unsatisfactory proposition. Planners throughout the socialist world have pronounced the securing of a higher standard of living to be one of the main tasks of development. If this objective is not achieved by (very optimistically estimated) gains in labor productivity, either the goal will have to be discarded once again or resources will be channeled from investment. It is quite possible that regimes enjoying little popular enthusiasm would regard the latter policy as too risky. This constraint on potential investment resources argues for more ambitious attempts to attract resources from the nonsocialist world.

The capital shortage problem of the centralist world is compounded by the need to import technology-laden capital goods to reduce the severity of the East-West "technology lag," a phenomenon that would render capital imports desirable even in the absence of an investment resources problem.[43]

Though the political objectives of individual or groupings of western states in their relationships with Eastern Europe are not appropriate matter for this chapter it should be mentioned that the desire of nonsocialists to provide capital for socialist development cannot simply be assumed. If provided at all, one must ask how this should occur. Western credits to the IBEC would likely enhance Soviet domination in Eastern Europe.

Although Stalinist mistrust of the West and willingness to suffer through the onerous difficulties of autarkic development are strictly historical phenomena in the era of Brezhnev's *Westpolitik*, it is inconceivable that the centralist world savors the prospect of the inevitable growth of its economic dependence on the West. Additionally, economic interaction with the West may imply another negative consequence—inflation. The domestic economy can be sheltered from this possibility, of course, by merely retaining the traditional command trade apparatus domestically, but this, once again, militates against the adoption of currency convertibility, multilateral trade relations, and the more rapid growth of social product these imply.

It is to be expected that advocating the retention of the old apparatus would imply an emphasis of the benefits rather than the costs of such a policy. Konstantinov and Larionov insist that, in the planned economy, currency convertibility simply cannot be combined with a spontaneously functioning market mechanism. "The planned regularity of the development of the national economies, of the socialist international division of labor and of foreign trade precluded convertibility of the capitalist type, which frees money from its real (not nominal) base and opens the door to currency speculation and inflation.[44]

Such dilemmas are the stuff of which bloc planners' headaches are born. The following chapter will demonstrate some of the ways in which these (primarily) economic difficulties are compounded by intransigent political realities.

Notes

1. Egon Neuberger, "Central Planning and Its Legacies: Implications for Foreign Trade," in *International Trade and Central Planning*, Alan A. Brown and Egon Neuberger, eds. (Berkeley: University of California Press, 1968), pp. 349-383.

2. For a typical treatments of Ricardo by socialists see Günther Kohlmey, "Wahl von Produktionsstandorten und internationale Mobilität von Produktivkräften in der Wirtschaftsintegration der RGW-Länder," *Wirtschaftswissenschaft*, Vol. 20, No. 9 (September 1973), pp. 1298-1311; and M.W. Senin, *Sozialistische Integration* (Berlin: Dietz Verlag, 1972), pp. 305-311.

3. H.W. Schaefer sees the integration movement and the Complex Program as a clear reflection of "the fading hopes of reform and the growing acceptance of a step-by-step integration process." See his *Comecon and the Politics of Integration* (New York: Praeger, 1972), p. 172. The reforms, of course, can be (and are often) seen as being *complementary* to the reform endeavors. See Senin, *Sozialistische Integration*, op. cit., p. 232. Usually this occurred more in the period before the reforms had bogged down and integration issues become predominant in the literature.

4. Kormnov and Cheburakov refer specifically to the signing of treaties pertaining to eighteen scientific-technical problems, thirty-five centers of cooperation employing in excess of 500 scientific researchers, six scientific coordination councils and two multinational production units, "Interatominstrument" and "Interetalonpribor" (instruments for comparative measures). See their "Sovershenstvovanie Upravlenia otraslevoi Integratsiyei stran-chlenov SEV," *Voprosy Ekonomiki*, No. 7 (1973), pp. 103-112.

Neues Deutschland, no. 29 (November 1973), reports on a communiqué issued by the economic commissions of the GDR and the People's Republic of Poland, reporting on meetings held in Warsaw, November 26-28, 1973, to establish general conceptions for the main lines of development of economic relations between the two countries until 1980. Emphasis is to be on cooperation in chemistry and seaport industries, and a mutual project for cotton spinning ("Friendship") in Zawercie. Emphasis in plan coordination is to be on stable deliveries of raw materials and combustibles, and a division of labor in metallurgy, chemistry, light industry and construction, and electronics.

5. Karl Morgenstern, *Sozialistische Internationale Arbeitsteilung* (Berlin: Akademie Verlag, 1972), p. vii.

6. Sandor Ausch, *Theory and Practice of CMEA Cooperation* (Budapest: Akademiai Kiado, 1972), p. 217. Ausch points out that "even CMEA countries with less developed engineering industries have submitted to coordination only a small part (3, 10, or 25 percent) of their planned total investment."

7. See Franklyn D. Holzman, "La Théories du Commerce extérieur des économies centralement planifiées," *Revue de l'Est*, vol. 3, no. 3 (July 1972), p. 16.

8. One wonders if the Soviet penchant for megaplanning, probably utilizing the traditional imperative (balancing) methods and supplemented with the techniques of mathematical programming, will continue to stultify economic interaction of the eastern states. It has been suggested that the Soviet-type mentality is willing to sacrifice some (probably large) degree of efficiency for the purpose of retaining some degree of economic control (political influence) in the planned economies. See Chapter 8.

9. See Dimitur Vasilev, "The International Socialist Division of Labour and Its Role in the Increased Profitability of Bulgaria's Foreign Trade," *East European Economics*, vol. 8, no. 1 (Fall, 1969), pp. 96-98.

10. Erich Kern and Klaus Werner, "Probleme der Koordinierung der Pläne für eine längere Perspektive zwischen den RGW-Mitgliedländern," *Wirtschaftswissenschaft*, vol. 19, no. 11 (November 1971), pp. 1620-1621. Kern and Werner suggest laws of two types: (a) agreements with specific mutual purchase and delivery obligations and (b) agreements pertaining to definite national development assignments.

A similar Russian view is that, in the attempt to coordinate their economies, structural development through increased mutual planning activities in CMEA, it is necessary that the planning organs involved, not to mention the countries themselves, accept the responsibility to see that commitments are indeed honored. See Yu. Shiryayev, "Sotsialisticheskaya sobstvennost v usloviyakh ekonomicheskoi integratsii stran-chlenov SEV" *Voprosy Ekonomiki*, no. 7 (1973), pp. 94-102.

11. One of the GDR's most prolific writers on integration, Karl Morgenstern, observes that each socialist country participating in the division of labor must ask "the question, which branches of industry should be brought into existence in industrializing or in already industrialized socialist countries, which industrial branches should be retained, deliberately promoted or deemphasized and possibly even eliminated in the long run." See his "Probleme der Ermittlung und der Durchführung effektiver Varianten der sozialistischen internationalen Spezialisierung und Kooperation," *Wirtschaftswissenschaft*, vol. 21, no. 10 (October 1973), pp. 1457.

12. See Werner Gumpel, "Die Auswirkungen der Wirtschaftsreformen auf den RGW," in *Die Wirtschaftsordnungen Osteuropas in Wandel: Ergebnisse und Probleme der Wirtschaftsreformen*, Band II Hans Höhmann, Michael C. Kaser, and Karl C. Thalheim, eds. (Freiburg in Breisgau: Rombach, 1972), pp. 158-159.

13. See Holzman, "La Théories du Commerce," op. cit., p. 14.

14. While, as is generally known, intrabloc trade has grown with respectable rapidity in recent years, trade relations with Western countries likewise continue to assume increasingly more significant proportions. The Czechoslovakian case is noteworthy in this regard. The percentage share of Czechoslovakia's trade with other socialist countries declined from 73.2 percent to 70.0 percent in the years 1965-1970. In the same period, the western share of the same trade increased from 17.9 percent to 22.4 percent.

See Franz-Lothar Altmann, "Tschechoslowakei," in *Die Wirtschaft Osteuropas zu Beginn der siebziger Jahre*, Hans-Hermann Höhmann, ed. (Stuttgart: Kohlhammer, 1972), p. 140.

15. See Alec Nove, "East-West Trade," in *International Economic Relations: Proceedings of the Third Congress of the International Economic Association*, by Paul Samuelson, ed. (New York: St. Martin's, 1969), p. 108.

16. Willi Kunz, "Zur ökonomischen Integration der Länder des RGW," *Einheit*, no. 8 (July 1970), p. 1047. His quote is a citation from V.I. Lenin, "Ursprünglicher Entwurf der Thesen zur nationalen und zur kolonialen Frage," *Werke*, vol. 31, Dietz Verlag, Berlin (1959), p. 135.

17. Economists have long compared corporations and their management problems with the problems of directing a centrally planned economy. For a good treatment of these difficulties at the corporate level, see Alfred D. Chandler, Jr., *Strategy and Structure* (Cambridge, Mass.: MIT Press, 1962).

18. In a classic article on the excessive bureaucratization of the Soviet Union before the reform era, Smolinski referred to the projections of Soviet cyberneticians that, by 1980, the entire Soviet population would be required for the planning process, even if computerized, if its growth continued as it had in the previous period. See Leon Smolinski, "What Next in Soviet Planning," *Foreign Affairs*, vol. 42, no. 4 (July 1964), pp. 602-613. Czechoslovakian economists especially emphasized the necessity of utilizing market processes in the economic reforms. They rejected the possibility that computers would enable planners to make, for example, the necessary calculations for price planning. Their scepticism was based on the fact that the mathematical theory of optimum processes has not yet been perfected, and that the statistical data required to calculate prices is imperfect and too slowly gathered. Such information does not reach the center soon enough to generate calculated prices appropriate to the momentary state of the economy. See O. Kýn, B. Sekerka, and L. Hejl, "A Model for the Planning of Prices," in *Socialism, Capitalism, and Economic Growth*, Essays presented to Maurice Dobb, C.H. Feinstein, ed. (London: Cambridge University Press, 1967), p. 102.

19. For more extensive discussion, see Werner Gumpel, "Die Auswirkungen der Wirtschaftsreformen auf den RGW," in *Die Wirtschaftsordnungen Osteuropas im Wandel: Ergebnis und Probleme der Wirtschaftsreformen* vol. II, "Analysis wirtschaftlicher Teilordnungen: Funktionswandel der Systemelemente, Hans-Hermann Höhmann, Michael C. Kaser and Karl C. Thalheim, eds. (Freiburg in Breisgau: Rombach, 1972).

20. This goal is largely associated with the now deceased Vajda. See Imre Vajda and Mihaly Simaik, *Foreign Trade in a Planned Economy* (London: Cambridge University Press, 1971), p. 87. Simply and directly, he long held that "in order to bring about multilateral trade and payments

and a transferable currency, controlled and planned socialist market economies and a corresponding foreign-trade system must be brought into being in the CMEA countries."

21. Ibid., p. 90.

22. Tibor Kiss, *International Division of Labour in Open Economies With Special Regard to the CMEA* (Budapest 1971), pp. 10-11.

23. Georges Sokoloff points out that this disassociation of the triumvirate's elements "équivaut à l'ajournement du projet." See his "Structures internes et coopération internationale des économies socialistes de l'Est européen," *Économies et Sociétés*, vol. 5, no. 1 (January, 1971), p. 258.

24. For samples of the views of two of the best known GDR economists espousing this view, see Karl Morgenstern, "Probleme der Ermittlung," op. cit.; and the senior author: Gunther Kohlmey and Gerhard Kraft, "Volkswirtschaftliche Akkumulationskraft and sozialistische Integration," *Wirtschaftswissenschaft*, vol. 19, no. 8 (August 1971), pp. 1193-1206.

25. Yu. Shiryaev, "Razvitie nauchnykh osnov sovmestnoi planovoi deyatelnosti stran SEV," *Planovoe Khozyaistvo*, no. 4 (April 1973), pp. 65-66.

26. As a typical example one might cite Karl Morgenstern, "Erfordernisse und Wege zur Weiterentwicklung der sozialistischen internationalen Spezialisierung und Kooperation," *Wirtschaftswissenschaft*, no. 5, (May 1970), p. 1449. He expresses regret about the attempt merely through a large number of individual measures, "usually unrelated *(losgelöst)* to each other," to solve the problems of integration. The attempt "to promote specialization and cooperation without having defined and coordinated the fundamental directions of relationships in the division of labor among the CMEA countries, and without ordering individual planning measures, where these bring about reaction *(Rückwirkungen)* in later attempts to profile fundamental directions, must in many cases necessarily cause additional difficulties later, or even doom some projects to failure."

27. The work by Sorokin and Alampiyev is typical. "In our view," they instruct, "greater success will require increased centralization of planning activity" if the lag in several branches of industry behind their counterparts in capitalist countries is to be overcome. See their *Problemy ekonomicheskoi integratsii stran-chlenov SEV* (Moscow: Ekonomika, 1970), pp. 62-63.

28. See J.M. van Brabant, *Bilateralism and Structural Bilateralism in Intra-CMEA Trade* (Rotterdam: Rotterdam University Press, 1973).

29. See ibid., p. 41.

30. For a recent book on the basics of CMEA international banking institutions, see Diethard Stelzl, *Die Internationalen Banken des Rates für*

gegenseitige Wirtschaftshilife (Munchen: Olzog Verlag, 1973).

31. If bilateralism makes little sense economically, it remains true that there are also political and administrative arguments that should not be ignored. Wiles, *Communist International Economics* (New York: Praeger, 1969), p. 324, reminds us that "bilateral arrangements between small STE's (Soviet Type Economies) have the supreme advantage that they involve no imperialism. Sovereignty is sacrificed, as in all international treaties, but voluntarily and to a body in which each country has equal weight. Moreover, administratively all bilateralism is very much easier."

32. M.W. Senin, *Sozialistische Integration* (Berlin: Dietz Verlag, 1972), p. 209.

33. These problems will be treated more thoroughly and analytically in Chapter 11.

34. Research has shown, however, that, in fact, the trends observed in CMEA import prices are identical to those prevailing in world markets, while the export prices of the centrally planned economies have not been noticeably related to world-market prices. See Paul Marer, *Postwar Pricing and Price Patterns in Socialist Foreign Trade: 1946-1971* (Bloomington: Indiana University Press, 1972). Searching investigations by the Hungarians are also of interest here. Sandor Ausch, *Theory and Practice*, op. cit., p. 94, reveals that a large volume of socialist trade is merely transacted at national prices of yesterday, in which actual costs of current national inputs are not correctly reflected. Research directed by Ausch has revealed "after a study of the domestic prices and rates of price equalization subsidies applied to the products of some enterprises that the prevailing 'socialist world-market prices' almost exactly (at most with differences of 5 to 10 percent due to bargaining) correspond to the inland prices, whereas they considerably differed from the prices of the capitalist world market."

35. See ibid., p. 109. Ausch indicates that even in the cases where agreements are made to divide up capitalist markets among the CMEA countries, these agreements are often not respected. Moreover, "in other cases, CMEA agreements dividing up the sources of imports cover the *whole* export surplus of the countries in question, and therefore prices are bound to be pushed up even if the agreement is observed."

36. See Kiss, *International Division of Labour*, op. cit., p. 103. Kiss adds that "differences in their internal economic mechanisms also prevent them from entering into export cartels to strengthen their competitive position."

37. See Paul Marer, *Postwar Pricing*, op. cit., and Edward A. Hewett, *Foreign Trade Prices in the Council for Mutual Economic Assistance* (London: Cambridge University Press, 1974).

38. See Zygmunt Knyziak, "Economic Criteria of the International Specialization of Production in Socialist Countries," in *Economic Development for Eastern Europe*, Michael Kaser, ed. (New York: St. Martin's, 1968), p. 127.

39. See Kiss, *International Division of Labour*, op. cit., p. 79.

40. See, for example, Morgenstern, *Sozialistische Internationale Arbeitsteilung*, (East Berlin: Akademie Verlag, 1972), pp. 53-54.

41. See van Brabant, *Essays on Planning Trade and Integration in Eastern Europe* (Rotterdam: Rotterdam University Press, 1974), p. 95. He makes the believable statement that "if no additional funds are put at the bank's disposal, the investment activity of the following decade will be influenced negligibly by the bank's investment policy, for its resources will be essentially tied up in a few selected projects."

42. See Stelzl, *Die Internationalen Banken*, op. cit., p. 87. After 1964, the U.S.S.R., East Germany, and Poland all expressed official regret over the disappointing effect of the International Bank, so that, in 1970, the International Investment Bank was founded.

43. Happily, much of the work done on the problem of importing technology can be found in a single volume. See especially part II of S. Wasowski, ed., *East-West Trade and the Technology Gap* (New York: Praeger, 1970).

44. See their "Valyutno-finansovye otnoshenie i sotsialisticheskaya integratsiya, *Kommunist*, No. 7 (1973), p. 101.

10

Socialist Integration II: Political Constraints

Economic aspects of the Eastern European integration drive were treated first (in the previous chapter) because that particular brand of integration is primarily economic in nature. The position seems defensible that an immediate, satisfactory resolution of all the *political* difficulties confronting CMEA would not begin to guarantee the success of economic integration, so long as the fundamental economic problems remain unresolved.

Nevertheless, these two kinds of integration roadblocks will remain or be resolved together. The economic issues cannot be dealt with unless some solutions can also be found for fundamental political problems: (a) agreeing to what extent the interests of "sovereign," individual countries should take priority over the interests of the community of states; (b) determining how community politics can best account for variability in national size (degree of trade dependence), opportunities for geographic integration, and the level of economic development; and (c) permitting the increased exposure of community members to Western influences, while still maintaining desired CMEA cohesion.

Largely, though not exclusively, these problems arise from the fact that the CMEA integration project is dominated by a superpower whose interests often differ from those of the smaller associated states. That this is the case will become apparent as the three basic problems listed above are treated in greater detail below.

Sovereignty: The State vs. the Community

It might be of some use to observe that sovereignty has both political and economic components, both of which assume importance in the process of economic integration. Several of the economic issues already treated have apparent (and therefore not explicitly discussed) sovereignty implications.

The degree of interdependence in international trade (the degree, in other words, to which autarky is repudiated) has an obvious bearing on a nation's freedom of policy action. The fact that East Germany, for example, is required by formal trade contracts to direct about one-half of its

---

See the title footnote to Chapter 9.

machine tool exports to the Soviet Union cannot help but influence the degree of independence enjoyed by East German planners.[a]

As in the case of integration, most sovereignty issues have both political and economic components (the relative weights of which would be impossible to specify).[1] Of primary importance for an integrating nation's political sovereignty is the fact that the implementation of integration schemes requires limitations on the jealously guarded prerogatives of national economic planners. By its very nature, integration requires at least some minimal, probably very considerable, community control over the resource allocation processes of member countries. When member countries balk at relinquishing this control, the process of integration is threatened. The question is, therefore, whether group economic interests should be considered of greater importance than those of individual CMEA members.

The question reminds us that politics is of paramount importance in the external relations of any sovereign country. This is no less true for socialist countries. It might even be said that CMEA, because its members, up to this point, have not been prepared to sacrifice national planning prerogatives, remains a more political than economic organization.

If it could be done at all, only the Soviet Union could exercise the political influence to coerce individual socialist states to cooperate in integration. In reality, the Soviet Union's power is finite—there are political limits beyond which the Soviets cannot (and probably do not wish to) go.

Wiles holds that "one of the worst misunderstandings is to present the CMEA as simply an extension of Soviet power. It is, on the contrary, by its very nature a brake upon the more extreme manifestations of that power."[2]

Nevertheless, Soviet influence is sufficient to generate the constant feeling that disclaimers must be made about Soviet power. Frequently, it is even denied that CMEA integration implies limitations on the sovereignty of individual socialist countries. A sophisticated version of this position holds that the integrative process, though it may affect the form and content of sovereignty, does not imply that it must be reduced.[3] Each national government plans its own economic development, though in the matter of determining what investments will achieve structural developments corresponding to community specialization preferences, sovereignty takes a new form "through the acceptance of common resolutions with other governments or their representatives."[4]

When resources are allocated to integration, a nation loses power over

---

[a] Or take the somewhat analogous case of the relationship of Opel in Rüsselsheim to General Motors in Detroit. Surely, many of the decisions taken in Rüsselsheim correspond to policy preferences one would find in Detroit, though they may be taken strictly on the basis of economic consideration pertinent to Rüsselsheim operations. This does not, of course, deny the possibility of Detroit also giving direct suggestions from time to time.

the sole determination of what happens to them, since the other seven countries participate in the decisions. But now, however, such a country can participate in decisions pertaining to the resources supplied by the other seven countries. "Consequently, the extent of its rights have not been constrained at all; they remain as before. Only the form of the realization of these rights has changed."[5]

As is commonly known, Rumania has consistently been willing to utilize whatever influence she could bring to bear in preventing encroachments by CMEA on the rights of individual members.

It may or may not be an exaggeration that Rumanian demands for "respect for sovereignty and national interest" were the greatest obstacle to Soviet pursuit of the single plan concept of economic unification (especially under Khrushchev) in the 1960s.[6] In any case, it is doubtful whether Rumania really stood alone on that issue. The Soviets were probably aware that other CMEA members found it unnecessary to argue the sovereignty case openly, only because a vociferous spokesman was already getting the job done.

Ceausescu, of Rumania, finally came around to accepting the Complex Program for integration in the centralist world, only because it contained nothing new in the way of integrative technique that would threaten national independence,[7] and because integration was defined (or rather left undefined) so as not to "affect national independence and sovereignty, nor lead to common planning and superstate forms of organization."[8] An acceptable formal definition is not to be found anywhere in the Complex Program. For our purposes, a general one such as van Brabant's is worthwhile. He defines integration as "a process aimed at the conscious elimination of barriers to trade and economic cooperation between economic units belonging to at least two different national states. . . . As a result [of integration], relative scarcities between any pair of goods and services are expected to converge to identical values."[9]

The strong position taken by the Complex Program against intervention "in the interior affairs of member states" is extremely impressive.

Socialist economic integration, it is proclaimed, "occurs on a completely voluntary basis and is not connected with the creation of supranational organs. It does not affect the question of internal planning, or the financial and economic accounting activities of national organizations." Moreover, the activity of the international economic associations (organizations) may in no case "constrict the interests of individual member countries of CMEA or those of the member countries of CMEA as a group." [10]

The unanimity requirement of CMEA, its foremost institutional sovereignty safeguard, demands that substantive decisions and recommendations adopted remain unopposed by all the brother states. However, as has become evident, establishing institutional limitations to assure that only unanimously desired economic processes be undertaken is tantamount to guaranteeing that substantial integration will not occur.

What can be the practical meaning, then, of the tremendous increase in organizational and literary output pertaining to economic integration in Eastern Europe in recent years?[b] The skeptical viewpoint might be that it is really little more than a smoke screen to camouflage dissatisfaction with the outcomes of the reform period.

To assume a more sympathetic stance regarding the possibility of a fortuitous union of national independence and international integration is no easy task. The contradiction in terms here ("integration" *and* "independence") should be apparent, but the pursuit of its policy implementation in postwar Eastern (and Western?) Europe is a matter of history. It might be worthwhile to attempt to coin a new term for the phenomenon. Might we consider *inter-independence (unabhängige Verflechtung)*? Some evidence that such a union is genuinely being pursued is available, however, even if it is scanty. First, a recent single exception to the unanimity principle is possibly significant, at least symbolically. For substantive questions facing the International Investment Bank (confirmation of annual accounting, disposition of earned revenues, appointment of management, etc.), unanimous action is still required, but all other actions require only a three-fourths majority.[11] Second, CMEA's "principle of interestedness" implies that certain mutual integration projects can be undertaken by a limited number of "interested" members. Others need not participate in such projects, but they cannot veto them in CMEA councils. Unfortunately, it is doubtful that these rather minor organizational innovations can be considered substantive new integration possibilities.

Regional and Developmental Integration Considerations

Accounting for Variability in National Size

It has been observed that economic integration must "create, ultimately, between the various areas belonging to an *economic region*, the same type of relations that exist within the national economies."[12] A great diversity of economic problems faces the member states of CMEA: the Soviet Union has vast natural resources, a large market, and depends little on foreign trade; Poland, East Germany, Hungary, and Czechoslovakia are de-

---

[b] The literature produced by the Soviet publishing apparatus pertaining to the desirability of socialist economic cooperation reaches well back into the 1950s, so the vast *increase* in published output on integration (rather than its initial appearance) is of interest here.

veloped industrial states with high trade dependence; Bulgaria and Rumania are developing countries. Even casual observation makes it apparent that CMEA is a political union attempting to achieve economic integration. Machowski has observed that it would make more sense from an economic standpoint, for example, to encourage East Germany, Poland, Hungary, and Czechoslovakia to form an economic unit—a Central European Economic Union (*Mitteleuropäische Wirtschaftsregion*).[13] This is evident, Machowski holds, on the basis of these countries' similar economic structures, resource endowments, labor-market conditions, national economic history, geographic proximity, and so on. Naturally, this suggested grouping is also not strictly a geographic or an economic one, but at least, in part, it is once again a political one. For example, sovereignty considerations make it unfeasible to exclude southern Italy from the EEC. Clearly, the same national-regional developmental phenomena (e.g., in Czechoslovakia) appear in CMEA. They would merely be minimized in the political groupings suggested by Machowski. Virtually nobody expects that such a notion could receive de jure currency in the contemporary Soviet world, but the principles of the Complex Program open the way for at least a partial de facto realization of the concept. [14]

For Eastern Europe, the question of the formation of an *economic* region is, in large measure, a question about the manner in which national size is to be accounted for by policymakers. The Complex Program is fortuitous in that it makes possible increasingly intimate economic relationships among the small, trade-dependent states of CMEA on the basis of multilateral plan coordination and joint production projects.[c]

As an example of independent activity within CMEA, East German and Polish projects are of particular interest. On the basis of the Complex Plan's advocacy of "common planning of individual branches of industry and production types," the two countries are jointly (capital costs being equally shared) developing a huge textile operation. Additionally, an experiment in free tourism has been undertaken. The latter had to be modified, since planners failed to foresee and prepare for the flood of people anxious to take advantage of the absence of all customs, currency, and other restrictions. When a Polish buying spree threatened to severely aggravate the shortage conditions of East German consumer goods supplies, the modifications adopted restored the tourist situation to something more like what planners had originally expected.[15]

Extending from the kinds of relationships developing between East Germany and Poland, the four central European countries mentioned could (on the basis of the principle of "interestedness") extend the degree of economic interaction, working in a de facto fashion towards the develop-

---

[c] Coordination of plans is described by the Complex Program as the "main method of organizing cooperation and intensifying the international division of labor."

ment of institutions that might one day permit the evolution of an integrated region of planned-market economies, obviously with the achievement of currency convertibility and trade multilateralism.

This would not be without benefits for the Soviet Union. In early phases, such a union would present the possibility of spreading East Germany's relative affluence over a substantial share of the northwestern CMEA region. Later on, as the union became substantially stronger, rising levels of national welfare there could be tapped for the entire CMEA area in two ways. First, capital assistance (already expected to some degree from East Germany and Czechoslovakia) could become a meaningful possibility for the developing members of CMEA. Second, the Soviet Union might begin to hope for better cost-sharing outcomes in the Warsaw Pact.[16] Finally, the U.S.S.R. desires to operate on a bilateral basis in her trade with the EEC. Rumania has sought special status as a developing country in dealing with the EEC. Why should the smaller central-European socialist states not be permitted to face the difficult task of dealing with the EEC (which is expressing unwillingness to see Western European members dealing individually with nonmember countries) as a bargaining group?

Unfortunately, probabilities are strongly against intensified integration along central-European lines and, consequently, perhaps, against integration in eastern Europe in any form. It is likely that the political costs to the Soviet Union of such a development would prevent its occurrence. In the first place, the Soviet Union has little desire to see East Europeans enjoying a level of affluence that is denied the Soviet people. This source of aggravation is probably already extant owing especially to the economic success of East Germany. More important, however, would be the accretion of countervailing political power to the Soviet Union's reluctant allies.

Accounting for Varying Developmental Levels

Similar in nature to the problems of regional integration facing CMEA are the considerable difficulties arising from differences in the level of development of member countries. The Complex Program refers to the necessity of a step-by-step equalization of levels of economic development though nothing substantial is said about how this is to be achieved (other than through "maximal mobilization and effective use of countries' own efforts and resources as well as by utilization of the advantages of the international socialist division of labour").[17]

Socialist economic literature insists that the perpetuation of deep-rooted differences between CMEA members would inhibit long-run optimization of growth for the socialist world as a whole, not to mention that of individual members.[18]

Since the level of development is usually defined in terms of per capita incomes and since the best socialist performance is usually achieved where population growth rates are lowest, the equalization goal will clearly not be achieved through the means provided by the Complex Program. Moreover, it is *not* a foregone conclusion that community welfare can be maximized in the short or intermediate run by policies consciously designed to force posthaste equalization of development levels.

Ostensibly, conscious planning techniques (including intra-CMEA capital assistance and educational, manpower, and management training programs) could beneficially reduce development level disparities in the long run. A standard growth model would cast doubt upon the welfare implications of policies designed, however, to assure extensive short- and intermediate-run capital flows (e.g., from East Germany and Czechoslovakia to Rumania and Bulgaria). In East Europe, capital poverty conditions suggest a priori that potential capital earnings may be larger in the more developed socialist states. Additionally, the "residual effect" of the growth equation—the technological and organizational possibilities—may likewise be substantially higher in the more developed countries. For a maximization of community welfare in less than the long run, one would do well to supply capital to those countries equipped to use it best and to develop mechanisms to distribute the greater earnings throughout the socialist world. The distribution problem for this approach, however, may also be of little consequence, so long as the socialist system remains largely what Leontief has described as an "input-input system."

It may be that the bearers of political and economic power acted wisely (as opposed to having fortuitously failed to act) in neglecting to develop means to pursue the goal of development leveling. In any case, this largely ideological aspect of socialist literature has recently seemed more a formality than a pressing issue.

However, putting the question of leveling aside, how will the integration effort account for discrepancies in the development of CMEA members? The more advanced socialist countries (East Germany and Czechoslovakia) are interested in developing specializations based on "efficiency" while the less developed countries show more interest in diversification, industrialization, and exploitation of all their resources, whether or not this may be efficient.[19] The ideology of the Soviet strategy of industrialization is most convincing to socialists, especially those who still have the process before them.

For the more developed socialist states, an attempt to achieve integration with partners undergoing a retarded industrialization program may entail some high costs. As was earlier observed, relying on supplies from abroad (*Fremdversorgung*) may mean incurring more expense and/or inconvenience than simply producing a (possibly higher quality) product at home. But even more seriously, when the East Germans, for example, forego the opportunity to integrate their economy technologically upwards into the more advanced and demanding world market, the corresponding technological *niveau* cannot be achieved. On the other hand, of course, the East Germans are fully prepared to cooperate in CMEA for political reasons. East Germany perceived in an intensified integration milieu an opportunity, through (technologically downward) CMEA integration, to increase East German political weight and consolidate the political basis of its international recognition.[20] Moreover, it is convenient to have guaranteed markets for products that would not sell so readily in the West.

Another development problem is created by the scarcity of foreign currency in the less developed CMEA states, who must hope to export raw materials for good returns, so that the foreign currency essential for capital imports will be available. They are attempting, to the dismay of their more developed brother states, to direct a larger share of their exports of raw materials to Western markets. Facing a constricted supply, the more developed CMEA countries are coerced to use scarce foreign exchange in Western markets for the necessary basic materials. For these countries, integration also comes to mean purchasing "increasing quantities of finished goods (mainly machines), regardless of quality or price, and often regardless of the real needs of their own national economy."[21]

But what about the needs of the less developed socialist countries? Interestingly, Bogomolow has suggested that, of the two integration alternatives facing these countries (to forego the benefits of specialization until a higher level of development has been achieved or to begin immediately to specialize in the integrative framework), immediate participation is best *if* (a) a mechanism exists for making good specialization choices and (b) technical assistance, credits, and other assistance are available for the developing countries.[22] Bogomolow would doubtlessly have a different view from that of most nonsocialist analysts about the availability of such assistance in contemporary CMEA. Rumania's resistance to integration, however, may well be an indication that, lacking these prerequisites, the nonintegrative development alternative would really be preferred.

Western Contacts and East European Cohesion

It has become fashionable, in recent times, for Soviet writers to begin works bearing on international problems with the observation that the economic relationships being developed among the socialist countries "by no means imply a repudiation of economic connections with nations of other types."[23] The statement is not surprising, of course, in the light of the manifest desire of the socialist countries to develop economic, scientific, and technological ties with the developed capitalist states.

But it is also true, as has already been observed, that in direct conflict with such statements, the Soviets are not above heralding the need to pursue integration "in the struggle against imperialism and its policy of undermining the positions of world socialism."[24]

The contradiction can easily be explained as representative ideological matter, not necessarily related to contemporary policy intent. It is mentioned here because it reflects, in addition to an ideological question, a genuine policy dilemma for CMEA as an institution. To what extent should the socialist states pursue economic excellence through methods of regional autarky? To what degree is interaction of the CMEA states as a collective with the Western economies prudent policy? For the East European community, the question of autarky vs. interaction is similar to the question of economic contacts with the West treated above from the perspective of the single socialist state.

Clearly, this is the headache of the Soviet Union. Though loyal socialists in all countries probably also feel concerned with the problem, the elicited response will, in large measure, reflect the fact that in a crisis CMEA, to some degree, can serve as an institutional arm of Soviet foreign policy. The Russians must find a way of receiving required technological transfusions from the West into the bloc without souring blood relationships tediously nurtured in postwar Eastern Europe. How an influx of Western capital and commodities can be obtained without increasing the velocity and magnitude of centripetal forces in the CMEA region probably remains a matter of speculation in Moscow.

Conclusions

In spite of the establishment of some common interests and affinities under Soviet leadership in postwar Eastern Europe, CMEA remains a long way from the achievement of the integration called for in the Complex Program. Strong centrifugal forces militate against progress towards any form of economic union.

Even though individual CMEA states see the need to increase the effectiveness of external ties, there almost seems to be more avid interest in doing so with Western countries. Important uncertainties are still attached to the proposition of further specialization within the bloc, including problems of supply consistency, product quality, and technological adequacy of imports.

Of the constraints facing the community as a whole, fundamental economic problems are of supreme importance. Even if no headway were made on some of the thorny political problems facing the CMEA region, integration could be noticeably enhanced by a more satisfactory attack on the problem of overcentralization in socialist national planning mechanisms. The intractability of planning bureaucracies generates higher costs of information, coordination, and administration in the integration process, simply guaranteeing that less integration can occur.

The process of physical planning through plan directives and the resultant "commodity inconvertibility" results in inefficiency domestically. It is possibly even more costly in international economic relationships, since it stultifies the development of value, monetary, and financial improvements that are even more essential for international planning and integration. Central planning requires the continued utilization of separate domestic and foreign pricing systems, not to mention the dichotomy between socialist and world-market prices. The unavailability of comparable allocative prices means that it remains impossible to establish cost comparisons indicative of potential production specializations for participants in integration. Additionally, the use of artifically adopted prices not reflecting conditions of East European economic scarcity (i.e., underpriced scarce raw materials are exchanged for overpriced, relatively abundant heavy-industry goods) has given rise to the interesting terms of trade "exploitation" of the Soviet Union by the East Europeans. Additionally, scarcity of capital, technological inadequacy, and problems of raw materials, all cause behavior militating against progress in integration. Removing these economic obstacles is a necessary condition for greater progress in CMEA integration. Complete success, however, would require solving the problems of political constraints on CMEA integration.

When we turn to politics, the sense of urgency is somewhat less. Still, the resolution of political problems, particularly that of sovereignty, is, likewise, a necessary condition for complete success in integration.

The East European states are endowed with enough political sovereignty to veto the idea of implementing a single economic plan for the entire CMEA region and to block substantive proposals for integration. They enjoy too little sovereignty, however, to integrate in CMEA subgroupings more profitable to the smaller member states. For the time being, it appears that socialist countries will be able to continue national pursuits of often conflicting individual interests, viz., those of a superpower, those of smaller (more highly trade-dependent) states, and those of developing countries. The disparateness of these interests will very often prove detrimental to the attempt to integrate.

When one reviews the number and intensity of problems and forces hindering economic union, it is difficult to avoid the conclusion that integration will simply not be achieved in the foreseeable future. This does not mean that CMEA will disappear and the economic order in East Europe will dissolve. It does mean that we have not seen the end of attempts of the magnitude of the reforms of the 1960s and the Complex Program of the present to find some innovation that will render economic difficulties more manageable.

Surveying obstacles to integration also lends increased weight to an interesting proposition. The socialists emphasize economic integration as a policy *goal*, saying very little about the largely hypothetical stage of the single plan and political unification. This is in contrast to the EEC's adoption of economic integration as a *vehicle* to reach the goal of political unification. Even if one assumes that the goal of the EEC will never be obtained (or is not even being seriously pursued), this comparison is not merely a matter of semantics. The significant point is that the EEC's economic integration incorporates forces of automaticity. As time passes, West European markets are automatically becoming more integrated, and the possibility of the withdrawal of individual members, for example, continually becomes more costly and less conceivable. The element of automaticity is completely lacking in CMEA. Each step toward integration can be achieved only after tedious negotiations, countless bilateral agreements, and inordinately involved planning arrangements. The proposition is, then, that the integration process is proceeding very slowly, because the East Europeans simply do not want integration very badly.

Abandoning a longer range perspective now, there remains an important logical conclusion bearing on inter-CMEA relations over the next few years. Because of the imposition of the Stalinist (heavy-industrial) development pattern on the satellites and because of international trade pricing techniques adopted by CMEA countries, the Soviet Union finds its economic ties with Eastern Europe increasingly costly and less rewarding. As the Soviet Union makes this discovery and turns to the West in search of ways to alleviate domestic economic difficulties, the bloc countries are following suit. It is most likely that developing relations with the West will enhance centrifugal political, economic, and cultural forces in Eastern Europe. What means are at the disposal of the Soviets to preserve cohesion and loyalty in the CMEA region? Economic assistance seems unlikely, since the Soviets are coming to perceive that too much of that has already been given. One hopes that some pleasant alternative will be found, or that the Soviets will be able to accept a position of less influence in East Europe.[25] It is, unfortunately, very likely, however, that a more recalcitrant Soviet Union may have to be dealt with. Because of the logic of the current economic situation in CMEA and the Soviet Union, it may be necessary to face the future of interbloc relations with some concern.

Notes

1. The issue of legal ownership of the individual national states in the overwhelming amount of the means of production could have been mentioned as yet a third component. The issue is of particular interest as joint production endeavors are entered into by CMEA members. See Yu.

Shiryaev, "Sotsialisticheskaya Sobstvennost. . . ." For the sake of simplicity the authors are inclined to treat the ownership questions as the legal reflection of the economic and political components. We are fully aware of the fact that this is not entirely so.

2. See P.J.D. Wiles, *Communist International Economics* (New York: Praeger, 1969), p. 315.

3. A.P. Butenko, *Sozialistische Integration: Wesen und Perspektiven,* (Berlin: Staatsverlag der DDR, 1972), pp. 58-59.

4. Ibid.

5. Ibid.

6. For at least part of the interesting history, see Hertha W. Heiss, "The Council for Mutual Economic Assistance—Developments since the Mid-1960's", in *Economic Developments in Countries of Eastern Europe* (Washington: Joint Economic Committee, 1970), pp. 528-542.

7. H.W. Schaefer, *Comecon and the Politics of Integration* (New York: Praeger, 1972), p. 172, indicates that the program did not expand on the nature or methodology of joint planning. It also failed to "decide on the regulation of direct ties or on the regulation and authority of joint organizations."

8. Ceausescu's quotation is cited in ibid., p. 113.

9. See J.M. van Brabant, *Essays on Planning, Trade and Integration in Eastern Europe* (Rotterdam: Rotterdam University Press, 1974), p. 39.

10. See *Mnogostoronnee ekonomicheskoye sotrudnichestvo sotsialisticheskikh gosudarstv: sbornik dokumentov,* P.A. Tokarevoi, ed., second ed. (Moscow: Yuridicheskaya literatura, 1972), p. 31. Kompleksnaya programma dalneishego ugubleniya i sovershenstvovaniya sotrudnichestva i razvitiya sotsialisticheskoi ekonomicheskoi integratsii stran-chlenov SEV."

11. See Heinrich Machowski, "Organisatorische Probleme der wirtschaftlichen Zusammenarbeit im Rat für gegenseitige Wirtschaftshilfe," *Vierteljahreshefte zur Wirtschaftsforschung,* no. 4 (1970), pp. 286-287.

12. Sandor Ausch, *Theory and Practice of CMEA Cooperation* (Budapest: Akademiai Kiado, 1972), p. 30.

13. Heinrich Machowski, "Die Funktion der DDR im RGW", in *Die DDR vor den Aufgaben der Integration und der Koexistenz* (Tutzing: Akademie für Politische Bildung, 1975), pp. 3-19.

14. Machowski himself holds that this would begin in the form of "Ad-hoc Arbeitsgruppen" (ad hoc groupings in CMEA). See the article coauthored with Fritz Franzmeyer, "Willensbildung und Entscheidungsprozesse in der Europäischen Gemeinschaft und im Rat für

Gegenseitige Wirtschaftshilfe," *Europa Archiv*, vol. 28, no. 2 (1973), p. 60.

15. See Machowski, *Die Funktion,* pp. 16-18.

16. A glance at statistics serially published in *The Military Balance* (The Institute for Strategic Studies, London) shows that the official financial situation in the Warsaw Pact closely approximates that in NATO. The superpower of each alliance devotes around a tenth of national output to defense endeavors—often over two (sometimes even over three) times as great a percentage as that which the smaller allies spend for defense purposes. For a survey of Soviet defense outlay estimates, see Herbert Block, "Value and Burden of Soviet Defense," in *Soviet Economic Prospects for the Seventies*, A Compendium of Papers submitted to the Joint Economic Committee, (Washington D.C.: U.S. Government Printing Office, 1973), pp. 175-204.

17. P.A. Tokarevoi (ed.), *Mnogostoronnee ekonomicheskoe sotrudnichestvo*, op. cit., p. 30, 34.

18. J. Novozamski, "The Development of the International Division of Labor Between Countries at Different Economic Levels," in *Economic Developments in Countries in Eastern Europe*, op. cit., p. 147.

19. The relative scarcity of raw materials existing in the bloc is, to some extent, a result of this preference. See M.C. Kaser, *Comecon*, second ed. (London: Oxford University Press, 1967), chap. 10.

20. See Werner Bröll, "Die wirtschaftliche Rolle der DDR im RGW: Das Spannungsverhältnis von System, Strukur und Integration," in *Probleme des Industrialismus in Ost und West*, Werner Gumpel and Dietmar Keese, eds. (München: Gunter Olzog Verlag, 1973), p. 332.

21. Ausch, *Theory and Practice*, p. 195.

22. See O.T. Bogomolow, *Theorie und Methodologie der internationalen sozialistischen Arbeitsteilung*, (Berlin: Verlag die Wirtschaft, 1969), pp. 83-84.

23. See G.L. Shagalov, *Problemy optimalnogo planirovaniya vneshneekonomicheskich svyazei* (Moscow: Nauka, 1973), p. 5.

24. See Schaeffer, *Comecon and the Politics*, op. cit., p. 188. The quote comes from Pravda, July 30, 1971.

25. Since this chapter was in preparation, CMEA has taken some steps moderating these conflicts of interest. At a January 1975 meeting of the Executive Committee in Moscow, the Council ruled that trade prices henceforth will be adjusted annually on the basis of world-market prices averaged over the preceding five-year period. Annual adjustment will permit CMEA raw materials and fuel prices to lag those prevailing in world markets to a substantially smaller degree, but the five-year average clause will modify the immediate impact significantly. See Jochen Bethkenhagen

and Heinrich Machowski, "Auswirkungen der neuen Aussenhan-
delspreise in RGW," Duetsches Institute fur Wirtschaftsforschung,
Wochenbericht, vol. 42, no. 17 (April 24, 1975), pp. 136-138. To the extent,
of course, that this removes weight from the economic burden of the Soviet
Union's bloc leadership, it increases the incentive of the other states to
reduce their increased load by seeking increased Western contacts. If such
contacts do not lead to liberalization tendencies perceived by the Soviets to
be in opposition to their interests (and are consequently tolerated), the dire
tone of these concluding remarks will prove, fortunately, to have been
excessively pessimistic.

11

Socialist World Market Prices: Optimality Considerations for Nonmarket Interaction

The Nature and Difficulties of International Socialist Pricing

According to some widely appreciated Russian humor, it would be necessary, in the event of a world wide victory of Marxist-Leninist socialism, to retain at least one capitalist country. This would serve to provide a set of market prices as a basis for future foreign trade among communist countries.

It is generally known that Eastern Europe claims to base its foreign-trade negotiations on prices prevailing in the world market, though they are allegedly "cleansed" of monopoly and cyclical effects and averaged over a five-year period. Exactly how they are formed and the effects of this price formation are less well known. Even East European authors recently tend to disclaim that actual price policies are as might be expected from the socialist price formation rules adopted in 1958.[1] Moreover, though one can imagine the socialists dislike relying on capitalist prices, knowledge is not widespread about their discussions on improving pricing practices and finding the means to escape from this embarrassing dependence.

The intent of this chapter is (a) to describe the process and effects of price formation techniques in socialist international trade and (b) to offer some analytical suggestions for improving these techniques. After pricing practices are briefly treated, a discussion of the conflicting socialist proposals to solve the pricing dilemma will follow. The economic effects of prevailing pricing traditions will then be reviewed (together with the problems of level and structure they imply), after which the question of an independent price basis (IPB) for CMEA countries will be addressed. These brief sections will serve as the necessary background for the final section, which will treat questions bearing on reformation of the socialist pricing system.

In spite of the reform era of the 1960s, foreign trade is still almost the exclusive business of the state. Trade is conducted by the foreign-trade monopoly (FTM), usually on the basis of bilateral barter arrangements established in multiyear trade contracts and, in particular, in the more

The material in this chapter was originally published with Jozef M. van Brabant as coauthor. See "Non-Market Pricing in the Socialist World Market," *Kyklos,* vol, 28, no. 2, pp. 77-95.

operative annual trade plans which are an integral part of the overall annual economic plans. Since prices play a minor role in constructing economic plans, it is apparent that trade flows are *not* in response to prices, which is in contrast to practice in Western economies where prices serve as the main catalyst of allocatory decision making. Trade contracts, by and large, reflect import and export requirements stemming from disequilibria in the material balances of each economy.

In the traditional socialist economy, foreign-trade enterprises produce the commodities contracted for export and sell them at domestic prices to the FTM. Where foreign-currency earnings fail to cover domestic costs, a subsidy is involved. Likewise, imports purchased by the FTM are sold to domestic enterprises at prices prevailing in the home market. The price difference is again treated as a state budgeting-accounting matter. This system has been slightly modified in some of the reformed economies, such as Hungary, Poland, and Czechoslovakia. For certain commodities (especially investment and durable consumer goods), prices on the domestic market are related to those prevailing in foreign markets. This is particularly so when the imported products are noncompetitive or when they amount to a large share of domestic consumption.

The process of establishing prices in this basically barter trade situation has been described by others and can be treated very briefly here.

Once the FTMs have begun negotiations, several institutional arrangements guarantee that prices will be Pareto nonoptimal though nonoptimality is actually already assured through the utilization of price averages from world markets in past periods.

As super monopolies representing entire economies, the FTMs are interested more in establishing desirable commodity structures and final trade balance than in attempting to develop rational sets of relative prices. Prices, therefore, receive relatively little attention and are adjusted mostly en masse at the time of general price revisions—occurring only every six to eight years.[2]

Coordinating trade plans based on physical planning indicators has given rise to a tradition of arranging not only bilateral balances of commodity values, but of commodity patterns in trade negotiations as well. The attempt is made to trade identical shares of raw materials, as well as intermediate and final products. Each socialist country considers machinery and equipment as "soft" goods and raw materials as "hard," and each wishes to increase its exports of machinery.[3]

Accepted pricing principles include a ruling that any commodity price arising from bilateral negotiations can be considered a "document." Precedents favorable to a given country are easily established, of course. As a purchaser, one deliberately concedes a high price in negotiations for reciprocal price concessions. Moreover, one can import at high prices a token amount of some good one hopes later to export in large quantities to a third party.

The CMEA technique for treating transportation costs also serves to introduce bias. Actual transport costs among East European countries are *not* significant in trade pricing. Rather, it is assumed that a CMEA country wishing to make a purchase from a socialist country would otherwise be forced to make it in a capitalist market, paying the associated freight costs. Traditionally, freight costs saved by making the purchase from a "brother country" were shared (halved) by the buyer and seller. The purchaser would simply pay half of this cost to the seller.[4] At least for raw materials, this principle has been modified in recent years. In flows using third partners for transit or international trade, one adds only half of the fictive transport costs (deducting actual freight charges).[5]

When the transaction occurs, currency payments are made at officially established exchange rates which also fail to correspond to economic reality.[6]

These adverse outcomes are, however, not the only sources of distortion generated by the institutions of planning convenience. The fact that the socialist economy is constantly plagued with foreign-exchange scarcity also has implications that are relevant here. In the first place, foreign-exchange pressures force CMEA members to schedule international sales and purchases, especially those characterized by seasonal regularities, in a manner that is unfavorable from the pricing standpoint. Moreover, foreign-exchange needs results in competition among socialists. They either fail to divide up available capitalist markets among themselves or do not respect market-sharing arrangements that may be achieved. Substantial price losses are sometimes incurred in attempts to underbid socialist competitors. Capitalist firms exporting commodities subject to significant price variations of a seasonal nature will periodically cease making deliveries. Though continually under the pressure of convertible currency shortages, socialist firms do not do so. In certain products, where socialists produce a large share of world output, contracts are transacted immediately after harvest (with socialist countries competing among themselves), so that substantial losses are incurred.[7]

It is often observed, in both bourgeois and socialist economic literature, that the irrational socialist pricing system is one of the most fundamental causes of international trade problems in the CMEA region. It is impossible for economic agents to make simple price calculations or comparisons under the current system. Planners cannot construct planning indicators based on economic costs, cannot make investment calculations including rates of return, etc. Apparently, anything less than "total reform of both pricing and planning policies" does not offer much hope that rationality can be introduced into socialist foreign trade.[8]

The Options for Change

The reform movement of the 1960s and more recent endeavors to intensify Eastern European integration (through a "complex program" of increased trade and interstate plan coordination) are evidence of socialist economic directors' awareness of the need to improve foreign-trade pricing.

In addition to the status quo, three other pricing models are of interest to theoreticians and planners in the centrally directed economies. The first possibility could be to move toward a reform model of the socialist market type, though this solution would be difficult to achieve. Not only are the concerned countries somewhat weary of and disillusioned with reform endeavors in general, but international pricing reforms would also require the cooperation of all CMEA countries and would fail to achieve consensus so long as jealousy of individual national sovereignties remains as it has been.

Still, the reform approach retains its significance for the future. This is because it is the midway station to the other two possible models, each of which is substantially more utopian (if not eschatological) than the reform model.

The Hungarian utopia is that of real market-type relations between "planned market economies," while the Soviet eschatology entails visions of a "megaprogrammed computopia." Since each of the four possible approaches can be expected to influence international interaction in East Europe, they bear brief explanation from the standpoint of the pricing problem.

In the case of the status quo model, socialists are forced to weigh the advantages of central control and sheltering the domestic economy from adverse world-market influences against the costs of the growing inefficiency of overambitious, bureaucratic centralism.

The institution of the foreign-trade monopoly is designed to permit trade but, at the same time, to keep central control over production, distribution, and also scarce foreign exchange. Having foreign-trade enterprises produce at domestic prices, selling imports at domestic prices, and providing for external foreign-trade balance through bilateral transactions permits microeconomic insulation against imported inflation. However, this market dichotomy does not completely forestall the influence of imported inflation on the domestic economy. Whenever the state has to step up subsidies to foreign-trade enterprises, it transmits potentially inflationary impulses if not to prices, at least to private incomes. Still, the socialists claim that current world inflationary woes are sufficient reason to reject any thoughts of dismantling the foreign-trade monopoly.[9]

Although the existence of the FTM prohibits prices from exerting any major allocatory functions, the combined minor functions of foreign-trade prices are significant enough to merit attention. This will remain so as long as the foreign sector is largely a residual one, filling gaps left open by the domestic production mechanism and disposing of unneeded (and unexpected) surpluses.

If a domestically unavailable input is needed to open a bottleneck, any potential import will be more closely scrutinized where lower priced alternatives are available. To finance such an import, of course, something else must be exported, and noticeably high- or low-foreign-trade prices may likewise influence this decision.

Generalizing, if the physical planning process signals a potential disequilibrium, planners are forced to consider new bundles of final outputs. Foreign-trade prices are bound to influence the planners' choices.[10] Prices are also likely to play some role in the geographical distribution of imports and exports, even if foreign-trade decisions have been made by other than price criteria. Nevertheless, so long as socialist prices play a role subsidiary to physical allocation, there is no point in trying to produce prices designed to direct international production and trade processes.[11]

As economies become more complex, centralized planning becomes increasingly less capable of efficient operation. In spite of the efforts of the largely unsuccessful reform movement, reform pressures continue to exist. Apparently, these can be suppressed for substantial periods of time in the socialist economy, but if announced desires to improve consumer welfare can be taken seriously, change may become inevitable. Since the intent of this article is to present some price reforms suggested by economic analysis, the reform model requires brief mention at this point.

Before the economy can be either programmed completely or turned over to the greater automaticity of market-type institutions, it will likely be forced to take a middle road in which priority (structurally determining) industries remain under close central supervision while less critical industries are granted greater decision-making power. This implies the development of market or quasi-market (liberal-socialist) institutions to allocate resources for nonpriority sectors.

The Soviet long-term pricing solution would be to generate optimal (shadow) prices and trade flows through programming. To what extent this goal should be associated with the Leninist vision of a single economic plan for a socialist world is difficult to say. But even the optimistic Soviet mathematical school would not maintain the time is near when super computers and programming methodology will permit detailed planning even for a single country, not to mention the entire CMEA region.

Finally, we come to the Hungarian approach, i.e., establishing "planned market economies" through the CMEA region and conducting trade on a multilateral basis, using scarcity prices and convertible currencies. Under current political conditions, of course, this is strictly utopian, even though Hungarian reform is not as radical as conservative socialist forces suggest. After all, CMEA's Complex Program also calls for eventual currency convertibility and multilateralism (the latter already pursued, however inadequately, by CMEA policies and financial institutions). Even the Russians occasionally acknowledge the idea that these things eventually will be achieved.[12] However, it is difficult to find any Soviet economists who advocate (as do most articulate Hungarian economists) the utilization of market institutions to achieve the objective.

The widely publicized Hungarian reform experiment includes market-like techniques in pricing. Take, for example, their treatment of transportation costs. Rather than including the arbitrary socialist transportation cost in the price in advance, they simply have the (Hungarian) purchaser pay the actual hauling costs, predisposing them, other things equal, to purchase from the producer who is nearest.[13]

Unfortunately, the campaign conducted by the Hungarians during the reform era failed to remove the emotional anxiety socialists experience when any "market" concept is invoked. Referring to *planned* market allocations and emphasizing that even the so-called market countries trading on main world markets deliberately influence market processes to achieve desired results (implying that socialists could too) failed to allay entrenched suspicions.[14]

Constructing planning institutions to perform functions otherwise left to markets does not result in optimal performance, but it does make it possible for socialist economies to continue to conduct business with each other. It is interesting that some of the raw material scarce CMEA countries specializing in machinery production are granting modest credits to the less-developed socialist countries needing capital to expand their extractive industries. The latter countries are desirous of developing machinery and industrial production, rather than exclusively producing under-priced raw materials. The need for special credit institutions to stimulate the output of goods in extremely high demand (i.e., to serve as a concealed price increase) reflects the inability of CMEA prices to affect resource allocation.[15]

Given the socialist preference to maintain firm central control, even at the cost of a substantial degree of efficiency, one cannot hope that the market solution represents an actual possibility for the near future.

Problems of Level and Structure of East European Prices

Since CMEA countries are unwilling to accept their own domestic prices for trade purposes, another pricing system becomes essential. As indicated, this is allegedly the "cleansed" world-market price (WMP). According to Hungarian and Western findings, however, after negotiations most transactions actually occur "at national prices of yesterday," rather than at prices found in any capitalist world market.[16] Even domestically, these prices did not accurately reflect present input costs.

Additionally, the overall price level in East Europe is higher than that prevailing in world markets, and machinery and industrial equipment are significantly higher priced than primary goods and raw materials.[17] The overall higher level can be explained primarily as a result of the fact that the socialist countries attempt to trade strictly with each other whenever feasible. This means that less foreign exchange has to be raised than is the case for transactions on exterior markets. At the same time, however, these reciprocal socialist demands permit sellers to push contractual prices toward the upper limits of "documentable" price zones in negotiations.

In contrast to the overall price level, the artificially high level of machinery and equipment (as compared to raw materials) cannot be explained on the basis of economic logic. We would expect these price level positions to be reversed if prices were established on the basis of comparative costs, since CMEA members specialize in machinery and equipment.

Underpricing of raw materials reflects, once again, the fact that socialist prices are not of primary importance in allocation. But even more importantly, raw materials prices also reflect an aversion towards net export balances in primary products because of the Soviet Union's deteriorating barter terms of trade. Soviet authors have claimed, since the early 1960s that as a deliverer of primary inputs, the U.S.S.R. is subsidizing East European industry not only because of intra-CMEA price policies but also because of the relatively high cost of producing raw materials in the U.S.S.R. and transportating them to the Western borders. In addition, the Soviets claim they exchange underpriced raw materials for machines that are not only overpriced, but are also below the technological and quality levels obtainable in world markets.

The recipients need this form of assistance, since they have come to rely on it to offset their relative inefficiency and scarcity of capital and reserves. Its sudden withdrawal would have "serious consequences" and remains unthinkable until the economic efficiency of these countries can be increased either through economic reform or through greater interaction with economies west of the Elbe.

Clearly, this anomalous price structure tempts socialist raw materials suppliers to look west for higher available prices and the opportunity to earn scarce foreign exchange. Concrete examples are not difficult to find. After 1958, for example, when East European coal exporters were encountering strong competition with oil, the export prices of Polish coal sold in the west consistently reflected the level of oil prices as the Poles attempted to maximize foreign-exchange earnings.[18]

The Soviet Union is no less anxious today to profit from potential petroleum sales in the West. In the face of dramatically high prices prevalent in Western markets, it must be difficult for the U.S.S.R. to accept the political realities that have dictated that the Soviets supply the brother countries with fuel and raw materials.

This price structure also cannot help but affect, over time, the flow of raw materials from Bulgaria and Rumania. They, too, would prefer to market more of their primary goods in the West. Further, they would prefer to pay for the machinery they import from the CMEA area with machinery exports. They have no comparative advantages here, but they desire to industrialize and have no desire to pay for their imports with underpriced raw materials.[19]

The Socialist Independent Price Basis (IPB)

Basing price negotiations on world-market prices is objectionable to many East Europeans for more than ideological reasons. The desire of nearly two decades to work out an independent price basis (IPB) reflects, in part, the objective of achieving more favorable terms of trade. In part, it also expresses the aspiration of greater independence from world markets.

Formal discussion on the creation of autarkic IPB possibilities has been pursued with less enthuiasm in this decade. Economic motives, planning interests, and international conditions remain basically as they were during the course of the IPB discussion, but no methodology for a separate socialist pricing system that permitted compromise and implementation could be constructed.

Bulgaria and the Soviet Union contended that an IPB would permit prices to reflect unique production and technological conditions prevailing in East Europe, so that CMEA members would shape their actual trade patterns to conform with ''natural and economic conditions of commodity production'' encountered there.[20]

The differing levels of national productivity in the community could be bridged by establishing realistic exchange rates for domestic currencies, so that incidences of low national labor productivity would not tend to put upward pressure on prices.[21]

The East Germans support continued insulation of socialist prices from the influences of the world market, though Brendel and Faude express the view that the current system is sufficiently different from the world market as to represent a unique phenomenon.[22] Because CMEA prices are based on different foundations (e.g., stop prices and world market prices of different base periods), they reflect the particular needs and aspirations of CMEA countries, diverging from WMPs with respect to both level and structure.

Whereas all East German economists may not accept this evaluation, the main point Faude and Brendel wish to establish most certainly represents the majority viewpoint. It is that continued central pricing control and insulation from inflationary WMP tendencies are essential for the stability and continuity of international cooperation in socialist Europe.

The fundamental cause of the failure of the IPB concept is twofold. To the extent that the East European economies wish to integrate into the world market, they cannot maintain an autarkic system of foreign-trade pricing.[23] Economists representing Hungary and Poland, in particular, emphasized this point from the outset of the discussion. For trade-dependent countries relying fairly extensively on extra-CMEA markets, it appeared that accepting a separate price basis would threaten to sever their connections with the world market and thereby present "grave difficulties."

In view of the importance of preserving stability and relative autarky at home, this is perhaps the lesser cause. More important is that any concept of an IPB different from current world-market prices implies constructing intra-CMEA prices on the basis of internal prices in one or most East European economies. Since the U.S.S.R. is by far the largest trade partner and also commands other influences to sway her partners, an IPB for East Europe would be heavily influenced by the preferences of Soviet planners regarding absolute and relative prices. With few exceptions, the East European economies do not wish to import and become dependent on Soviet price irrationalities.

Towards the end of the official IPB discussion, it appeared almost as if the participants could be categorized as to where they stood on the issue of economic reform. Those favoring more liberal measures rejected the IPB and its negative implications for greater interaction with the West on the basis of WMPs. Countries that had scarcely modified their central planning mechanisms favored retaining the techniques of economic insulation.

The latter sentiment failed to convince the more liberal reformers that acceptable answers to methodological questions could be found. How should one estimate production costs in one socialist country for comparison with those prevailing in others? How could such cost estimates be converted to a single currency base? How can agreement on the treatment of transportation costs be achieved? And when these tasks are done, how does one account for pricing problems arising from trade with nonsocialist countries?[24]

Keeping the more conservative forces in CMEA from implementing the IPB did not assure a resolution of socialist pricing difficulties for the smaller, trade-dependent socialist countries. Besides, given the recently intensified desire to strengthen Soviet economic ties with the West, the notion of separatist pricing becomes more unappealing anyway.

Still, something urgently needs to be done about the inflexible, Pareto nonoptimal pricing traditions of socialism. The objective of the following section is to offer suggestions designed to bridge the gap between present practice and either the planned market economy or the "computopia" of the future.

Suggestions for a Reformation of CMEA Pricing

If anything approaching genuine scarcity pricing could be achieved, it would be a fairly simple matter to establish realistic official exchange rates. These are, of course, currently lacking in Eastern Europe.[25]

The price revisions of the 1960s helped bring price structures more into line with actual production costs, though the socialists admit that substantial "inadequacies" remain. Additionally, "numerous" differences remain in the structures of prices and production costs in the CMEA countries.[26] In the transition period between current arbitrary pricing and more rational pricing in the future, one would have to attempt to establish workable exchange rates and international trade prices.

Soviet economists admit that methodological substitutes for scarcity prices ("instruments for evaluating the economic effectiveness of specialization variants in CMEA") have simply not yet been developed. Kormnov and Cheburakov suggest that member countries could establish prices for new products on the basis of minimal production outlays in multinational socialist production units with detailed specialities, i.e., from cost accounting in some of CMEA's joint cooperative ventures.[27] Establishing rational prices for commodities already being produced presents a more difficult problem. This must be accomplished, however, if broad international cooperation and detailed specialization is to be achieved in East Europe. Perhaps this could be done, even though individual countries are unable or unwilling to present good information for such purposes, by taking advantage, once again, of cost experience gained in collective ventures.

Such measures may be of assistance in getting started on the road to reform but cannot be expected to accomplish much more. Once the break is made from undeviating commitment to command techniques, concepts and institutions of reform become appropriate.

It is quite certain that planners will retain control over priority industries for some time. This is to be expected so long as the exigencies of ideology and the preferences of the directors remain as they are. Moreover, current planning technology is much more suited to the direction of a given number of significant industries than to directing the totality of productive endeavor. Logic would suggest that any real reform attempt would ultimately imply quasi-decentralization, i.e., loosening controls on all but priority industries.

The structurally determining industries, as the name suggests, are those for which directors most keenly desire to control not only current performance, but also the level and types of investments they undertake. These industries include those characterized by substantial economies of scale, those requiring massive investments, and those producing commodities of national specialization within CMEA under the foreign-trade ministry. These three industry types are clearly not mutually exclusive. Declining (comparatively disadvantageous) industries, singled out for extinction by planners and developing import substitution industries, would likewise fall in this category. These would also continue under central control.

Peripheral, nonpriority, or nonstructurally determining industries would be substantially released from the "petty tutelage" of the planning agencies. Rather than issuing detailed planning directives, one would assure at least minimal correspondence between enterprise behavior and social objectives.

The rules (together with underlying theoretical considerations) to be presented here are in the spirit of the Lange-Lerner tradition. Having the benefit of several additional decades of experience with socialist economic practice (beyond that of Lange and Lerner), rules can be designed to be more in keeping with the needs of the command economy in transition.

The marginalist, Lange-Lerner pricing rules have been shown to be insufficient where enterprise earnings have to be taxed to provide funds for national objectives. As we observed in Chapter 4, Baumol and Bradford have shown that where such revenues are essential, rational (quasi-optimal) prices *must* deviate from marginal costs. The deviation of each commodity's price from marginal cost must be inversely proportional to its price elasticity of demand if Pareto optimality in the presence of a revenues constraint (i.e., quasi-optimality) is to be achieved.

The socialist debate about the "correct" Marxian surplus value (profit markup) has failed to incorporate rationality considerations, though this could easily be done.[28] The markup is applied in some way to production costs, where the product price p is the sum of per-unit capital costs and depreciation c, unit labor costs v, and the given profit markup m.

Utilizing a simple form of the Baumol-Bradford theorem, the quasi-optimal surplus value in the partial equilibrium case or when cross elasticities are zero, is achieved when

$$m = k(p/\varepsilon_d) + MC - AC \qquad (11.1)$$

As usual, MC and AC represent marginal and average costs respectively, ε_d is elasticity of demand, and k is defined as $1 + \lambda/\lambda$, where λ is the Lagrange multiplier. This expression indicates that, when the price elasticity of demand is low, the revenue-providing profit markup will be higher than when demand is elastic.

To the extent that foreign trade is conducted in hard-currency (Western) markets, the profit markup could be tied to incentive considerations. Peripheral industries' earnings of scarce foreign exchange represent a windfall for the economy, since the primary foreign-exchange earners are under central control. The state could share earnings with the enterprise by permitting it to retain some portion of the total. Consider the ratio of the enterprise's absolute share of net revenues (profits) m_e to the public's share m_p. One could set m_e/m_p higher for foreign-exchange earnings than for net revenues earned domestically. Further incentive would be provided by letting the ratio rise along with foreign-exchange earnings. Specifically,

$$m_e = n(m_p\sigma) \tag{11.2}$$

where σ represents the percentage of total sales in hard-currency markets, and n equals some constant (smaller than 1). Relating this to the quasi-optimal surplus values or profit markup gives

$$m_p + n(m_p\sigma) = k(p/\varepsilon_d) + MC - AC \tag{11.3}$$

so that the sum of enterprise and public net revenues is equal to the quasi-optimal profit markup.

With the introduction of quasi-optimal prices, the problem of determining where comparative advantages lie becomes quite manageable. International trade can be conducted for a given commodity when

$$c + v + BBm < p_x - t \tag{11.4}$$

where BBm represents the Baumol-Bradford markup as given by equation (1), p_x is an export (socialist or world-market) price, and t represents the additional costs of producing a commodity for a foreign market, i.e., net transportation costs and the additional costs of foreign operations. Crucial here is the correct calculation of c and v and the selection of trade markets.[a] We shall assume at this instance that (a) c and v are the real costs of capital and labor per unit of output and (b) the highest return and lowest cost foreign markets can be chosen.

If the rules to be set forth here are to stimulate the "private" interest of enterprises in accordance with the "social" interest of the planners, a key assumption is that c and v correctly reflect real costs. If they do not, the peripheral enterprises may behave contrary to the social interest. If prime costs are biased downward (which is likely to be the case because of underestimated land rent and capital cost), peripheral enterprises will

---

[a] It is, of course, widely known that socialist enterprises or foreign-trade corporations are not, in fact, always free to select trade partners according to highest return and lowest cost considerations. If the markets singled out for trade are uniform in prices, then the rules can still be applied. If output slated for trade is constrained in one market while free in another market for the residual, then the entrepreneur can still solve the problem as a discriminatory monopolist, provided the foreign markets are perfectly separated.

produce more than in the optimal case, and their profits will *appear* larger from the enterprise's point of view. As long as planners wish to control price and production policy in key industries servicing peripheral branches, prices in these autonomous industries are highly likely to be irrational from the allocatory point of view. However, in view of existing rules and allocation processes, in some cases it may still pay to let enterprises maximize according to apparent costs and actual revenues.

Where the producer faces the option of producing commodity (subscript) 1 or commodity (subscript) 2, both of which could be marketed abroad, and where the following condition holds

$$\frac{c_1 + v_1 + BBm_1}{p_{x_1} - t_1} < \frac{c_2 + v_2 + BBm_2}{p_{x_2} - t_2} \tag{11.5}$$

it is appropriate to produce commodity 1 with its greater comparative advantage.

It is, of course, true that the smaller, peripheral industries cannot be expected to have gathered extensive experience in such matters as calculating marginal costs or running projections on demand elasticities, and so on. Moreover, these industries have never been forced to be concerned with questions of economic efficiency under the socialist planning tradition. It is, therefore, worthwhile to present some simple behavioral guidelines that would cause both of these enterprises, at once, to achieve more efficient operation and to act in the best interests of the planners or (more sympathetically) of the society.

The behavioral rules would incorporate Baumol-Bradford efficiency considerations and can be simply presented. At the same time, they maintain the tradition of the socialist "telescopic faculty" (which demands planned constraints on current private consumption so that current and future social needs can be satisfied). The peripheral enterprise producing new goods or attempting to find the quasi-optimal price after the initiation of the decentralizing price reform receives the following instructions:

1. Gradually increase output until it is apparent that total costs of production tend to approach total sales revenues, i.e., until net revenues begin to decline.
2. Gradually reduce output and adjust the price upward, clearing the market. Continue this process so long as net revenues continue to rise.

When all the enterprises in a given industry follow these rules, they will mutually constrict the total supply. Whether the participants are aware of it or not, the outcome is a simulation of collusive or monopolistic behavior. Whereas such behavior may be undesirable (and perhaps not permitted) in some of the structurally determining industries enjoying economies of scale or producing a commodity protected from foreign competition, it is not inappropriate for the decentralized, nonpriority industries. The upward price bias implied by such behavior is not only suggested by the Baumol-Bradford theorem, but is also appropriate for the socialist objectives of conservative consumption.

A traditional objection to monopoly behavior is that (the higher price and restricted output aside) resources are underutilized and, therefore, at least in part, are shunted into other industries. Competing there as a part of an expanded supply causes them to enjoy a lower compensation. In the socialist scarcity economy characterized by "tautness," factors need not fear reduced returns and these outcomes can be viewed as simple conservation of resources.

As a matter of fact, the downward bias implied by monopolistic and monopsonistic "exploitation" of the labor factor might prove to be a boon. Freeing consumer goods of central control might prove to be a strong stimulus to these heretofore suppressed industries. In the process of rapid expansion, their attempt to bid resources away from other sectors could prove to be a source of strong inflationary pressure.[b]

Additionally, planners have tended to favor greater concentration of industries with their ease of control and potential for scale economies, but they must fear accumulations of potentially competitive power.[29] It is likely that the rules suggested would permit the behavior preferred by planners while avoiding the undesired power accumulation. They would generate monopoly outcomes, but this would occur only through unconscious cooperation on the part of individually unimportant, dispersed decision makers.

The rules can also be extended to the foreign-trade sphere. Again, the objective is to maximize total net revenues. These are the sum of domestically earned profits NR_d and net revenues earned in world markets NR_x, given respectively as

$$NR_d = [p_d - (c + v)]q_d \qquad (11.6)$$

$$NR_x = [p_x - (c + v + t)]q_x \qquad (11.7)$$

where q_d is the volume of output marketed domestically and q_x is the volume marketed beyond national borders.

Generally speaking, the maximization of these revenues requires price discrimination behavior. This is possible, as usual, where markets having differing demand elasticities can be kept separate and where the monopolist equates the marginal revenues encountered in the home and foreign markets to the marginal costs. The sum of net revenues is

---

[b]This was pointed out to me by Lester Thurow. I thank him for reminding me of the general equilibrium effects of decentralization. These efforts are treated for the investment problem on pp. 89-91.

$$NR = R_d(q_d) + R_x(q_x) - C(q_x + q_d)$$

where R_d is the domestic revenue function, R_x is the foreign revenue function expressed in net domestic earnings, and C is the domestic cost functions. To maximize, the partial derivates must be equated to zero:

$$R_d'(q_d) - C'(q) = 0 \qquad R_x'(q_x) - C'(q) = 0$$

Rewriting, one finds

$$R_d'(q_d) = R_x'(q_x) = C'(q)$$

or marginal revenue at home and abroad must be equal to marginal cost. In order for this to be a maximum, the second order conditions must be such that marginal revenue in each market is rising less rapidly than the marginal cost of total output.

To deal with specific cases, one must specify whether competitive or noncompetitive conditions prevail in the foreign market in question. Take first the case where the domestic industry may be interested in entering a purely competitive foreign market. The industry is, in effect, a monopoly industry domestically (by following the price rules previously suggested), but a price taker in the external market. To begin with, it may be assumed that $p_d \not> p_x$, since the industry would otherwise require protection from foreign competition. It is likely that periphery industries could not expect such protection in the long run and would find themselves on the way to extinction.

Where $p_x - t > p_d$, foreign trade is, of course, to be recommended. The price discrimination equilibrium solution requires that marginal revenues from separate markets be equal and that their sum be equated to the marginal cost of the total output. Enterprises initiated into the quasi-decentralist reform and desiring to engage in foreign trade would be instructed to sell the greater share of output abroad until the constricted domestic supply and rising price no longer result in rising profits.

This behavior will cause an increase of domestically earned marginal revenues to the level of those earned abroad. To achieve this behavior, it may be necessary to permit the relevant domestic producers to enter into an association to cooperate in exploiting the revenue-generating potential of foreign markets.

The equilibrium positions of this model can best be seen by reference to Figure 11-1. The notation is as usual, though superscripts n and t have been added to denote nontrade and trade values respectively, and subscripts m and c refer to competitive and noncompetitive situations. The c^t on the vertical axis represents unit costs of production after the introduction of trade.

Encouraging the industry to behave noncompetitively before the intro-

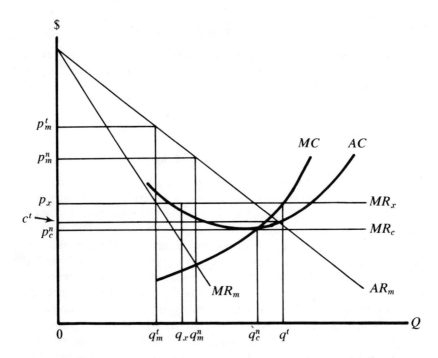

Figure 11-1. Optimal Discrimination in Socialist Foreign Trade

duction of foreign trade causes the industry output to shrink from q_c^n to q_m^n. The domestically competitive, nontrade price p_c^n is naturally lower than the noncompetitive one p_m^n. When trade is introduced, total output rises from the competitive, nontrade level q_c^n to q^t. This output is divided between the domestic market q_m^t and the export market q_x, so that $q^t = q_n^t + q_x$. Note that, after the industry begins to conduct foreign trade, the domestic (monopoly) price rises to p_m^t; the purely competitive export price is given by p_x. Discriminatory pure profits are given in Figure 11-1 as $(p_m^t - c^t)q_m^t + (p_x - c^t)q_x$. These could be divided by the state and the enterprise, as was suggested above. Figure 11-1 ignores, for the sake of simplicity, the additional costs of producing for foreign markets. It might be observed, however, that foreign competition will not invade the domestic market so long as $p_m^t < p_x + t$.

Moving now to the other extreme, let us investigate the case where the domestic producer becomes aware of an opportunity to enter a foreign market without competition. (The GDR, for example, as the exclusive socialist producer may sell an item to Rumania, which, for lack of foreign exchange, cannot make the purchase in Western markets.) The optimization requirements can also be approximated simply in this case. The domestic industry is instructed to:

1. maximize net revenues domestically (following the procedure given earlier);
2. enter the foreign market with a price moderately above the domestic one, gradually constricting the export supply and adjusting the price upward, clearing the market—continuing this process so long as net revenues continue to rise;
3. transfer output from the domestic to the foreign market, so long as net revenues continue to rise.

Under certain conditions, foreign demand may be such that the export price would have to be lower than the domestic one. In such a case, the profitability of conducting foreign trade may not be as readily recognized. The producer would be instructed, in this case likewise, to maximize net revenue first at home, then to enter the foreign market with a price sufficiently below the domestic price to attract some buyers, then continuing to reduce prices as long as profits continue to rise.[c] Though such behavior may appear externally as dumping, it is in fact merely price discrimination.

The final and most difficult case is the one in which imperfect competition is encountered abroad. Lacking a universally accepted model of oligopoly, economic theory is not as yet able to suggest the simple planning rules that such a theory would hopefully imply.

Nevertheless, knowledge of the Baumol-Bradford theorem and the planner's preference for tautness indicates some appropriate guidelines for foreign-trade pricing behavior under oligopolistic conditions.

In the first place, the industry continues to perform in a manner that attempts to satisfy the profit maximization conditions presented above, though this may be a difficult task in the uncertainty of the foreign oligopoly environment. It is obvious that other objectives entering into the "bourgeois" economic analysis (e.g., maximizing total revenues with a satisfactory profit constraint, maximizing the share of the market, and maintaining a high degree of prestige for the individual enterprise or its managers) tend to fall short of satisfying social (or planner's) goals.

As a matter of general policy, the industry should be instructed to enter the external market with prices reflecting the Baumol-Bradford departure from competitive behavior. Entry will lead to one of three possible outcomes—active international collusion, some kind of market sharing or tacit collusion, or some form of unstable equilibrium rich in the uncertainty characteristic of imperfect competition.

When the possibility of international collusion ("cooperation") arises, the industry would be encouraged to behave in the cartel setting as it does domestically. From the political viewpoint, this may prove acceptable only

---

[c] The two cases considered here do not exhaust all the possible outcomes. Other possibilities can, however, be treated in a similarly simple way.

so long as planners do not fear an accrual of power to the international cartel and its national representatives.

Market sharing or other tacit collusion may well imply that the firm must operate as a price taker in the sphere of economic action permitted by implicit agreement. The industry would then behave approximately as shown in Figure 11-1, hoping that the volume of possible export sales will be such as to permit equation of marginal revenues in foreign and domestic markets and to equate the marginal revenues of domestic and foreign markets to marginal costs.

In the noncollusive, uncertainty case, the exporting industry will doubtlessly have to organize to plan a strategy for the foreign market. Price wars or other such outcomes of oligopolistic confrontation à la Cournot or von Stackelberg may be encountered. The industry must attempt to make an accurate appraisal of its competitive staying power and the lengths to which it may be willing to pursue potential earnings in the relevant export market.

It is possible that some foreign-trade experience, independent of the central direction of socialism, would permit such industries to achieve what many Western export industries have proved to be possible—to perform better than the economic theories of oligopoly which try to explain their behavior.

The monopolistic rules presented here for domestic decision making in nonpriority industries bear some resemblance to essential features of actual price formation in these enterprises in traditional socialist economies. Instead of a quasi-optimal markup, planners have tried to add to the average industry cost and normal profit markup various kinds of turnover taxes. Revenue objectives may be paramount in some instances, but, in a substantial number of cases, turnover taxes have been selected in order to equate domestic demand and supply. The case diverges from the quasi-optimal one above in some essential aspects, for it is largely not the enterprise that selects output and price but some planning agent. Since planners probably lack the detailed knowledge available to the individual enterprise, price-output directives are likely to be suboptimal. If the entrepreneur is instructed to act as stipulated above, the socialist economy could achieve better enterprise performance without that segment of the planning bureaucracy that is currently preoccupied with nonpriority industries.

Notes

1. Soviet authors themselves have lately expressed doubt about the vaunted principles of socialist world-market prices. See, for instance, N.

Mitrofanova, "Perspektivy dalneishevo sovershenstvovania vneshnetorgovykh tsen sotsialisticheskikh stran," *Planovoye Khozyaistvo*, no. 4 (1974), pp. 41-49.

2. See Sandor Ausch, *Theory and Practice of CMEA Cooperation* (Budapest: Akademiai Kiado, 1972), pp. 87-88. Also see footnote 25 of Chapter 10.

3. Ibid., p. 86 and B. Csikós-Nagy, "Some Theoretical Problems of the Price System in CMEA Intertrade," in T. Földi, and T. Kiss, eds., *Socialist World Market Prices* (Leyden: Sijthoff, 1969), p. 105. Tibor Kiss, *International Division of Labour in Open Economies–With Special Regard to CMEA* (Budapest, 1971), p. 223, reminds us that (as will be seen in greater detail below) raw materials are underpriced. If the small socialist countries raised these prices, they would have to increase substantially their payments to the Soviet Union.

4. Ausch, *Theory and Practice,* op. cit., p. 82. He further observes: "If a CMEA country able to export a certain kind of material agrees on a high price with another country which is, from this point of view, in an unfavorable geographical situation and must pay high freights, this price will be extended also to other, similarly situated countries. The same extension takes place when two partners agree on relatively high prices concerning one or several materials which are irrelevant in this particular bilateral relation but are highly important for the supplying party in its trade with other CMEA countries."

5. See V. Shanina, "Voprosy tsenoobrazovania na vneshnetorgovye perevozki mezhdu stranami-chlenami SEV," *Ekonomicheskie Nauki*, no. 10 (1973), pp. 84-89.

6. Trade accounts are recorded by CMEA in *numéraires* called "national devisa units." Interstate socialist trade occurs on the basis of "devisa rubles" (also referred to as "accounting" or "transferable rubles"). The CMEA countries convert transactions from devisa rubles to national devisa units at official exchange rates. There is also a dollar/devisa unit exchange rate, which (as is widely known) overvalues the purchasing power of the socialist currencies vis-a-vis the dollar. See Paul Marer, *Postwar Pricing and Price Patterns in Socialist Foreign Trade (1946-1971)*, (Indiana University, 1972), pp. 2-4.

7. Ausch, *Theory and Practice,* op. cit., p. 107-109.

8. The view expressed on this matter by A. Boltho is similar to ours. See his *Foreign Trade Criteria in Socialist Economies* (London: Cambridge University Press, 1971), pp. 93-94.

9. Typical in this regard are G. Brendel and E. Faude, "Wesenszüge und Entwicklungstendenzen des RGW-Preisbildungssystems," *Wirtschaftswissenschaft*, vol. 21 (1973), p. 1292. As was mentioned above,

CMEA-type price negotiations can also have an inflationary bias. Hewett (see below) has also referred to this phenomenon, labeling it "bilateral inflation." In bilateral trade negotiations, prices for commodities being traded can "simultaneously increase for the sole purpose of placating both sides without affecting the net barter terms of trade."

10. As Edward A. Hewett puts it, the optimal approach for the planner in the traditional socialist economy is to rank surpluses according to the ratio of the domestic to the foreign price from the lowest to the highest, "then commence exports in that order until imports are just paid for. This is the only way to minimize the domestic cost of foreign exchange and thus the domestic cost of the final outputs." See his *Foreign Trade Prices in the Council for Mutual Economic Assistance* (London: Cambridge University Press, 1974), pp. 129-130.

11. Ausch, *Theory and Practice,* op. cit., p. 188, indicates that "thousands of 'foreign-exchange rates' exist, their number about equalling that of the various articles entering into foreign trade. It is obvious that such 'foreign-exchange rates' are unable to affect exports, imports and the balance of trade or to change the present situation where value and exchange value of the various commodities continue to be measured by meticulously established proportions of barter in kind."

12. Cf. the German translation of M.W. Senin's *Sozialistische Integration* (Berlin: Dietz Verlag, 1972). Given the more orthodox Soviet eschatalogical view of the programming computopia, it is hard to believe they are anxiously pursuing thoughts of decentralization that would permit the achievement of convertibility, etc.

13. See Wladyslaw Sztyber, "Theoretical Basis for the Reform of Sale Prices in Socialist Economies," *Eastern European Economics,* vol. 9 (1970-1971), p. 123.

14. Csikós-Nagy, "Some Theoretical Problems of the Price System in the Trade Between CMEA Countries," in *Foreign Trade in a Planned Economy,* I. Vajda und M. Simai, ed. (London: Cambridge University Press, 1971), p. 110, refers to "deliberate price policies" exerted in world markets, and indicates that these markets are "often used only as a technical medium to ensure that the price tendencies which are thought to be correct assert themselves." CMEA development preferences would be achieved through such prices along with a customs tariff system. He observes (p. 111) that "the national tariff systems of the CMEA countries are actually functioning, although instead of customs duties they operate through export subsidies and import levies."

15. For the details see Jozef M. van Brabant, *Essays on Planning, Trade and Integration in Eastern Europe* (Rotterdam: Rotterdam University Press, 1974), pp. 179-182.

16. Ausch, *Theory and Practice,* op. cit., p. 94, and his colleagues found "after a study of the domestic prices and the rates of price equalization subsidies applied to the products of some enterprises that the prevailing 'socialist world-market prices' almost exactly (at most with differences of 5 to 10 percent due to bargaining) corresponded to the inland prices, whereas they considerably differed from the prices of the capitalist world market." See also N. Mitrofanova, "Perspektivy dalneishevo," op. cit.

17. S. Ausch and F. Bartha, "Theoretical Problems of CMEA Intertrade Prices," in Földi and Kiss, *Socialist World Market Prices,* op. cit., p. 109, calculate that the average discrepancy between the levels of the CMEA and world-market prices are 25.9 percent for machines, 15.4 percent for raw materials, and 1.7 percent for agricultural goods. These findings are in line with work done by Hewett, *Foreign Trade Prices,* op. cit. and Marer, "Postwar Pricing," op. cit., who have measured changes in CMEA prices over time. They emphasize the negative implications involved for the net barter terms of trade of the Soviet Union.

18. Heinrich Machowski, "Zur Preisbildung im RGW-Intrablockhandel: Das Beispiel der Polnischen Steinkohle," *Osteuropa Wirtschaft,* vol. 14 (1969), pp. 89-112.

19. Adam Zwass, *Preisbildung im RGW-Intrablockhandel,* unpublished manuscript, Vienna, 1972, has emphasized this problem.

20. A. Lutov and V. Ivanova, "The Necessity of an Own Price Basis in the Trade Between Socialist Countries," in Földi and Kiss, *Socialist World Market Prices,* op. cit., p. 129, are representative.

21. Ibid., p. 200.

22. Brendel and Faude, "Wesenszüge," op. cit., pp. 1288-1292.

23. This is the view of the Polish economist, A. Bodnar. See his "Price Problems in the Trade Between CMEA Countries," in Földi and Kiss, *Socialist World Market Prices,* op. cit., p. 47.

24. For a more detailed discussion of these questions see Hewett, *Foreign Trade Prices,* op. cit., pp. 165-175.

25. O.T. Bogomolov, *Theorie und Methodologie der internationalen sozialistischen Arbeitsteilung,* (East Berlin: Verlag Die Wirtschaft, 1969), p. 118., takes this position, affirming quite correctly also that it is "especially necessary" to establish a course by which monetary sums expressed in national currency units and reflecting socially necessary labor costs can be calculated in comparable foreign-exchange values.

26. Ibid., pp. 122-123. To overcome the problem, Bogomolov suggests the construction of special indices that, unlike prices, cannot be biased through various influences. He suggests using indices of production costs and investment quotas as a basis for developing such indices. Of course,

these measures are also subject to nominal value changes or changes arising from purely financial forces.

27. Efforts have already been made to utilize large quantities of cost data to develop special "conversion coefficients". See Yu Kormnov and M. Cheburokov, "Sovershenstvovanye Upravlenia Ostraslevoi Integratsiyei Stran-Chlenov SEV," *Voprosy Ekonomiki*, no. 7 (1973), p. 110. They can only suggest that such efforts be increased to solve the problem of converting (or recalculating) from these data national (normative and actual) production costs into a collective currency (transferable ruble) value.

28. Bogomolov, *Theorie and Methodologie*, op. cit., esp. p. 119, is particularly vocal on the inadequacies of profit markup practices in socialist pricing. He makes explicit reference to the way the revenue-providing (and consumption-influencing) turnover tax is applied in the markup. Diverse practices in this regard give rise to the nonuniformity of pricing structures in the socialist countries and result in the necessity of maintaining separate domestic- and foreign-price levels. These practices have also resulted in the low level of capital-goods prices and the relatively high level of consumer-goods prices.

29. Georges Sokoloff has presented a good discussion of the problem. See his "Structures internes et coopération internationale des économies socialistes de l'Est européen," *économies et sociétés* vol. 5, no. 1 (January 1971), pp. 227-261.

Index

Index

About the Author

Phillip J. Bryson is Associate Professor of Economics at the University of Arizona. He has presented papers, given lectures and published scholarly articles in the United States, Canada, Germany, Great Britain, Switzerland and France. Much of the research effort of this book was done in West Berlin at the East European Institute of the Free University, where Professor Bryson was a Research Fellow of the Alexander von Humboldt Foundation. He is a member of several honorary societies, the American Economic Association and the Royal Economic Society.